MANLEY BEASLEY:

Man of Faith —
Instrument of Revival

Ron Owens

What some are saying
about Manley Beasley's biography

I have been teaching on prayer for thirty-six years, and have twice typed all the prayers of the Bible into my computer, yet I keep discovering that I hardly know the beginnings of what God considers true prayer. With all my many notes, I took a major step forward in prayer principles when I read Ron Owens' biog-raphy, Manley Beasley: Man of Faith, Instrument of Revival.

Although I have taught on faith and practiced faith as much as I've known how, I needed the details Owens has given us on Beasley's life to make real faith as concrete as it was in Beasley's life. Although I knew Manley and heard him speak several times, Owens has given us the comprehensive tool to drive home the authenticity of God's nearness and our immedi-ate access to Him. Owens has skillfully, step by step, exposed the authenticity of one man who constantly realized the impor-tance of God's direction in every area of life. Every Christian should read this book.

—T. W. Hunt
former seminary professor, author, and speaker

Sitting at the feet of this great man of God was an honor I will always treasure and one of the greatest building blocks of my faith. The tears flowed as I read Ron Owens' account of his life because he captured the essence of Manley's life and faith. I sensed I was there once again. The words, "God won't hurt you," will forever ring in my ears as Manley's challenge to me during some of the darkest days of my life and his name, to me, will always be synonymous with faith.

—Kaye Dunn-Robinson
pastor's wife and widow of evangelist Ron Dunn

Manley Beasley was the greatest man of faith I ever knew. While many of us talk about faith and preach about it, Manley was a living example of the faith life. His ministry and life message have greatly influenced me to believe God for the impossible. Manley was a part of a defining moment in my life, one that altered the course and direction of my ministry for the past nineteen years. Manley is one of the great giants of faith in Christian history.

—Michael Catt

senior pastor, Sherwood Baptist Church, Albany, GA, and executive director of Sherwood Films, creators of *Facing the Giants* and *Fireproof*

I was fifteen years old when I heard Manley Beasley for the first time. There was something about his manner and message that inspired a new awareness of God like I had never experienced. I remember the overwhelming conviction that the man I was listening to had actually been with God.

During my formative years as a teen-ager his counsel and leadership were instrumental in leading my family to make decisions that ultimately resulted in my call to the ministry and even who I married. Manley was a true catalyst for the faith of thousands of leaders, and it would be impossible to measure the exponential impact his faith has had through those he has influenced. I am so thankful that Ron Owens has written his story. It is my prayer that every generation will not only learn about the message of this man, but be challenged by the rare kind of faith that occurs when someone becomes totally dependent upon God's power.

—Reggie Joiner

founding staff of North Point Community Church, Alpharetta, GA
founder and CEO of *The reThink Group*

Now that I have read this book, I have finally met Manley Beasley and heard him preach; and what an experience it has been! I wish I had known him personally and heard him pray and preach the Word. Ron Owens has given us a tender but powerful account of the life and ministry of this remarkable servant of God. Reading this book and obeying the truths presented ought to help us grow in our faith and obedience. I pray that our Lord will give the book a wide and enduring ministry.

—Warren W. Wiersbe
author, former senior pastor of Moody Church, Chicago, and former director of the Back to the Bible Broadcast

I saw Manley for the last time in 1990 as he was preparing to deliver his final message to the Southern Baptist Convention, about a month before his coronation. We talked about the Solemn Assembly held the night before at New Orleans Baptist Theological Seminary where God had moved so mightily. He would have been so pleased the following year when more than 20,000 people participated in a whole session of the Convention to meet God in Solemn Assembly.

Manley was a unique gift of God to the church. He showed how to count it all joy to suffer for Christ. He was always discipling and mentoring present and future leaders. He taught many thousands of us another level of faith. I am excited about sharing this book with many people who are facing suffering as well as the many others who need to follow his example of learning to have faith based on a word from God.

If you don't read another book, you don't want to miss this one. You will meet God as you read it and be challenged to follow the God Manley Beasley followed and glorified in life and death. I plan to have it near me when I prepare to enter the valley of the shadow of death.

—Avery Willis
former senior VP of the Southern Baptist International Mission Board
executive director of the International Orality Network

I've known Manley Beasley for nearly 50 years. Ron Owens has done the impossible. He has made Manley the man live in this book, and he has made the message of Manley come alive. As I read this outstanding book, I felt that once again I was standing in the presence of Manley and hearing him teach.

—Jimmy Robertson
director, Milldale Baptist Conference Center, Zachary, LA
and president of Fires of Revival

Manley ministered to me and my family on many different levels over the years. Of all the things he said to me that I shall never forget had to do with his definition of victory, or success, in the Christian life. "Son, victory is coming to the place where what is said of you is what is written about you in the Bible." What a blessing it was to know and interact with someone whose life lived out that which was written of him, and how pleased I am that this book will introduce him to those who were not privileged to have known him.

—Jon Moore
Jon Moore Evangelistic Association, Euless, TX

Ron Owens has done a superb job in his biography of Manley Beasley. Manley is one of the most unforgettable people I have ever met and Ron Owens makes it clear why he was just that. Ron leaves no doubt but that Manley was a chosen vessel endowed with spiritual power and uncanny spiritual insight. As badly as we need another one, I seriously doubt that God will raise up another Manley Beasley in this generation. Thank God for a book as near to making Manley live again as anything written could do.

—Roy J. Fish
distinguished professor of evangelism, emeritus,
Southwestern Baptist Seminary, Fort Worth, TX

Ron Owens has done a monumental work in this biography of a most remarkable man. I have known few men as intimately as I knew Manley Beasley. He was a man of contagious faith. He not only taught it, he lived it, and others caught it because he taught it and lived it.

He was a man of prayer—bold, direct and expectant prayer. When he prayed one would tend to go away wanting to pray like Manley did. He was a man of great suffering without complaint, of quiet confidence without pride or presumption, of great strength while plagued by great weakness in his body.

We loved him much, we love him still, and our ears still ring with the piercing sound of his voice with one-liners we will never forget. Thank you, Manley, for being a model of song in the storm. Thank you, Ron, for making Manley come alive again in this splendid biography.

—**Jack Taylor**
president of Dimensions Ministries, Melbourne, FL

Like no one else, God used Manley Beasley to teach me the importance of trusting God with specific faith. Bro. Manley gave me a vision for deep intimacy with God and sensitivity to the Holy Spirit. This book is absolutely a must read for every believer and leader.

—**Greg Frizell**
prayer and spiritual awakening specialist
Baptist General Convention of OK

This book is dedicated to

Marthé Ann Beasley,

Manley's devoted wife and caregiver

Published by
CrossHouse Publishing,
P.O. Box 461592
Garland, Texas 75046-1592
Printed in the United States of America
by Lightning Source, LaVergne, TN
Library of Congress Number 2009920287
ISBN 978-1-934749-42-5

CONTENTS

Foreword

Manley Beasley was still in his twenties when I first met him. He was preaching a revival meeting at the Castle Hills, First Baptist Church, in San Antonio, TX, where my good friend, Jack Taylor, was pastor. Jack told me about this young man and urged me to come. What followed was an encounter that began a friendship that lasted until Manley's death in 1990.

He was an imposing figure in those days. His jet-black hair and his fiery passion for the Lord set him apart. I will never forget the first night I met Manley. After listening to him preach, Jack and I took him to the motel. He insisted that we come in for a season of prayer. And pray we did! I had never heard anyone pray like Manley Beasley. He would pace the room as he prayed, accenting many sentences with a breathless, "whew!" He talked to the Lord with an intimacy that I had never known. In many ways that encounter with Manley shaped my own walk with the Lord with an indelible stamp that is still there today.

In those years Manley would preach the crowd away. His preaching was so challenging and so hard, calling for repentance and godliness, that many could not stand to hear his messages. At Castle Hills that week, after large crowds on Sunday, the crowds dwindled each night, but by the end of the week revival had come. That week began a move of God in that church that deepened and matured for years after that. The stories that surfaced from that week are still like experiencing the Book of Acts all over again! And the impact of that week is still reverberating around the world today.

During the years that followed, Manley lived with multiple

diseases that should have killed him quickly. However, God had different plans for him. As his strength would fade, he often preached as he sat on a stool behind the pulpit. And sometimes he would leave a hospital where he was a patient, preach in the evening, and return to the hospital—all against the instructions of the doctors! He seemed to preach each message as if it would be his last, and indeed it might have been. But he preached on and on with an urgency that few men have known.

Then one day one of my greatest privileges became a reality. I became Manley Beasley's pastor. The last 13 years of his life he and Marthé were members of First Baptist Church of Euless, TX, where I was pastor. Those were blessed years for Carol Ann and me! We saw a living parable unfold before us each day. We watched a man whose life was one of faith in God and complete trust in Him. As the years passed his message became more and more focused on the reality of trusting God, having faith in His providence, and relying solely upon God for daily strength. We watched the children grow up and leave the home, each of them serving the Lord in a unique way. And we watched the faithful love of a man and a woman and their journey of faith.

His life message became that of the life of faith. Where most would strategize ways to meet the needs of their lives, Manley relied only on prayer. He never asked for money or sent out a list of needs. He simply went to the Lord for his provision and the Lord always met his needs. His message was so profound that many times it would require careful re-listening to catch the depth of his message. How often we would look at one another and ask, "What does that mean?" But upon examination of the message and the character and conduct of Manley, the meaning would soon emerge in a transforming way.

To the end he remained a faithful proclaimer of the Word of God and an incredible and loyal friend. He found himself in disagreement with some who were close friends. Even in the midst of disagreement, however, his love for them was great and his friendship strong. He was the prototype in our generation of a man of God who walked with God in simple, yet profound faith. This book is about the man and his message. You will be amazed at the life of Manley Beasley. You will be astounded at the obstacles he faced and overcame in his earthly pilgrimage. And you will be blessed at the message of his life and ministry that is found in these pages.

This is a must read for every believer. We must not allow the remarkable life of this gifted and godly man to fade from our memory. His story is the story of the faithfulness of God to those who walk with Him. More of us need to walk in faith as Manley did, and future generations need the record of Manley's life and message. I commend this book to each reader, and express my deepest gratitude to Ron Owens for bringing Manley's life story to all of us.

Jimmy Draper
president emeritus of LifeWay Christian Resources

Foreword

The wind shifted suddenly to the north, turning the spitting rain into an icy sleet as I waited for the evangelist to exit the airplane. He was already three days late for our "revival meeting" scheduled that first week in December 1972. He had phoned me each of the previous days to say that health considerations were keeping him in the hospital. He urged me to continue holding the services, however, until he was strong enough to preach himself. Finally, he had arrived.

I was at the gate, waiting in eager anticipation for our evangelist's appearance. This had been the first series of revival services I'd scheduled as the new pastor of Eastwood Baptist Church, Tulsa, OK. I'd been on the field for less than four months and was anxious for this first meeting to succeed. But the evangelist's illness, the hectic pace of the Christmas season, and the reluctance of the congregation to add one more event to an already crowded schedule was now creating a gnawing sense of foreboding in my heart. Ron and Patricia Owens, our musicians for the week, were doing all they could to encourage the folks to "hang in there," but on Tuesday evening the crowd was considerably diminished. Now, a cold blast of wintry air was only heightening my sense of foreboding as the sleet began gathering on the tarmac.

The evangelist appeared at the plane's doorway. Looking frail and gaunt, he pulled at the fur collar of his tan overcoat, wrapping a scarf up around his neck. My heart sank as two flight attendants helped him down the stairs and into a waiting wheel chair. I was certain that we'd be heading to the closest hospital.

Stretching out his hand that was even then becoming stiff and hardened by a disease he would battle until his death, Manley Beasley greeted this preacher whose confidence was rapidly fading.

"Well, brother, what are you believing God for during these days?" he asked, as we drove away from the airport. It was a question with which I was becoming increasingly familiar; a question he'd asked each time we'd spoken, including the day I'd first called to invite him to our church. As the ice began to thicken on my car window, I couldn't help but reply, "I'm trusting we'll even be able to meet this evening."

"Oh, we'll meet all right," laughed Bro. Manley, "Otherwise I wouldn't be here. And we'll probably have just the folks in attendance that God will use to do His work in your church."

Bro. Manley was only with us for three nights that week, preaching his message of faith, while seated on a cafeteria stool placed in the center of the platform in the church's auditorium. A history-making ice storm limited the crowd to about as many people as it takes to flag down a railroad hand-car, but that message of faith brought the same folks back each of those three nights. And Bro. Manley was correct! Over the years, God used those people to keep Jesus squarely in our focus, and the message of faith became the church's operational principle during those incredibly exciting years of spiritual growth.

Bro. Manley possessed a remarkable capacity for communicating and illustrating out of his own life the important truth that faith is made complete by the volitional choice to act in obedience to God's revealed will. Citing the example of those on the roll call of faith (Heb. 11) he would remind his hearers that faith was not simply a matter of thinking, or of feeling, but acting in obedience to God's Word. He was fond of reminding audiences that sometimes believers must "act like it is so, when it is not so, so it can be so."

From that December in 1972 until the day of his death, Manley Beasley became a friend and mentor, both by his personal choice and mine. Each successive year brought meetings together, some by deliberate choice, others by what can only be called divine arrangement. Bro. Manley's message of faith never changed, but this preacher's life was changed as I began learning what it means to walk by faith. Long ago, someone commented that every man is a product of the books he reads and the friends he keeps. Bro. Manley was both a mentor and friend who willingly allowed me the privilege of drawing wisdom from the book of his life. Read on, and you will discover in this biography of his life that the same privilege can be yours!

Tom Elliff
senior vice president for spiritual nurture and church relations
International Mission Board, Southern Baptist Convention

Acknowledgements

There are many to whom I owe a deep debt of gratitude for helping make this biography a reality, only some of whom can be listed here.

• Those who faithfully prayed over the course of the research and writing—intercessors like Lucy Esch, whose prayers have been a gift of priceless worth.

• The Beasley family—to Marthé and Debbie, who gave up hours of their time to be interviewed over and over, and to Manley Jr., Stephen, and Jonathan for their invaluable contribution of memories from those special years when a husband and father was with them. And to Manley's youngest sister, Pat Pylate, who went the extra mile to research dates and events and provide many documents and photos without which the book could not have been written.

• My wife, Patricia, who patiently listened to me read every word of the manuscript many times over, and whose counsel and encouragement helped make the book what it is.

• J. L. (Skeet) May, whose enthusiasm for the project and practical support over the months of writing meant more than he will ever know.

• Manley's "Milldale family," Jimmy Robertson, Sonny Holland and Danny Greig, for their encouragement and counsel.

• John and Judy Rownak for always "being there," and especially to Judy for the hours and days spent in transferring Manley's sermons from cassette to CD.

• Emerson and Betty Paulsen, who spent hours listening to me read, asking questions, representing those who had never met or heard Manley.

• The many who wrote this biography with me through their personal memories and testimonials to what Manley meant to them. They are the ones who have really told Manley's story. And a special thanks to those who submitted tributes that we were not able to include due to space constraints.

• Those who graciously took the time to not only read the manuscript but to write a response.

• Jimmy Draper and Tom Elliff, for being willing to write the forewords.

• Finally, to Manley, who is one of the many who now make up that great "cloud of witnesses." *Thank you for living a life whose fragrance did not end at your home-going, but continues on in the lives of the many who were touched by yours. That fragrance will continue to live as the story of your life and message is passed on to subsequent generations. To God be the Glory!*

Introduction

The challenge of writing anyone's biography is the capturing of not only the historical facts of a person's life but the essence of who that person was. And when it comes to the life of someone like Manley Beasley, you are faced with an individual *whose life was his message and whose message was his life.* The message of prayer, faith and dealing with adversity that Manley lived and preached was forged in the foundry of experience; the terminal diseases he carried in his body for years, the hospitalizations, the months in intensive care, and then, and then only, was the message passed on through his preaching, his writing and his interacting with people in the myriad of ways he was used of God to minister.

Who and what Manley was is well articulated by his brother-in-law and fellow minister of the Gospel, Mike Gilchrest, while moderating Manley's Memorial Service, July 13, 1990, at First Baptist Church, Euless, TX.

"Manley's whole heart was set on glorifying God in his mortal flesh and his union with Jesus. It was like a marriage intimacy and relationship that was so unique it was almost mystical. And this relationship was for better or for worse, in sickness or in health, until death took him into the presence of God.

Manley was not just an instrument, he was a servant. There is a difference. An instrument is anyone God uses whether he is right with God or not. A servant is one whose heart is set on being obedient to his master. Manley was meticulously obedient to Jesus. Pharaoh was an instrument, Paul was a servant. Manley was a servant.

Another characteristic of the life of Manley was that he preached, not for motivation, but for transformation. He preached for change. Most preachers preach to motivate. Motivation lasts from three to seven days. Change lasts for a lifetime. Manley did not provide information as much as he gave revelation. That is why hundreds are here today to give life-changing testimonies, not of a man, but what God did through a man who walked with Him.

Through the years my wife Patricia and I have been privileged to be associated with a number of God's choice servants whose lives validated their ministry. Among them was Manley, in whom the fragrance of the life of Christ pressed through his humanity. His passion, like the Apostle Paul, was to be identified with and conformed to the image of his Lord, even when it meant conformity to His sufferings and death.

This book does not follow the line of traditional biographies, though it does contain biographical information. This is a "message-driven" biography that incorporates excerpts from messages Manley brought to churches small and large, to international conferences and from the stage of national conventions. It is also a collection of "snapshots," of family remembrances and testimonies of those whose lives would never be the same after having encountered Manley on their journey. This, I believe, is what Manley would have wanted. It is, in fact, where this book had its "genesis."

I am not one who gives much thought to interpreting dreams, or to think that God might speak to me through this medium, though Scripture does say that *"old men shall dream dreams!"* Some time back, however, I did have one that startled me. There were three of us in this dream; Manley, Skeet May, who had been a close friend of Manley's, and chairman of his board, and myself. Manley was talking directly to me. I cannot recall anything he said except for his last statement: *"Son"* he said. *"Write about the message. Write about the message."* At that, he stood up and walked toward a closed door through which he passed, without opening it. He was gone. I turned toward Skeet. We looked at each other for several moments before Skeet said: *"That's what you are to do, Brother Ron. That's what you are to do."* I phoned Skeet the next morning to tell him about the dream. His response was, *"That's what you are to do, Brother Ron. That's what you are to do."*

The Beasley family has been very helpful and supportive throughout this whole effort. They of all people knew Manley best, and they of all people want his and their Lord to be honored. So, this is also the story of family, of mothers who prayed, of miraculous conversions, and of children who have followed in their parent's footsteps. And this is also the story of a partnership, a marriage of two opposites whom God brought together for His glory. A wife and caregiver who was there through thick and thin, laughter and tears, over mountains and through deep valleys, stirring the waters and helping carry the load.

And so it is that this book is offered, in an attempt to pass on the message of this "out-of-the-ordinary life" to those who were not privileged to know or hear him personally. It is also to remind those of us who did know and love him, that there was a man sent from God whose name was Manley Beasley.

Ron Owens
January 2009

Manley Beasley

Prologue

Summer 1949
First Baptist Church, Port Neches, TX
Sunday AM

"That looks like the young Beasley boy."

"It can't be. He took off a couple years ago . . . unless he's come back"

"His mother signed him up with the Merchant Marines, or something like that."

"How could she? He would have been too young."

"He was getting into a lot of trouble at school and she worked it out somehow."

"I don't know what he's been doing. I do feel sorry for her though."

"They say he's not too bright and that he was failing school. He was having trouble just reading and writing. I hear that one of his teachers in Mississippi told him that he was never going to amount to anything."

"Shhhh. Bro. Webb is about to say something."

"We are grateful for those who have responded to the invitation this morning. This young man you see standing beside me is Manley Beasley. You all know his mother, our faithful member, Vera Mae Beasley. Well, Manley has been away for some time but has now come back home. Some of you remember his coming several weeks ago during our "revival" meeting to pub-

licly declare his faith in Christ. Now Manley wants you to know that the Lord has been speaking to him about becoming a preacher, and he asks us to be praying for him."

"Well, I'll be. Who'd of ever thought . . .?

"I have the feeling that he is going to need a lot more than our prayers. Hmm . . .."

SECTION ONE
The Early Days

There are interesting parallels in the life of Manley Beasley to other men in history who, though having run away from God in their youth, would one day become trophies of His grace. Among these are St. Augustine, John Newton, Fyodor Dostoyevski, the great Russian author, and in more recent years, the Scotsman, James Alexander Stewart, who had a significant influence on Manley. Then there is Franklin Graham, about whom Ruth Graham writes in her book, *Prodigals and Those Who Love Them.*

Of the similarities in these lives, one rises to the top—they all had godly mothers who taught their sons the ways of God at an early age and who faithfully prayed for them. Yet, in spite of this early spiritual nurturing, all of these mothers, with the exception of John Newton whose mother died when he was only seven, suffered the agony of watching a child turn from what they were taught, to choose the ways of the world—some running away from God for years.

This section, *The Early Years,* is as much about faithful, godly mothers as it is about their children. It is the story of Manley's mother, Vera Mae, who in the face of what would seem insurmountable odds, never let go of a promise that God had given her. It is also the story of Marthé's mother, Beatrice Hanson, through whose obedience her offspring are not only walking with the Lord but most were, and are, being called to ministry related vocations. May this be an encouragement to

25

those parents and grandparents who are presently grieving over a wayward child. Don't give up. The God whose grace was sufficient to turn around the life of a prodigal like Manley Beasley is still performing miracles today.

1
A Prodigal Returns Home

"Prodigals are as new as tomorrow's headlines and as old as the Garden of Eden. For some reason they are usually thought of as teenage boys, but prodigals are not limited in gender, race, age or color. They have one thing in common: They have left home . . . and they are missed."

—Ruth Bell Graham[1]

The life-choices her son was making weighed heavily on Vera Mae Beasley when she told her pastor that she needed to talk with him right away. Manley had again left home, headed for yet another voyage somewhere across the seas. This last visit at home had not been a happy one. He had again been drinking with his friends. She was in desperate need of a word of counsel. She needed someone to talk to. *"God, how far are you going to let Manley go?"*

Pastor Webb dropped by the next day, a Monday. Once more Vera Mae walked him through the story of her wayward boy who, at the age of 14, had left home as a Merchant Marine to sail the oceans of the world. She talked about his drinking and gambling. She described how discouraged she felt when he returned home for brief visits between tours. She told her pastor that all she had to hold on to was the promise she'd received from the Lord at Manley's birth and again when he was dying at the age of two—the promises that he would live and that he would grow up to be a preacher.

The pastor's heart went out to this dear mother who once

27

again was having her faith severely tested. He knew their only recourse was to turn to the One who surely had the answer. Opening his Bible to Matthew 18:19 he read the hopeful, promising words of the Savior, the One who knew Manley best, the One who knew where he was at that very moment. *"Again I say unto you, that if two of you shall agree on earth as touching any thing that they shall ask, it shall be done for them of my Father which is in heaven."* The mother and the pastor went to their knees, claiming this promise and asking God in His mercy to stop Manley wherever he was. They did not know that when he had left home that weekend he headed for the *Port of New Orleans*. At that moment he was looking for a ship on which he could work his way back to the Orient.

Manley would later recall how, that Monday, perhaps even as his mother and Pastor Webb had been praying, he suddenly was overwhelmed with a desire to return home. He couldn't shake the urge, so he counted his money and found that he had just enough to buy a bus ticket from New Orleans to Port Arthur. He could hitchhike home from there. He would not understand until later that this desire was the prompting of God, the Holy Spirit, the One who had pursued him around the world and now was about to accompany this wayward, chosen child, on his last few miles *home*.

Home! In God's providence a youth-led "revival" was being held at First Baptist Church, Port Neches, that week. Manley was persuaded to attend the Friday evening service. He had not been to church in so long. Several of the young people then talked him into joining them the next morning for a "breakfast service." He agreed, not so much due to their persuasiveness, but because his first cousin, W. C. Beasley, a decorated World War II hero, would be the speaker. He listened intently. He really admired his cousin.

Manley returned to church that evening. Cecil Pemberton,

one of the young people in the church who had recently surrendered to preach, was the speaker. At the end of the message an invitation to respond publicly was extended. As the invitation was coming to a close, Lee Wilkerson, that year's Baylor University Homecoming Queen, left her place in the choir to go stand beside a handsome young man in the congregation. *"Are you ready to give your heart to the Lord, Manley?"* she asked. He said nothing. His mother prayed. Lee took his arm and the next thing he remembers, he was standing at the front.

In looking back, Manley recalls his having already begun to cry out to God for forgiveness as he had listened to his cousin, W. C. Beasley, share his testimony that morning. Now, as he took the hand of pastor Webb, no question existed in his mind that the transaction had been completed. *The prodigal was finally home!*

For his mother, however, this was but the first step in God fulfilling the promise He had made to her—a promise that only a few of her prayer partners knew about, a promise that had never been shared with Manley because, as she told her friends, *"I don't want another 'mother-called' son in the ministry."*

There He Stands

Now, *there he stands* . . .. It must have been through tears that Vera Mae watched her boy walk to the front of the church again, a few weeks later, this time to tell the pastor that he felt God had called him to be a preacher. *There he stands*—the son who had been born with the umbilical cord wrapped around his neck, that little baby who was almost as black as coal, who was not able to breathe. That little boy whom the doctor said would not live. Now *there he stands.* You can almost hear her whisper: *"God, I promised you that if You would let him live I would give him entirely to You. And you let him live. Oh God!"*

Now *there he stands* . . . the same child who was so sick

when he was two years old that the doctor gave him little hope of recovery from, what was then, an incurable fever. *"But this cannot be the end for my baby."*

As Manley's older sisters, Henry Mae and Joyce, watched him lie dying in his crib, Vera Mae slipped out of the house. She had to get alone with the Lord, if but for a few minutes. She desperately needed to hear another word. What she actually said while walking down the lane is only speculation, but surely she reminded her Lord of His promise to her at Manley's birth. What is not speculation, however, is what she heard in her spirit by the time she reached the end of the lane—not only was Manley going to live, but he was going to live to be a preacher!

With this promise in her heart, Vera Mae rushed back to the house. The doctor met her at the door with the news about a new vaccine that had recently been approved by the government. He had just heard from Jackson. If they could have it sent right away via *The Rebel,* the train that ran between Jackson and Rockport, perhaps Manley would live. Vera Mae and the girls gathered around Manley's crib and prayed. *"Have it sent, doctor."* She knew, she knew that one way or the other, vaccine or miracle, that fever was not going to take the life of her little curly-haired son.

2
Mountains, Valleys and Plenty of Boulders

"Our faithful God has promised
He will lead and guide us daily by His mighty hand;
He knows exactly what His children need
and works according to His perfect plan.
There have been mountains we've been asked to climb,
some rivers have been wide, some skies been grey;
The valleys have been deep and dark at times,
but without fail our God has led the way."[2]

The Neches River, winding 416 miles from Van Zandt County in northeast Texas to the Gulf Coast, transverses an area once inhabited by the Attakapas Indians. These Native Americans were nicknamed the "Flatheads" by explorers who observed their disfigured craniums, the result of the lacing of boards too tightly to the skulls of their infants. Despite the efforts of the Spanish to colonize this river basin, white settlers did not really enter the region until the 1820s. Stephen F. Austin, on his first trip to Texas, wrote in his diary in 1821 that the Neches *"affords tolerable keel-boat navigation."* It was on this river that the Port Neches settlement was planted, a settlement that continues to be linked to the past by the Attakapas burial mounds still dotting the surrounding landscape. To this historic corner of Texas the Beasley family was about to move.

Henry and Vera Mae had lived all their married life in

Rockport, MS. He was 16 and she 15 when they vowed to be faithful to each other 'til death would part them. When Vera Mae took those vows, however, she didn't realize what life had in store for her. Despite not having gone beyond the eighth grade, Henry soon became a successful businessman in this small community on the Pearl River, located just sixty miles south of the State Capital of Jackson. He developed a 40-acre farm where he grew tomatoes and other vegetables, which were shipped by truck all over that part of the United States. Life treated them well. They eventually were blessed with five children; three daughters, Henry Mae, Joyce and Patricia, and two sons; Manley and Kenneth.

But then things started to take a turn for the worse. Henry became addicted to alcohol. Sometimes, under its influence, his personality changed. Though he never seriously harmed the children, his dear Vera Mae suffered greatly. When sober, however, he lived the life of a hard-working man. Ironically—and providentially—in spite of his weakness, he instilled in his children a strong work ethic. He taught them the importance of honesty. He even taught them the principle of tithing, which he himself practiced, even to the point of giving to the church 10% of the syrup he produced as a sideline.

Regrettably, Henry's addiction began to affect his business. Eventually he lost the 40-acre farm, the trucks, and their lovely "house on the hill" where Manley was born. The family loved that house, but now the family was forced to move from the countryside to a place that Grandpa Harris owned in the town of Rockport proper. Though this was difficult, especially for the children, they still had Grandpa Harris' large house and farm on the Pearl River to visit.

During these tough days Vera Mae experienced a growing concern for Manley. The influence of her husband's lifestyle was beginning to have an effect on her young son. He started to skip school, run with the wrong crowd, and get into more and more serious trouble. She didn't know what to do. Then, one day, Henry announced that they were going to move to Texas. Move? Away from Rockport? Was this the answer to her prayers? *This could be the best thing for Manley,* Vera Mae thought. *It will get him away from the influence of his wayward Rockport friends.*

The move was largely precipitated by Henry's losing the family business, along with the encouragement of several of his sisters and their families, who had previously moved to Port Neches in order to get in on the oil refinery boom. And so it was, in the spring of 1945, just as World War II was winding down, the Beasley family headed west where Henry had a job waiting.

"We looked like the Beverly Hillbillies," recalls Pat, the youngest child. Henry, Vera Mae and the three children, Kenneth, Manley, and Pat, traveled in a "very old" car, followed by the other two children, and a cousin, who drove his "very old" flatbed truck with slats on the sides to hold things on board. The furniture was fastened every which way to the flatbed, and all the chickens, in makeshift coops, were tied to the sides. The cow and the pig, who would become a big part of the family, were purchased when they reached Port Neches. Vera Mae arranged to have them kept in a fenced-in area about two blocks away. The chickens had the back yard to themselves.

When they arrived at the Neches River, they saw a bridge unlike any they had ever seen before. It was the *Rainbow Bridge* which, back then, was the tallest bridge in the South. When Vera Mae realized they were going to have to cross it, she slid down on the floorboard of the car, closed her eyes, and stayed there until they had reached the other side.

Though Henry's drinking continued after their move to Port Neches, his strong work ethic enabled him to maintain his job. He was able to confine his drinking to evenings and weekends.

But Vera Mae's hope that this move would be good for Manley — getting him away from the rough crowd he was running with in Rockport, was not to be realized. Manley became increasingly rebellious. During the year of their move he ran back to Rockport twice. On one occasion he ended up in jail. The Rockport authorities, who knew the Beasley family, arranged to have Manley escorted back to the Texas line, where he was turned over to his parents.

These were very difficult days for Manley's mother. She was broken-hearted over what was happening to her son. If it had not been for the sustaining grace of God and the promise He had given her that her boy would one day grow up to be a preacher, she would not have been able to survive. But survive she did. She stayed the course, a testimony that was not lost on Manley who one day would be called on to face his own severe tests in which he too not only was able to stay the course but be victorious in the trials. Vera Mae taught the children to live that kind of life, not just in word but in action.

"We watched her pray when no one was looking," her children testify. *"We watched her reading her Bible. Her faith was very simple; she believed what God's Word said and she practiced it. She kept her focus on Him, otherwise her circumstances would have defeated her. Mama prepared all five of us for the adversity we would each face one day."*

When Vera Mae died, a Catholic neighbor dropped by to say: *"I believe that when they coined the word Christian in the New Testament, they had someone like Mrs. Beasley in mind."* She never wanted to get up in front of people and talk, but she didn't have to. The life of Jesus pressed through her everyday living. She was a living epistle read by all who watched her live.

3
From Shore to Sea and Back Again

"True Faith bids eternal truth to become present reality."
—Manley Beasley

The year 1946 was one year after the atomic bomb was dropped on Nagasaki; one year after the surrender of Germany and Japan to the Allies; one year after the United States joined the United Nations; one year after Franklin Delano Roosevelt died; one year after Harry Truman became President. It also was the year Winston Churchill made his famous Iron Curtain speech, and the year Benjamin Spock's book *Child Care* was first published. It was the time and Port Neches was the place, where Lee Hazelwood, who went on to write the hit song, *"These Boots Are Made for Walking,"* was about to graduate from high school.

During 1946 the United States Merchant Marines was making major activity adjustments. During the war years, each ship—armed with 3-inch and 4-inch guns on bow and stern with 20mm guns on each side manned by six to ten navy sailors,—braved the hostile waters of the Atlantic and Pacific meeting the colossal demand of supplying the Allies with provisions that were essential for victory. Now they were getting back to doing what they had initially been commissioned to do when that steam-propelled vessel, *Savannah,* left the Port of Savannah, GA, on May 22, 1891, with a cargo of goods destined for regions beyond.

And 1946 was the year that Manley's mother began to cry out to God for wisdom. What was she going to do with her son who was showing signs of heading toward a life of crime, though thankfully, to that date, his run-ins with the law had been relatively minor? She was also increasingly concerned over the school situation. Manley had had serious learning problems back in Mississippi, where one of his teachers told him that he was never going to amount to anything.[3] Now that they were in Texas where the standard of education was even higher, what hope was there of his making it through another grade?

Unknown to Vera Mae, Manley was suffering from dyslexia, a condition no one knew anything about back then. Dyslexia results in people having difficulty with language skills such as spelling, reading, writing, and sometimes speaking. It is a condition that often leads to problems in school, in the workplace, and even in relating to other people. It leads to stress, and many dyslexic students become so discouraged they do not want to continue in school. And this was exactly what was happening to Manley. He was becoming so frustrated and angry that he began to lash out at the school system and the society he thought were to blame for what was happening to him. And so it was that a loving mother, not knowing what else to do, agreed to let Manley see if he could join the Merchant Marines. He applied, and was accepted, but only after lying about his age. He gave them a 1929 birth date rather than 1931, the year he was actually born.

This was a whole new world for young 14-year-old Manley Beasley as he moved from the flatlands of East Texas to the rolling waves of the ocean. He departed June 13, 1946, aboard the GUNNER'S KNOT, headed for Yokohama, Japan. Though he no longer had to face the frustration of not being able to keep up with his school peers, he would now be confronted with the challenge of adjusting to the life of a sailor. He would have to quickly learn the discipline and requirements of life at sea. And learn he did, as attested by his eventually becoming the ship's cook and his several years of service while circumventing the globe two times by age 16.

These would also be years when God's grace would be extended in great measure to this teen-ager, for in God's providence, in the midst of the rough and tough existence of a sailor, God was pursuing this wayward child. God was holding on to him, preparing him, even in his rebellion, for that day when he would be used to touch countless lives around the world.

Manley did not talk a lot about his years of sailing around the world, because he did not want to dwell on the past. Some of his experiences, however, would surface from time to time in conversations with family and friends. Once he told about how his ship found itself in the midst of a "left-over" World War II minefield. He prayed, they survived, though the prayers God listened to were more likely the ones of his mother, Vera Mae, who was on her knees daily, interceding for her wayward son.

He was grateful for the things he learned—immensely indebted to God's hand of providence and calling, but not proud of times such as when he missed his ship's departure in a Japanese port due to his being under the influence of alcohol. A kindly, older Japanese lady took him in until his ship returned several months later.

As hard as these years were on Manley's mother, she clung to the promise that one day her son would be a preacher, and on this she rested. She had received the promise and held on to it even—or especially—in those times when her faith was severely tested. Her message was not unlike the message that Manley would one day preach—that, the nature of faith is three-dimensional: intellectual, emotional, and volitional. He taught that the volitional part of faith is *acting as if a thing is so when it is not so in order for it to be so because God says it is so.* This he would say, puts you at the *disposal* of Christ, allowing Him to be the Lord and Master of the situation.

Manley's Message

·   When you grasp this principle of faith, you will begin to understand that sin itself, in the life of a believer, is the result of unbelief. It means that you have chosen not to trust Christ and because of this, you can't work the works of God because you are not at His *disposal.* The only person who is pleasing to God is the person who is walking in the will of God and who is standing on His Word.

The Bible says that signs shall follow them that believe. Are there signs that follow you? ***Faith is not what God is going to do, or what He has done, but it is what He is doing!*** What are you personally believing God for right now? Food? Clothing? Home? Well, that's fine, but it is not the kind of faith I am talking about. Some of the biggest devils in town have better homes, better clothes, better cars, and better food than you have. Those things come under the mercy of God. The point I am trying to make is this: Faith is so acting on the revealed Word of God that God has to perform a miracle to keep it. Oh that the only explanation for our lives would be that God is at work in us.

A dear lady, a lawyer's wife, approached me one day in Jackson, MS, where I was in a meeting. She told me about a childhood friend in town who was lost. She said: *"I have been calling her every day and the maid tells me she is not in, but I know she is. She won't come to the phone; I want her to be saved so badly I can't stand it. She and her husband owned a big casino in Las Vegas and I have prayed and prayed for her. God recently burned that thing down and He brought her back to Jackson. Her husband is a big gambler and he is connected with politics. I can't get to her. What do you think I should do?"*

I said: *"I am going to tell you two things. First, you need to go home and make sure that you are right with God. When you know there is nothing between your life and God, come back to see me and I'll tell you the second thing."* The next morning she came back. Her eyes were swollen and I could tell she had been weeping. At the end of the service she came up and said: *"Preacher, as far as I know there is nothing between me and my Savior. What is next?"*

I stuck out my hand and said, *"Sister, the Bible says that when two agree as touching anything He will do it. Will you agree with me that God is saving her soul right now?"* She pulled back and said: *"I can't even get her to come to the meetings."* *"That's not your business,"* I said. *"Your business is to believe God."* She said: *"How is God going to do it?"* *"That is not your business either,"* I said. *"Your business is to believe God. Will you agree with me that God is saving her now?"* She began to tremble because she could not understand it.

That was Thursday morning. I said: *"Lady. HOW God saves that woman is not your business. WHEN He saves her is not your business. Once you come to the place of faith, you enjoy it just like it is already being done. Sometimes God gives assurance that by a certain time He is going to fulfill a promise, but that is not always the case. He says, 'Trust me, try me, and prove me.'"* She shook my hand.

That night—no gambler's wife in the congregation. Friday night—no gambler's wife. But each night I would encourage the lady by telling her, *"It is happening right now."* I really don't know how she felt, but she would say, *"Yes sir. Yes sir."*

Saturday morning I thought about that lady. I prayed, *"Lord, you know that that gambler's wife needs to be saved, and I know the principle of trusting You. I am not about to doubt you, but, here is a baby in Christ who needs to learn this lesson of faith so, I am trusting you and praising you for saving the gambler's wife."*

39

That night I looked out and saw that lawyer, his wife and children, and right behind them is this woman wearing a big hat. I knew it was her. I preached on hell until you could smell it. When I came to the invitation God said: *"No invitation."* I said, *"Wait Lord. That woman!"* I begged God, to no avail, to let me give an invitation. I am sure the lawyer's wife did not know what to think.

Sunday morning came and the place was packed out and right over there to my left was this woman wearing that big hat. I had not preached more than fifteen minutes of an evangelistic sermon before that woman came walking to the front. I left the pulpit and stepped down to meet her. She said: *"I can't stand it. Since Thursday God has been killing me. I'm about to die. How can I know Jesus?"*

By that time the lawyer's wife was beside her friend. I asked her what happened? The lawyer's wife said: *"Yesterday she called me to say that she didn't know what was happening to her. Since Thursday she has been dreaming that she is going to hell. She asked me to take her to the preacher and she came last night and you didn't give an invitation."* I told her that that was not the issue. The issue was that the day she began to believe, she began to receive. You must put your faith into practice. The business of faith is to convert truth into reality. True faith bids eternal truth to become present fact.

Manley loved to tell the story of the conversion of the Scotsman, James Alexander Stewart, who was used in Manley's life in a very significant way over the years through his writings and personal times of ministry.

As a teen-ager, James was an outstanding football (soccer) player. His godly mother saw that it was becoming the passion of his life and nothing would dare interfere with his goal to become Scotland's best. She solicited friends and family to pray that God would arrest her son and turn that drive and ambition into a life that would honor Him. They prayed and prayed until one day Mrs. Stewart announced that God had told her that James had been saved.

Everyone rejoiced at the news, except James. Every time someone told him how happy they were to hear that he had been saved, he'd tell them that he was going to play football and go to hell. This did not dissuade his mother, however, who, though rebuffed by her son every time she brought up the subject, was resting on God's promise.

One day, in the midst of a football match it happened. Right there, on the field, James fell to his knees and cried out to God for forgiveness. He did not stay to finish the match but ran directly home to announce to his mother his conversion, who said: "*Yes, James. I know. That's what I have been telling you all along. You are saved!*"

The actions of a doer of the Word will coincide with his confession. James the apostle wrote that "*faith without corresponding actions is dead.*" When we act on the Word of God, we demonstrate our faith. God said: "*I watch over my Word to perform it . . . therefore be doers of the Word and not hearers only.*"

4
Life-Shaping Decisions

"All the way my Savior leads me, what have I to ask beside, Can I doubt His tender mercies who through life has been my guide?"
—Fanny Crosby [4]

We have decisions in all our lives that, having been made, set our future's course. We don't always understand at the moment to what degree this will be true, but in retrospect we can see their significance. Charles Haddon Spurgeon is credited with having said, *"We live life going forward and we understand it looking back."* And so it would be with Manley Beasley.

Pastor Webb was surprised at how soon it was, after his conversion, that Manley sensed God's call to be a preacher. He may have questioned the validity of such a quick decision on the part of anyone else, but being aware of the promise Manley's mother had been holding on to for years, he knew that this was no ordinary moment.

"Brother Webb, I believe God has called me to preach. What do I do next?"

What do you say to a young man who dropped out of school when he was 13 because of his not being able to keep up with his studies? What advice do you give someone who has little reading or writing skills? How do you counsel this most unlikely candidate for the ministry? Pastor Webb knew that his response would probably determine the next steps Manley would take. Actually however, unknown to either of them, God had already prepared the way for this "prodigal come home." Pastor Webb was about to be His messenger.

"Manley, you are going to need to go to school. You must improve your reading and writing skills. Though your memories of past school experiences are not the best, you must now take it seriously." Manley knew this, and he was ready to put forth the effort. But how? He would not be able to meet any college's entrance requirements. Going back to 7th grade was out of the question. How could he get an education? It was then that Pastor Webb added this encouraging word, a word that Manley held on to for the next several years; *"Manley, if God is truly calling you to preach, He will make a way for you to go to school."* As they went to their knees to commit Manley's future to the One who called, unknown to either of them God was already preparing the way.

Six weeks later, Dr. W. M. Ethridge, vice president of East Texas Baptist College in Marshall, TX, paid a visit to his pastor friend, Lonnie Webb, who told him about Manley. He arranged for them to meet. Dr. Ethridge was so struck with Manley's sincerity and depth of faith that he told him he would give him an opportunity to study at the college by waiving the usual high-school diploma requirement. He said that if Manley made it through the first year with passing grades, he would be allowed to continue. Manley registered that next semester and roomed with Pastor Webb's son.

That first year proved very difficult. It did not help that his father resented the fact that his son was going into the ministry. But in spite of this, Manley would retreat to Port Neches as often as he could for encouragement and counsel from his pastor and to pray with his godly mother. He struggled but persevered and ended the year with passing grades.

Not long after this another "life-shaping event" took place in Manley's life. It—or rather, she—came in the form of a fiery, vivacious lass from Keatchie, LA. Life would never be quite the same again for the Beasleys.

Manley meets Marthé

"There he stood at the screen door in his polyester suit with those wide lapels, standing first on one foot then the other. I had just washed my hair and had rolled it up in those old socks with the holes in the heels like they used to do years ago. I was something to behold, wearing cut-off jeans and one of my brother's old white shirts with these rags hanging down the sides of my head.

'Well,' he said. *'I have come to take you out to dinner.'*

'Really?' I said. *'Don't you see that I have just washed my hair? Anyway, don't you have a phone?'*

'Oh. I'm sorry. I guess I should have called you.'

'Yes,' I said. *'I think you should have. It would have saved you a trip.'*

'Well . . . won't you come?' he insisted.

'No, I'm not going anywhere like this.'

'You could just comb your hair and come on,' he said.

'No, I don't do that. Anyway, when I have a dinner date, it is set up ahead of time.'

'Well, if I make an appointment now, would you go out to eat with me tomorrow night?'

'I'm not sure. Call me.'

"I was visiting my brother who was on the staff of Central Baptist Church in Port Neches, TX. He had gotten to know Manley, who was then a member of First Baptist Church. He had begun to wonder if this would not be a good catch for his sister. He had shown Manley my picture but had said nothing to me.

"My brother was going off somewhere for several days, so he invited Manley over to his apartment to meet 'his lovely sister' who had come down from Louisiana where she was going to school. Well, when we met, Manley ignored me. He hardly looked at me. I thought, *'He probably thinks that I'm going to be like all those other twittering girls who have their eyes on him. Well, he can forget that.'* So, all I said was, *'I'm happy to meet you.'* Then my brother mortified me. He said, *'Manley, I'm going to be gone for several days. Would you take Marthé out to dinner one night?'* Manley said: *'I'm very busy.'* *'Well, that takes care of my brother's plans,'* I thought. *'He'll never come back.'*

"But now, there he stands, unannounced, at the screen door, so handsome, with that thick black hair. I sure was not going to let him know how I felt, however, though some time later he told me that the moment he had seen my picture, the Lord told him, *'That's the girl you are going to marry.'*

"He phoned the next morning to set up a dinner appointment for that evening. Remembering how sharp he had looked the night before, I got all dressed up. And guess what? He arrived in blue jeans! I asked him where we were going to eat and he named a seafood restaurant somewhere between Port Arthur and Galveston. I figured it was just some fish shack. We drove and drove for miles along the beach. There were no other cars, no people, nothing. I began to pray, *'Oh Lord, help. He's mad at me and he is taking me somewhere to dump me in the ocean.'*

"We finally arrived at *Grangers*, this big, famous fish place on the water. The waiter arrived at our table so Manley ordered us both their special shrimp platter. I did not like shrimp. I thought, *'What kind of person is this?* But I didn't say anything. We were served and Manley ate and talked for some time when he suddenly noticed that I was not eating.

'Is something wrong with your shrimp?'

'I have no idea,' I said. *'I don't eat shrimp.'*

'Why didn't you say something?'

'You didn't ask,' I replied. *'You just ordered shrimp, so I thought you knew something I didn't know.'*

'Well, I'll order you something else.'

'No,' I said.

'This is not frozen shrimp. he insisted. *'This is fresh, right out of the gulf. It's the best shrimp there is.'*

'Well,' I said. *'I guess I'll try them.'*

Bless my soul, my taste buds must have changed. I loved the shrimp. Every anniversary after that he took me out for a special shrimp celebration."

Marthé Ann Prince

Marthé Ann Prince was born in Keatchie, LA. Her father worked on an oil rig in the Gulf of Mexico—a dangerous occupation and one in which deaths were not uncommon. Her mother prayed and begged him to persuade his company to assign him to shore duty. The company eventually did.

Fred Prince was the eldest of six children. While Fred was still quite young, his father, Marthé's grandfather, walked out on the family. Her father soon realized that he needed to quit school to help his mother rear his younger siblings. She was not only a mother, but she also ran a boarding house in their hometown of Smackover, AR. These were very difficult days for the family. Marthé's grandmother, who was not a Christian, became rather bitter, not only toward her deserter husband but also toward God.

At 16, Marthé's father decided he wanted to venture beyond Smackover, AR, so he lied about his age in order to join the Marines. Before long he was shipped off to France. Fortunately for him, and in God's providence, it was right at the end of World War I. He soon returned home to meet Beatrice Hanson, who would become his bride and Marthé's mother.

As a young woman, Marthé's mother felt called to the ministry. Being a woman and a Southern Baptist, she could not understand that call. She would soon realize, however, that the call was fundamentally one of surrender to God's will, so she told the Lord that whatever He asked of her she would be ready to obey. And what a plan God had in store for her and for her offspring!

Marthé's mother would eventually bear four children, three of whom—her son and two daughters—would end up in the ministry. Her son became a preacher and her two daughters would marry ministers. Each one of them had children and out of twenty-four grandchildren twenty-one would be called into the ministry. These would have children, and out of the great grandchildren, eighteen are in the ministry. Only God knows how many of the great-great grandchildren, who are now coming along, will eventually hear the same call their great-great grandmother heard generations earlier—the call to surrender! Marthé's mother felt this would be the way God was going to fulfill the call He had placed on her life. She lived to see three generations of God's faithfulness. Marthé and Manley both shared the rich heritage of godly Christian mothers.

And so, from these two trees another branch was formed. Manley and Marthé were married on December 20, 1952, about a year after they met in her brother's apartment. They would set up housekeeping on the campus of Louisiana Baptist College, in Pineville, LA, where they pursued their education before moving on to Lamar State College of Technology, (now Lamar University), in Beaumont, TX.

When they arrived at Lamar, Manley discovered, much to his surprise, that though the school offered religion courses, none of them were in Bible. He immediately filed a complaint with the administration. The impact of that complaint is confirmed by his 1954 spring-semester transcript, which shows he had taken *Bible 231: Acts of the Apostles and Pauline Letters*. Manley would go on to graduate in 1955 with a *Bachelor of Science* degree with a triple emphasis—psychology, history, and Bible.

5
Family Matters

*"Family means putting your arms around each other
and being there."*

—Selected[5]

Heat, Humidity and Funeral Fans

"Mother, he crossed over my line."
"Now children. Stay inside your spaces."
*"Mother, he twinked me again. Stop that. See . . . look
what Stephen is doing."*
"You twinked me first."
"I did not."
"Yes you did. Twink, twink, twink."
*"Children, behave yourselves. Daddy is trying to think
about the service tonight as he drives."*
A few moments of silence, then—**TWINK**
Manley: *"If I hear one more twink, I am going to stop
the car and leave you by the side of the road."*

Every summer, Manley would pile Marthé and their four children (and all the luggage) in their car to spend ten "hot" weeks going from one camp meeting to the next. They traveled all over the south, up through the Carolinas and as far north as Pennsylvania—one week of meetings then on to the next *Brush Arbor*. In an attempt to keep some semblance of order among the three children in the back seat (the youngest, Jonathan, was up front with the parents), Marthé would tape strips of bright yellow tape on the seat so each would have equal space to sit in. The rules were simple:

   1. No invading of the territory belonging to the one sitting next to you. Stay inside your lines.

   2. No poking or touching each other, and especially, no "twinking!"

Twinking was a flicking, or a kind of snapping of the finger intended to cause a slight sting on the bare arm of your neighbor, always accompanied of course with the irritating sound, *twink*—a temptation most difficult to resist, especially for children in such close, non-airconditioned quarters for so many miles.

On this particular day, with the threat of being left by the side of the road hanging over their heads, the three "back-seat passengers" settled down, at least for the time being. Two-year-old Jonathan, however, standing on the front seat between his parents and having observed what had been transpiring, could not resist the urge that suddenly came over him. Looking at his father, who was driving, he reached over and said "twink," as he flicked the end of Manley's nose. As the back seat broke into hysterics, Jonathan, immediately repentant, cried: *"I'm sorry Daddy. I'm sorry, I'm sorry."* This of course broke the tension and all had a good laugh as they journeyed on—on to what Marthé described as *"more heat, humidity and funeral fans,"* on to the next "tent revival."

These summers on the road, though challenging, especially with four rambunctious children, were nevertheless good family times. They were at least together, which for the remainder of the year was not always true. Manley was often away in meetings. The children looked forward to making new friends at every stop. The two older ones, Debbie and Bubba (Manley Jr.), would sometimes be invited to lay over for an extra week or so with the family with whom they had been staying. Stephen and

Jonathan, the younger two, would travel on with their parents.

As in many multiple-child families, one usually had the most difficult time adjusting to what was not a normal family lifestyle. In the Beasley household this child was Stephen, the son most like Manley in many ways, and the one with whom Manley identified the most during the several years Stephen was struggling to find himself. Manley talked more with Stephen about his own past than he did with any of the other children, because he knew what his son was going through.

A Testimony

Stephen recalls some of those intimate father-son talks: *"I would ask Dad a lot of questions, but rather than giving me a direct answer he would try to show me how I could find the answer myself by turning to Jesus; by looking into God's Word. I said something one time about how nice it must be to have the kind of faith he had. His response to that was; 'Son, you can have all of God you are willing to pay the price for.' I guess I still struggle with that. Don't we all?*

"When Dad was still with us, I suppose it was kind of easy to piggyback on his faith, but as I look back what I probably miss the most was the feeling that, when you were in trouble, when you had a problem, as long as Dad was around and knew about it, things were going to turn out OK."

The feelings Stephen had for his Dad were similar to those Manley felt toward his mother, Vera Mae, as expressed in a letter written to her several weeks before her 71st birthday.

You were there . . .
March 23, 1977

Dear Mother,
It would be trite for me to say that I love you. With all that I

am and all that I ever will be, it is a constant expression, that I love you. You know, it's difficult for a boy to be able to put into words the feelings of his heart when he sits down and thinks about his mother. In fact, his mind is really incapable of formulating those feelings into words that can really express his feelings.

But as I sit here this morning, looking out at the oak trees, the birds, the squirrels and old Samson who has taken over my chair, like a flash my mind dances back over forty years of history. In fact, as far back as I can remember, in almost every scene, there is Mother! So, I guess what I'm saying is that I am especially grateful that you've always been there. I know there will come a day when you're not there in person, but I don't think too much about those days because I feel like they will take care of themselves when we get there. I just want to enjoy you while you are here.

You know, not only do I see you there, but I see you meeting the needs of my heart. Sometimes you acted as though you were not even aware of what you were doing, but you were meeting the needs. And those needs worked out to an eternal purpose in my life as time has proven. The amazing thing about what I see this morning is not only that you met the needs, but you met them with a disposition that only God Himself could have given you . . ..

I am being interrupted by an occasional newscast, the dog barking and the kids coming in, but I want to say that I am sure that there are other likenesses to God that are hanging around your door which at this point I don't have the insight to see. But, I want you to know that I appreciate you so much for just being there and meeting those needs through the God-like character I have seen in you over the years. And it does excite me that the Lord has left you with us to enjoy and benefit from all the treasures that have been built up inside of you.

The kids have just returned with all their exciting stories of our family's history. I encourage them to spend as much time with you as they can because these days are beautiful days. They are beautiful because we are still all available to each other. I trust that, in your old age, you will not allow any kind of bitterness to spring up in you, resentment or reaction to any problem, because the devil would like to mar a testimony of seventy odd years of a walk that is next to angelic. We are praying for you.

Love,
Your son,
Manley

Sibling Affection

The feelings of love and respect for Manley ran deeply among his siblings. Less than five months before his "homegoing" they got together to write a congratulatory letter to him for his 40 years of service to the Lord.

February 18, 1990
Congratulations Manley, for faithfully serving the Lord for forty years. We are proud of you as our brother, but even more so because you are our brother in Christ. In thinking of your life and your role in our lives, we feel much pride and thanksgiving that God has used you in so many special ways. God has used you to teach, to lead and to strengthen us as a family, as well as people all over the world. When we think of your life, we can see that God had a tremendous plan.

When you were a little boy, laying in that big bed, so very sick, God had a special new serum to save your life, because He had a plan for you. And we also remember when you were that young teen-ager looking for direction in your life. You tried whatever seemed to be an answer; sometimes it would almost work, at least for awhile; but God had a better plan.

In 1949 you were helping Joyce with Larry and baby Billie Elizabeth. You would go over every day to help give them their baths. You had not been saved long at that time and one evening you went over to tell Joyce that you were called to preach. There were no "maybe's" or "questions". God had called—you answered!

We saw a young man who struggled those first few months in college, with grades, money and preaching—but God had a plan. The grades changed; God's Word came alive; preaching was your life. The flame had begun to burn deeper and God's plan became a reality.

There has not been any looking back, only marching forward in the plan of God. Like a tree planted by the waters, your roots have gone deeper with God; your branches have touched the four corners of the earth. Only time and eternity will reveal the plan God had for one little boy who now is a giant man of God.

Congratulations for being available to God. We have all been blessed by sharing in your life. We love you.

Your family,
Henry Mae, Joyce and Bill, Kenneth and Nettie Joe, Patricia Ann and James, and all the nieces and nephews.

SECTION TWO
Man of Prayer

"When the glory of the Father is the goal of every prayer,
When before the throne of heaven our High Priest presents it there,
When the Spirit prompts the asking and the pleading heart believes,
Then, yes then we know for certain he who's asking will receive."
— Unknown[6]

Charles Haddon Spurgeon once said: *"It is a high privilege to be authorized to ask in the name of Jesus as if Jesus Himself asked, but our love to Him will never allow us to set that name where He would not set it."* [7]

Through the years that we were privileged to work with Manley, we never heard him pray a "casual" prayer. On occasions when he was asked to pray for someone, he would not do so immediately; he would want to know specifically how he should pray. Sometimes it wasn't the prayer the one requesting him to pray would have expected or wanted. He was never quick to respond with an, *"I'll pray for you."* He held the matter of prayer in too high regard.

Andrew Murray, author of over 250 books and pamphlets, many of them on prayer, stresses the priority and importance of prayer for the nurturing of the Christian and the empowering of the church. Throughout his works he talks of the deep, intimate communion with Christ that is available to every believer through prayer. This describes Manley Beasley.

6
In Your Hand
or In Your Heart

*"In order to appropriate something for our daily walk in Christ,
there are two essentials—to see what is already ours in Christ and
to be aware of our need for it. Upon these two factors rests the
ability to appropriate, to reach out in steadfast faith and receive
that which belongs to us in our Lord Jesus Christ."*
—Miles Stanford [8]

During the years he was the Beasley family's pastor, Jimmy
Robertson, one of Manley's closest friends and partners in min-
istry, experienced how serious and important prayer was to
Manley.

A Testimony

"I had the glorious privilege of serving as Manley's pastor
for six years. During those years he was my teacher. He taught
me many things, but the first and most important thing he taught
me was about prayer.

"The first time I had Manley in a meeting, after the service
he announced that we were going to stay at the church to pray.
We prayed until 1 AM. Next morning at five o'clock, I heard a
knock on my door and there stood Manley. I said: *'Is there an
emergency?'* He said: *'There sure is. We need to pray.'* We went
back to the church and prayed until noon. That was the beginning of a glorious revival in our church and community.

"I'll never forget what Manley did the third day of that

56

meeting. He wrote something on a piece of paper, sealed it in an envelope and said: *'Put this in your Bible, then read it after I am gone.'* He had written down everything he was trusting God to do, and I tell you, it was exactly what happened. I wasn't used to that. I had always preached and hoped something would happen. I would pray and hope to get an answer some day.

"Later, when the Beasley family moved to Milldale where I was pastor and directing the ministry of the Milldale Bible Conference, he called me one day and said: *'Tell Sonny Holland to get ready. We are going to pray.'* I told Manley that my brother had a camp on a small island on Lake Manchuc, a lake connected to Lake Pontchartrain, but that it was only accessible by boat and that there was no water or electricity. He said: *'We are going to go down there and pray.'* I said: 'How long do we need to prepare to stay?' He said: *'Until we meet God.'* I said: *'What do you want me to bring to eat?'* He said: *'Don't bring anything but a jug of water.'* I said: *'Bro. Manley, do you understand that we will be going out there by boat and that there will be no way back to the grocery store until they come after us?'* Manley said: *'That's wonderful.'*

"We went to the camp and we prayed. We studied God's Word, we fasted, and we stayed, as Manley put it, until God showed up. We left that camp, not hoping that something would happen, but knowing in our hearts that it was already happening. I understood that day what Manley meant when he would say: *'You either have the answer in your hand or in your heart.'* It was in our hearts that day as though it was reality, and it would soon be in our hands."

Manley's Message

When I say *praying something through,* what does that mean to you? Or, when I just say *praying,* what does that mean to you? There are many good definitions of prayer, but to me, *prayer is communion and communion is not just man talking to God but God talking to man.* In other words, if I am carrying on a conversation with you, I am not only talking to you, but you are talking to me.

Sometimes a preacher will say to me, *"Bro. Manley, we had a great prayer meeting."* I'll then ask him the question, *"What did you say to God?"* and he will tell me. Then I'll ask, *"What did God say to you?"* That usually confuses people. You see, if what you have said to God has not caused God to say something to you, there is no communion, so, have you really prayed? Prayer is more than a one-way conversation.

Check the prayers in the Bible and you will find that not only did they speak to God, but God spoke back. Even when Paul prayed regarding his thorn in the flesh, he prayed three times. He prayed until he had some kind of answer. *I believe that we are to pray until we have an answer in our hand or in our heart.* That is a broad definition, but it is specific enough to literally change your life. Sometimes when God talks to you, He places the answer in your hand. It is a literal answer. But sometimes that answer is in your heart. God speaks to you through His Word and you have that witness in your spirit and you really know what is going to happen.

Years ago, every evangelist who came to our town would go to my Daddy's house and lead him to make a decision. The decision would last two or three weeks and he would go right back into sin. They did this with good intentions because they knew I was praying for him. Then one day I went to the woods, determined to stay in those woods until God gave me an answer about my Daddy—either in my hand or in my heart. I stayed there several days and when I came out of those woods God had given me two verses. One of them was 1 John 5:14-15 that says: *"And this is the confidence we have in him, that, if we ask anything according to his will, he heareth us. And if we know that*

he hears us, whatsoever we ask, we know that we have the peti-
tions that we desired of him." That *"have"* does not mean that
you are *"going to have,"* it means that you *"have it right now."*
When I came out of those woods, I knew my Daddy was
being saved. You know what I did? I went and told Marthé first,
then I went and told my Daddy that he was being saved because
I had that perfect assurance—not yet in my hand, but in my
heart—that my Daddy was being saved. God had spoken.

In those days I was a pastor, and every Sunday when we
would have lunch with my parents, I would look at my Daddy
and say, *"I love you and you are not going to hell. I have an*
assurance that you are being saved." He did not know how to
handle that kind of witnessing. Everyone to that point had him
pray a prayer, but he would soon go right back to sinning. Let
me tell you, when you are born again, you do not go right back
to sinning. You are a changed person.

Some time later, when I was in a meeting in Houston, TX, I
was praying early one morning and the Lord said to me, *"This*
is the day." I walked out of that room, went straight to the pastor and said, *"My Daddy is going to be saved today."* He
thought I was crazy. But later that day Marthé called me and
said, *"I believe your Daddy got saved this morning."* He had
gotten under such conviction that he thought he was dying and
he had called a doctor. The doctor who came was a Christian,
and after thoroughly checking my Daddy out he looked at him
and said: *"There is nothing wrong with you physically."* And
right there my Daddy realized what was happening. He was
under such conviction that he thought he was dying. He was
saved that morning. Beloved, prayer is communion. When we
are ready to pray until we have the answer *in our hand or in our*
heart, we will begin to see God do what only He can do. That is
exactly what happens.

One of the most encouraging words I have ever received in

my life came from my pastor who ordained me. He knew about my past. He knew that, because of my dyslexia, I had not been able to learn to read and write as a young teen-ager. He knew I had dropped out of school in the 7th grade because I had been under so much pressure that I was about to go all to pieces. He knew how my mother, by the wisdom of God, let me join the Merchant Marines to travel all over the world, and before I was sixteen I had gone around it twice. But my pastor also knew of the power of prayer. When I was wondering how I was going to make it, he told me, *"Manley, whatever lack you have in life, if you are doing what God calls you to do, prayer will make it up."* I determined that from that point on, for whatever issue in life, I would stay on my knees until I had an answer *in my hand or until God spoke in my heart.*

The kind of prayer we are talking about releases God to do what He alone can do. This is the kind of prayer that comes to the Lord and stays before Him until an answer is *in your hand or in your heart,* whether it takes a day, a month or a year.

Note: In light of his reading difficulty, Manley had asked God to help him learn to read just well enough to understand the Bible. Not only was that prayer answered, but God gifted him with the ability to speed-read. Whereas most of us read one line at a time, Manley was able to understand the content of entire paragraphs at one glance. God sometimes answers our prayers above and beyond what we could ever ask or think.

7

Preparing the Way
Through Prayer

*"Prayer has its rise and its deepest source in the very Being of God.
In the bosom of Deity nothing is ever done without prayer—the
asking of the Son and the giving of the Father."*
—Andrew Murray [9]

A Testimony

"Manley came for a meeting to the church where I was pastor in Corsicana, TX," recalls Jon Moore. "I recorded everything he said. For months I went to sleep at night listening to
those tapes. So much of it was beyond my understanding at that
point in my life, but for years afterward I would run across
something in Scripture and the Lord would open my eyes to a
truth and I would say to myself, *'That's what Manley meant.'*

"I was privileged to travel with him from the summer of
1977 to the summer of 1978. I heard him say many times: *'Find
out what God is doing in relation to your life and join Him!'*
This was years before I heard the name Henry Blackaby, who
teaches the same truth. Manley told me that he personally would
not answer everyone's questions. He was convinced that too
many pastors tried to be their people's 'guru,' answering every
question they asked and trying to solve every problem they had.
From his perspective, by so doing, they were robbing their people of the experience of seeking the face of God for themselves
and 'praying through.' More than once I have heard him say

from the pulpit, *'I've already said more than you are going to practice,'* then he would sit down and the meeting would be over."

Phyllis, Jon Moore's wife, tells how Manley would sometimes appear harsh but recalls also how very tender he could be. "Our daughter, Kim, and our son-in-law, Bailey Draper, were told that they would never be able to have children. Many people were praying for them and they had, of course, asked Manley to also pray. One day their phone rang: *'Start getting the nursery ready,'* they heard a voice say. The Lord had given Manley a word and Bailey and Kim immediately began getting the nursery ready. They have two sons!"

During the time Manley's dialysis treatment was being administered at his home, Jon remembers going with Phyllis to just sit with him. "We asked many questions and he was always patient and gracious with us. We found him grieving over the lack of balance in a lot of the day's teaching; he categorized some of it as heretical. He said that some of what was being taught had just enough truth to deceive people and that so much of it seemed to be more self-centered and self-gratifying than God glorifying.

"Through the years, when we would go out to a restaurant with Manley and a group of friends, we recall how often we'd all be talking when suddenly Manley would start sharing. Almost as though on cue, everyone would put their utensils down, grab for a napkin, or anything they could find to write on, and begin taking notes. We picked up so many profound nuggets during those unexpected moments. Oh, how much we miss those days."

A Burden Change

During his college years, in addition to attending classes, Manley preached whenever and wherever he was given the opportunity. Upon graduation he was asked to pastor Hillcrest Baptist, a mission of First Baptist Church, Nederland, TX. It experienced unusual numerical growth during his four years as pastor, growing from a membership of 45 to almost 500 "active" members, most of whom he personally led to the Lord.

In the midst of being a pastor to this growing congregation he began to experience a "burden change." He found himself spending more and more time thinking about the spiritual condition of the church in America and the nation as a whole. During this period he came into contact with Charlie Miller, the director of Beaumont's Rescue Mission. Charlie had been converted in Chicago under the ministry of evangelist Paul Radar. At one point he worked with Billy Sunday in his evangelistic campaigns. Charlie shared Manley's concern and burden for the spiritual condition of America. He soon became his prayer partner.

Charlie, who had now lost his voice to a tumor, was God's instrument to help Manley grow in his understanding of the importance of prayer in the life and work of the ministry. They would spend entire nights on their knees praying for revival in America. It was during these formative years that Manley made the commitment to not just be a man who prayed, but a man of prayer. He never wavered from this commitment for the rest of his life. He never lost the conviction that for every mighty work of God someone has paid the price in prayer. Manley tells this story:

"I was in a revival meeting in a little mission church outside of Mobile, AL, some years ago. It would have seated about 150 people. When I stepped to the pulpit one night I felt impressed to do something I had never done before and have not done since. I asked the question: *'How many would like to be saved tonight before I preach?'* Fourteen adults in that little congregation raised their hands. I was shocked, so I told them that as I preached, to place their desire to be saved before the Lord as a prayer, because they could be saved during the sermon.

"There was such an awareness of the presence of God that night. It was so unusual that I asked the Lord to show me what was behind it. I knew from the study of the Bible, and revival history, that something had taken place—that in all probability someone had paid the price in prayer. *You may not realize it, but when you see God manifest Himself in some unusual fashion, you can be assured that someone has been praying.*

"The Lord answered my request in a very unusual way. The next day a lady came to the pastor's house to ask him to show her how to be saved. She was one of his church members, but she said that she was convinced she was not a true Christian. He asked her to explain what had happened to cause her to be so deeply convicted. Was there something in particular that God used to bring her to that point, other than the obvious work of the Holy Spirit? She said: *'Yes sir. There was something. It was my ten-year-old daughter.'*

A Child Shall Lead Them

"*'You see,'* she said. *'The other night when my daughter and I returned from the meeting, we each went straight to bed. The next morning I got up, fixed breakfast, then called my daughter. She did not respond. I called a second time and there was no response, so I went up to her room. I walked in and saw that her bed had not been slept in and I could not see my daughter. My heart just dropped. I walked around the end of the bed and found her lying on the floor, face down on top of a map. When she heard me she got up and I could tell she had been crying. 'What's the matter,' I asked. 'Nothing,' she said. 'Well you need to get ready for school,' I said. 'Mother,' she replied. 'May I stay home today? I didn't sleep at all last night.' 'Why?' I asked.*"

"She told her mother that when she had returned to her room

she had knelt down to pray for the meeting at the church. She said that as she prayed she became more and more burdened for the people and before she knew it she was not just praying for them but was praying for revival around the world. She said she went and got a map of the world, put it on the floor, and all night she had been laying on the map, praying for revival. Her mother said that when she picked up the map it was soaked with the tears of her daughter.

"Now I knew why we were so aware of God's presence that night. I knew that the pastor had not prayed like that. I knew that I had not prayed like that. The song leader had not prayed like that. God had found a ten-year-old child who was willing to pay the price. He had worked through her, even to the bringing of her own mother under the conviction of the Holy Spirit.

"What I miss more today than perhaps anything else is what the churches used to do years ago. The saints would spend the first few days of a *revival meeting* getting their own house in order, getting their lives right before the Lord, then they would begin to intercede for the lost. They would pray for their relatives and friends who needed Jesus and then, only then, would the evangelistic emphasis begin. No wonder there was such a sense of God's conviction and power in those meetings. Back then, many of those praying for the lost were children and young people. I remember seeing puddles of tears left at the altar by some of those children who were so burdened for their parents or friends. Before those meetings were over you would find boys and girls leading their parents down the aisle or walking alongside their friends. *The effectual fervent prayer of a righteous man availeth much!*" (Jas. 5:16).

Bonding of Hearts

During the early years of Manley's ministry a group of his *praying buddies,* some whose friendship went back to his college days, would go to a church a week ahead of the scheduled meeting and pray "on location." They would pray all over the church building, all over the grounds, even in the cemeteries located adjacent to many of those country churches. On one occasion, as the men were praying among the tombstones, some with their eyes closed, one of them fell backwards into an open grave! Fortunately he was not injured. That in no way dampened the zeal of these committed *prayer warriors* whose work of prayer, as Manley testified, played a major part in the mighty moving of God's Spirit during those days.

One of those *praying buddies* was Ed Greig. Ed and Manley had first met at *East Texas Baptist College* in 1950 where their hearts soon bonded in their desire to be totally sold out to the Lord. Ed was already married, with two children. Manley had not yet met Marthé, but when he did, he soon transferred to *Louisiana Baptist College* where she was in school. Ed and another friend of Manley's, Harold Brown, were not far behind. It was soon evident, however, that their conservative views were not going to be greatly appreciated on the LBC campus because the school, at that time, had taken a liberal turn, and the three zealots ended up causing quite a stir.

Manley did not let too much time pass before proposing to Marthé. He did so after taking a brief leave from his studies to make one more Merchant Marine voyage in order to earn enough money to buy the engagement ring he had his eye on. He returned; he proposed; she accepted; and they were married. Before long the three families sensed the Lord leading them to make a move back to Texas. Their academic records were forwarded to *Lamar State College of Technology* in Beaumont where they finished their educations. After that the three friends served as pastors of churches in the Nederland area, not far from Beaumont and Manley's home in Port Neches.

The Greig and Beasley families remained very close over

the years. Theirs became a relationship of mutual respect, love, and encouragement. Ed and Manley were true intercessors and unusually mature for men who were only in their late twenties. They took everything to God in prayer. Nothing was too small or too big to be prayed over.

Despite all the seriousness of ministry, they shared humorous moments in their relationship. One such time occurred when Manley was off in a meeting and Marthé had become quite ill with a high fever. Manley phoned Ed and Janell Greig to ask them to go and pray for Marthé. *"No problem, Manley. We'll go right over."*

When they arrived they discovered that Marthé was indeed sick, but they were not prepared for what happened next.

"Eddie boy, did you bring the oil?"
"No, Marthé. We didn't bring any oil."
'Well, you're supposed to use oil when you pray for the sick."
"Marthé, we don't have any oil."
"Well then, you can't pray for me."
"Are you serious?"
"I am."
"Come on, Janell. I'm not going to argue with her if she wants to stay sick."

So, Ed and Janell went back home where, in a few minutes, the phone rang. It was Manley again.

"Eddie, I'm sorry. I just talked to Marthé and she told me what happened. Would you please go back and pray for her? She is quite sick. She promised that she would not do that again, but just in case, take some oil with you this time."

The prayer partnership and friendship continued through the

years and was passed on to the next generation. Danny Greig, the eldest son, was saved under Manley's preaching and would go on to become director of the youth ministry at *Milldale Bible Conference and Campground.* He taught Debbie Beasley both to ride a horse and drive a car and often chauffeured Manley to his meetings. Danny would eventually succeed Jimmy Robertson as pastor of the Milldale Baptist Church.

Some would say that Manley and Ed were "called home" too soon—but our times are in God's hands. In talking with "those who remain" I have sensed a spirit of nostalgia. Janell, Ed's wife, put it this way: *"There was something different about those men back then that you don't see much of today—their walk of faith and the presence of God."* Danny added: *"History causes us to hunger for what God has done in the past, not so much a repeat of what happened, but something that you know God is doing."*

A Testimony

"Manley meant a great deal to me because of his living demonstration of 2 Corinthians 12:7-10. I was drawn into his life and message of victory in the midst of my own suffering. His teaching on faith challenged me to truly trust God during a time of opposition when I could not see any immediate victory, or get any answers. I learned from Manley that according to Hebrews 11, my faith was certainly the substance that I needed and the evidence of what God was doing in the unseen world. As a result of his preaching I believed with eyes of faith even though the physical and visible seemed to indicate otherwise."

—Hayes Wicker, pastor
First Baptist Church, Naples, FL

8
The Prayer of Faith

"You can have as much of God as you are willing to pay the price for."
—Manley Beasley

Among Manley's closest friends was fellow evangelist Bill Stafford. Bill and Manley ministered many times together in church meetings, conventions, and revival conferences. Manley entered the Stafford's life at a very critical time, as Bill shares in the following testimony.

A Testimony

"It was in the mid sixties when I ran into Manley in a hotel in Greensboro, NC—a tall, handsome man with beautiful thick black hair, wearing a Stetson hat. I had been hearing about him for over a year. People were reporting that everywhere he went a mighty moving of God's Spirit in revival occurred. Manley invited me to have a meal with him. That meal turned out to be the beginning of the most precious ministry relationship I have known—a relationship during which I learned what a mighty man of God Manley was and the discernment he had in dealing with people's problems.

"I was still in the pastorate at that time, so I invited him to hold a meeting in my church. This was during a period when my dear wife was dealing with serious depression, partly due to some things we had been experiencing in the ministry. I decided that the best thing for her, and for me, was to send her to spend a week with her relatives in California. Well, when Manley found out what I had done, he told me to have her get right back home. I admit that I was not thrilled, but I did what he asked.

"That week was the beginning of a turning point for Sue, who had become disappointed in, and disillusioned by, so many preachers and so-called Christians who acted like anything but followers of Christ. Manley handled her situation in such a way that hope began to replace bitterness, and her life was transformed as her trust in God was slowly restored. But it was not only a life-transforming time for my wife, it was for me also, because I was ready to quit. In my mind I had already thrown in the towel. I had had it. During that week, however, I began turning from trying to trust God, to the place of really believing Him. God met us both at our point of desperation. Manley then returned a year later for a meeting in which I felt God leading me to resign the pastorate and enter into a full-time traveling ministry. During that week God dealt very deeply with my wife and me as He prepared us for the years ahead.

"Manley seemed to take a liking to me. I think it was because he knew how hungry I was. It was not long before he asked me to do some meetings with him. I jumped at the opportunity because there were many areas in my life and ministry in which I needed to grow. I took every opportunity to just be with him, to sit under his preaching. When he stood in the pulpit he had an aura about him, a sense of the presence of God that I had never experienced before.

"I recall a meeting in Mount Airy, NC, in which we were both preaching. This was after he had become so ill. At that time he had to wear a brace just to hold his head up. After I had preached the first message, church leaders helped Manley to the pulpit, where he sat on a stool. He sat there for a few minutes before he started to talk about the sufficiency of Christ. He went on to say that he wondered whether his hearers could handle the truth they had been hearing, because they probably were not living up to the truth they already knew. He said if they were not ready to go on with God, they might as well have stayed home. I could tell that the audience was getting disturbed, but I had learned that God used Manley to sometimes rattle people into conviction.

"After a while he began getting into the message of the faith life. He had not been speaking for more than fifteen minutes before people started moving toward the altar. I couldn't believe it. Out of a crowd of 600 not more than half a dozen stayed where they were. I shall never forget the moaning and crying; people all over the place getting right with each other. We had not worked up an ounce of emotion, it had to be the convicting power of God at work. I just stood there watching. I had never seen anything quite like this before.

"After things had quieted down and people had returned to their seats, Manley said: *'I believe there are people outside, some who may right now be passing the church, who need to be saved. Let's pray that God will supernaturally draw someone right in here tonight.'* We all began to pray and no more than a few minutes had passed when the front door of the church opened and in walked a family. The pastor asked how he might help them. The father of this family told him that something had gotten hold of him as they were driving by. He said that he had felt compelled to turn around and bring his whole family into the church. They were all gloriously saved that night.

"After that, people from all over the area started coming to the meeting. They were even coming to the church during the day, wanting to be saved. The meeting had to be extended as conviction of sin settled all across that community. The holy presence of God was making Himself known. This is but one example of the manifest power of God at work. We saw it repeated over and over again—the unexplainable. Oh, how I long to see it again!

"If I were asked to describe who Manley was, I would have to say that he was a man who walked so closely to God, so surrendered to Him, that he was an enigma to the world and also to many Christians. When you were around him, you found yourself hungering for the things of God, because God was his life. I believe he was given to us so we could witness first hand the sufficiency of Christ lived through a broken vessel."

—Bill Stafford, Evangelist
Chattanooga, TN

Manley's Message

In Ephesians 6:18 Paul writes about *"praying always with all prayer and supplication in the Spirit, and watching thereunto with all perseverance and supplication for all saints"* In your study of prayer in the Bible you will notice that there is more than one kind of praying. There are, as best I can tell, five categories of prayer.

The Prayer of Confession

When I think about prayer, I think first of the *prayer of confession*. It is prayer that is fundamental to all other types of prayer. True confession is agreeing with God about a given issue. Interestingly, I have discovered that when I take care of a matter that needs confession, other things I have been praying about are often answered. It's as though God is waiting for me to get my confession up to date.

Someone who has influenced many of us over the years in this area is Miss Bertha Smith— affectionately and respectfully just called, Miss Bertha. She, and several other Southern Baptist missionaries had been profoundly impacted by God during the

Shantung Revival in Northern China in the 1930s. From that point on all those who had witnessed that visitation of the Holy Spirit would never be the same again. Everywhere Miss Bertha went, up until her 100th year when the Lord took her "home," she talked about *the holiness of God and the sinfulness of sin*— and with her, it was more than talk.

A young couple, who had gone to visit in her Cowpens, SC home, asked her how she was doing. She had told them that she was doing just fine. To their surprise, after they had left and had driven no more than a mile or two, here she came after them, honking her car horn. They pulled off to the side of the road. Miss Bertha had chased them down to confess that she had lied when she'd told them that she was doing fine because, just before they had arrived, she had burned the rolls and she was very upset. She asked that young couple to forgive her for not telling the truth. Miss Bertha understood the importance of "keeping sins confessed up to date."

The Prayer of Petition

Though it is true that the prayer of confession sometimes leads to the resolving of other prayer issues in your life that are unanswered, this will not always be the case. That leads us to another type of prayer—the *prayer of petition*. This kind of prayer stems from a need or a desire. Petition is simply "asking" God for something. We seek and we knock. This is the most prevalent prayer in the Bible. But what happens when our prayer of petition is not answered? What do we do then?

The Prayer of Thanksgiving

Let's now look at another type of prayer, the *prayer of adoration, praise, and thanksgiving*. This prayer is a spontaneous response in your heart when you see God for who He is and what He is doing. Marthé has taught me more about this kind of praying than anyone else. I saw this demonstrated in her life when the doctors told her that she had cancer. I was away in a meeting and when she phoned to tell me the result of tests the doctors had made, I told her I would catch the next plane home. She said *"No, come home after you have finished the meetings. I'm alright."*

When she met me at the airport that following Monday, her face just radiated the peace of God. I couldn't believe it. She kept praising and magnifying the Lord for what He was doing. She said, *"I may have cancer but I also have the victory. Jesus is Lord. He is in charge."*

This continued to be her attitude when, one week later, she went through another series of tests at M.D. Anderson Hospital in Houston. The doctors there advised her that they had found a "giant cell" tumor that had been eating away at the end of the thigh bone and that a secondary malignancy existed in one of her vital organs. Even as this diagnosis was being delivered, I was scheduled to speak at a *Fullness Conference* in Fort Worth, so I called the conference leaders to tell them that I would not be coming. I asked them to pray for us. That night the whole conference went to prayer, as did other friends around the country whom we had been able to contact. There's no way to know how many were petitioning God for Marthé's healing. All the while she was praising Him for His goodness. Back in our room we opened the Bible and were led to Psalm 128:2, where the words, *"it shall be well with thee"* jumped from the page. That was Thursday.

On Friday, a couple who did not know what had been happening contacted us to say that the Lord had told them to buy Marthé a new fur coat. They said they would put it in the mail. That blew my mind. Why if Marthé was going to die, would God lay it on someone's heart to buy her a new fur coat? I started laughing as I made my way to the doctor's office to get their final word and to learn what they were going to do.

The doctors advised me that they needed to do one more biopsy before determining what the next step would be. The biopsy was done that day. We had to wait another week for the results. While we waited, Marthé began reading Hannah Hurnard's book, *Hind's Feet on High Places*. She opened to the preface and read: *"The Lord God is my strength and He will make my feet like hind's feet and he will make me walk upon mine high places"* (Hab. 3:19). Marthé's mind went immediately to the Swiss Alps, where we ministered annually at a *Conference on Revival*. She thought, *"Either the Lord is going to give me an awfully good artificial leg or He is going to heal me."*

The following Thursday we both looked into the incredulous faces of the doctors—*"The new tests have shown conclusively that, though there had been a cancerous tumor, it is now benign. Mrs. Beasley, you are cancer free."*

9
Prayer's Highest Forms

"The mark of a godly man, or church, is that everything they do is God-initiated."

—Manley Beasley

Behind the Scenes

Manley had a number of "behind the scenes" interests and ministries that few knew about. One of those interests was helping young men determine God's will for their lives. His prayers for, telephone calls to/from, and counseling with these men were often able to assist them in staying on—or getting on—course.

A Testimony

Bro. Manley's excited voice greeted me on the phone. *"Philip, I have great news! I have just talked with the people at Liberty University and they are going to give you a full scholarship. All you have to do is show up in two days."*

I didn't know what to say as everything was already in place for me to attend Louisiana College. I managed to get out the words: *"I appreciate what you have done, Bro. Manley, but I feel God wants me to go to Louisiana College."* Although that may have sounded spiritual, I knew how hypocritical it was. I had not really prayed where I should go to school—I just wanted to go to Louisiana College. Bro. Manley had been praying, however. He had begun praying the moment he'd heard that I had stopped running away from God and had responded to His call to ministry.

I knew that Bro. Manley's concern with my attending Louisiana College had to do with its liberal leaning at that point, but for a dairy-farm boy who had never left the state of Louisiana by himself, the more important issue for me was attending a school that was close to home. I was not going to move a thousand miles away. After listening to Manley's urging I finally said what amounted to *"thanks, but no thanks."*

Fifteen minutes later, the phone rang again. Bro. Manley wanted to speak with my Dad. This was serious. Twenty minutes later, Dad sat me down. *"Son, you're the only one who can make this decision, but Bro. Manley is so concerned that you are making a mistake that he has been weeping on the phone."* I knew then that I had better start seeking the Lord. I needed a word from Him.

For the first time I did just that. *"God, how can I know where You want me to go to school?"* I had no sooner thought those words than in my heart I heard: *"Start reading in Timothy."* I read of Paul's admonition to his son in the faith to remain in Ephesus while he, Paul, went on to Macedonia. I then turned to Titus and there it was again—another young man doing what Paul asked him to do. The message could not have been plainer. God was giving direction for my life through Manley. He was my Paul. I was to go to Liberty!

My mother panicked. I was having to leave the next morning. She was sending her baby to a "far-off country." We left Wal-Mart at midnight and at daylight I pulled away from my childhood home in Tickfaw, LA. I waved goodbye to my parents. My mother was crying. My little Toyota pickup was filled with my belongings. I was headed for Lynchburg, VA, 1,000 miles away, and to a school I knew little about. What lay ahead was in God's hands. I kept hearing Manley's voice: *"Philip, when you get to Liberty, find a man named Vernon Brewer. He will help you."*

When I arrived on the campus I asked the first person I saw to direct me to his office. I walked in and said:

"Mr. Brewer, I'm Philip Robertson. Manley Beasley has sent me to you."

"Phil, welcome to Liberty! We are so glad you are here; we've been expecting you."

So much about any doubts I may have had about Manley's influence and connections. I was given a full scholarship. I have to say that those three years spent at Liberty are among the best years I have ever had. God used Manley to set my course, to impact my life with a worldwide vision. I will forever be grateful to my "Paul" whose name is Manley Beasley.

—Philip Robertson, pastor
Philadelphia Baptist Church, Deville, LA

A Testimony

"Manley was like a father to me. The Beasleys lived around the corner from my parents. As a young person I would spend a good bit of time over at his place. He and my father, Freddie Gage, went way back, both being in full-time evangelism for many years.

"One of the most impacting moments I had with Manley was in January 1986 when at the time I was an assistant football coach at Liberty University in Lynchburg, VA. I had gone there with my heart set on pursuing a career in the coaching profession. I found myself becoming restless and beginning to wonder about what I was planning to be. So while at home during the 1985 Christmas season I dropped by to visit Bro. Manley and to seek his counsel. I told him about the questions I was having. I'll never forget what he said. *'Rick, if God is calling you into the ministry, you are going to be miserable doing anything else.*"' I left his home that day, flew to New Orleans to partici-pate in the National Coaches Convention, and was miserable. I didn't want to attend any of the clinics to learn more about X's and O's or hang out with any of the other coaches. I just want-ed to get alone with God. I flew back to Lynchburg before the Convention was over. The next Monday I turned in my resigna-tion to the Head Football coach. I immediately enrolled in Liberty Seminary. I have been in full-time evangelism ever since my graduation.

"Manley helped me understand why I was experiencing the restlessness in my spirit. He helped me understand that I would not have peace until I surrendered to God's call. I treasure the opportunities I had to minister with him in several Convention settings during the last two years he was with us. He was one of my favorite preachers—one who had a special anointing on his life. I love the Beasleys. They are family to me."

—Rick Gage
Go Tell Ministries, Duluth, GA

Manley's Message

The Prayer of Intercession

The characteristics of this prayer are, *identification, substi-tution, and realization. Intercession* goes beyond confession, beyond asking and receiving. This prayer goes beyond praising and thanksgiving—it takes us into the realm of *identification* with that for which we are seeking an answer. An *Intercessor* will stay with it until the answer is received. It may take months or even years, but an *Intercessor* never gives up. *Whatever the cost, an Intercessor will not be denied. Intercessors are willing and ready to die so that, whatever they are praying for, might live. Intercessors are those who have come to the point of never making a request for which they themselves are not willing to be the answer.*

The Spoken Word of Faith Prayer

There is another type of prayer that some consider to be the highest form of prayer. I call it the *spoken word of faith* prayer. This prayer could also be called a *prayer of confession,* but not in the sense of confessing sin, but in the sense of confessing or declaring the reality of a personal word received that relates to some aspect of God's purpose and will. Mark 11:23 is an example of this kind of confession or spoken word of faith. *"I say unto you, that whosoever says to this mountain, 'Be removed and cast into the sea . . .'"* He is talking about a saint who has come to the full assurance in his heart of God's will concerning a matter. This saint has been brought to the full assurance of faith that a certain thing is the will of God. He is ready to speak it or confess it. *What this saint believes in his or her heart is the will of God, is then confessed with the mouth that something is so when it is not so, in order for it to be so because God says it is so. This is a word that has been received from God upon which the saint stands.*

Hebrews 11:13 says that *"these all died in faith not having received the promises but having seen them afar off."* They saw the promises afar off; they received a word from God and were persuaded of the promises. After being sure that it was a word from God they embraced the promise, they believed and acted on the promise. But they not only acted on the promises, they confessed that they were pilgrims and strangers. They confessed what they believed and God brought into living reality exactly what they confessed.

We're not talking about you running off and confessing anything and everything you might come up with out of your emotions, wishes, and hopes. You can only confess what you believe, in your heart, is a word from God, and you can only believe in your heart when you know the truth about a given situation.

I woke up one morning in 1970 with a great deal of swelling in my body. From that day on, for seven months, I died a little more each day. I knew I was dying and I would travel all over the place, even in my weakening condition, to have people fast and pray for me. I did not ask them to pray for healing but I asked them to pray for wisdom so that I could know the mind of God. I was looking for a *"report from God—a word from God."* For seven months I would go. For seven months people would come to our home. I heard no word until January of 1971, in Chattanooga TN. This is what I heard.

"Son, you are going to live to see your children's children."

Once I had received that word I not only had to believe it and claim it, but I had to confess it. The first thing I did was call my wife.

"Marthé, I am not going to die."

"How do you know?"

"God spoke to me last night through Psalm 128:6 that says 'you will see your children's children.' I'm going to live to see my grandchildren."

That was in January, and guess what happened after I had confessed that word from the Lord? I kept on dying for the next six months. For six solid months I kept confessing the word I knew I had received from God while I kept on dying. Six months of confession. Six months of dying.

Perhaps the biggest test came in early July in a Bible conference when my body was so collapsed that my oldest son, Manley Jr., had to carry me around like a sack of potatoes. I could barely lift my hand. Every day he would tie me into a big lounge chair at this conference because if they had not tied me down I would have fallen out. I would watch people begin to walk toward me and then turn the other way because they could not stand to see me in that condition—skin stretched over bones.

Then, during that week a test came in a different form. A

well-meaning, famous evangelist who was speaking at that meeting announced that he was going to *"pray for Bro. Manley and that God was going to heal him."* Don't you think that sounded good? Well, the Lord said to me, *"Son, don't get your hopes up. This boy doesn't really know what he is doing."*

At the next service that brother came to pray for me. He didn't know what to do. The Lord said to me. *"Go to the pulpit."* Six men picked me up and carried me onto the platform. My tongue was so collapsed that I could barely make myself understood. I said: *"Folk, I'll be back. I know you think that I am going to die, but I'm not going to die. God has given me a word. I'm going to live. I'll be back."* I made that confession in front of 2,000 people with six men holding me up. How did I know I'd be back? God had said that I would live to see my children's children and none of my children were married yet and none of them had any prospects.

You might say that this "confession" of a word from God opens the door to the Lord to perform His Word, but it also binds Satan because what you are confessing is what has already been happening in heaven. And if any of you are not sure that God keeps His promises, Marthé will gladly show you pictures of two grandbabies—two of what I call my "promises."

This kind of prayer is a battle. It has been for me. *"Say unto this mountain, be removed! Doubt not. Whatsoever you say . . . ."* It is a battle, but I believe this is the highest form of prayer we find in the Bible—the prayer of the *spoken word of faith*. Our warfare is not against flesh and blood. This prayer results in seeing the hand of God released and the "strongman" bound. When we rediscover what Christ accomplished at the cross and in the resurrection—the victories that were won, the true significance of what He did—our faith will increasingly embrace this kind of praying. I personally believe that Satan fears this *spoken word of faith* praying more than any other.

But just as with other kinds of praying, we may not always receive the answer immediately. Remember Daniel who was praying in the will of God but whose answer was delayed for 21 days due to the forces of the enemy. Daniel was right with God. He was praying in the will of God because he was praying Scripture. He certainly had faith; a faith that wouldn't faint. Why then didn't Daniel receive an answer to his prayer right away?

Was the answer delayed because God hadn't immediately heard Daniel's prayer? No. God heard and answered when Daniel prayed, but it took 21 days for heaven's messenger to get through the enemy line. This is an example of Satanic hindrance. When you have prayed in the will of God—when you are right with God—what are you supposed to do when you don't hear right back? You believe, you don't doubt, you stand on the word God has given you, you continue to pray and confess it. I confessed the promise God had given to me for six months. Actually, I am still confessing it because the doctors say that I am supposed to be dead.

Someone had a dream that they were being given a tour of heaven. They visited every building except one. The visitor asked why he couldn't see it. The angel said: *"I didn't think that you would want to see in it. That building houses all the undelivered answers to prayers of people who, when they did not get an immediate answer began to doubt and gave up too quickly— so the answer never reached them. They forfeited God's blessing."*

I can't give you a Scripture and verse that talks about a "storehouse of undelivered answers to prayer," but I can give you years of experience when I have known those times of defeat because of delayed answers due to the resistance of Satan—those times when I doubted and gave up on getting an answer. Those were times when I forfeited the blessing of God.

It takes a good deal of faith and courage to *"call into being those things that are not"* and to not give up as you wait until the answer is in your hand. But be encouraged—*that word which God has spoken to your heart; that word that has been confessed in faith, God will, in due time, accomplish it.*

SECTION THREE
Man of Faith

*Faith is the substance of what you are looking for
before it has even arrived.
God says it, that settles it, so go act upon it
and you'll have a faith that's alive.
To get in on what God has promised His children
depends on some action from you,
A faith that is living is more than just trusting,
it's doing what God says to do.*

*It's not enough just to say you believe it
if you don't intend to obey.
God has so clearly revealed in His Word
how He wants us to live every day.
You'll find that you don't have to wait until heav'n
to get in on what God has for you,
As you dare to step out in faith you'll discover what God
says He'll do, He will do.*[10]

The annals of Christian history are periodically dotted with the names of men and women who are considered to be giants of the faith—saints who were like cream that rose to the top of their generation. Not all of them, however, were recognized in their day as being unusually special. It has sometimes taken years of "hindsight" for the Christian community to catch up with the important role they played in their day, and the impact their lives would subsequently have on future generations.

These were followers of the Master who were not out to build their own kingdoms but were preeminently preoccupied with building the Kingdom of God.

When it comes to the subject of faith, the first person we may think of is George Müller, of Bristol, England, who, in his day, housed and fed thousands of orphan children, trusting God alone to provide their daily needs. His personal conviction was that he was to make his needs known to God alone, in prayer, and not to make public appeals. As we read the many stories of God's miraculous supply we marvel at his faith and rejoice in the great God he served.

But little did George Müller understand the impact his life of faith would have on future generations. The legacy he left has been of far greater blessing to the Body of Christ than even the work he accomplished while here on earth. The fragrance of George Müller's life has traveled around the world, inspiring and challenging thousands, if not millions, to a deeper walk of faith.

To those who knew him, or knew about him, Manley Beasley's name was also synonymous with the life of faith—that was his nomenclature. God called him to a pilgrimage that not too many are called to make. As hundreds, if not thousands, watched and followed him through trials and testings that no one would volunteer for, they saw a modern-day Job being tried, as by fire, and they saw him come forth as gold.

While in the furnace, God taught Manley many lessons. The study of what is the "walk of faith" became one of his life's passions. He walked it. As long as God gave him the strength, he taught it. This section is devoted to some of his teaching on this subject as well as to testimonies of those whose lives were eternally impacted by the sight of molten gold being shaped into the image of Christ.

10
What Is Faith?

*"True faith is that disposition of heart that invokes the activity
of a second party—God."*
—Major W. Ian Thomas [11]

During the 1970s and 1980s names like Exciting Eastwood,
MacArthur Boulevard, Castle Hills, First Baptist Euless, plus a
host of other churches, large and small, were like second homes
to Manley Beasley—places that his life and ministry touched on
a regular basis. Though much could be written about his relationship to many churches, a very special bonding developed
between Manley and a pastor, staff and congregation in Tulsa,
OK—a relationship that not only impacted that church and city
but extended to many other parts of the world. It is the story of
Manley Beasley and *Exciting Eastwood.*

In August 1972 Tom Elliff became pastor of Eastwood
Baptist Church. Having been exposed to the moving of God's
Spirit on the campus of Southwestern Baptist Theological
Seminary in the revival of 1970, Tom knew he would forever be
dissatisfied with business as usual. He began to wonder how he
could set the future spiritual course of these people that God had
put under his care. Eastwood was a church that had just been
holding its own for a number of years.

Tom had heard about Manley Beasley, who'd been at
death's door and who was being used of the Lord to create a
hunger for revival in the hearts of God's people. Tom contacted

him. A meeting date was set for the first week in December. He also arranged for Ron and Patricia Owens to lead the music. They arrived, but Manley didn't. He called Tom on Saturday to say he was in a Dallas hospital. Tom preached on Sunday. Manley called from the hospital on Monday—Tom preached Monday night. The same on Tuesday—Tom preached. Finally, on Wednesday, Manley showed up in a wheel chair, wrapped in a heavy winter coat, looking as though he should have stayed in the hospital. Then to top it all off, that evening Tulsa was hit with one of Oklahoma's worst ice storms in years. With Manley finally there, Tom was not about to cancel a meeting just because there were two inches of ice on the ground. Two hundred showed up for the service. Manley preached, sitting on a stool. He didn't have the strength to stand. When he finished he just sat down.

There was more happening, however, than met the eye. Tom recalls a conversation he had with Manley before that evening's service.

"What do you want, Tom?"

"What do you mean, Manley?"

"Son, what do you want to see happen here at Eastwood?"

"Manley, I want God to bless. I want to see people saved . . .."

The next morning Manley called from the motel and asked the same question. Tom gave him the same answer. Manley preached again that night, Thursday, sitting on a stool. When he finished, he sat down. After the service he asked Tom the same question: *"What do you want?"* Friday morning he called again. *"What do you want, Tom?"* This time, Tom responded:

"Bro. Manley, I've been listening to you and now I think I know what I really want. I want to see Jesus. I want to experience the fullness of His life living in me. I want this personally and I want it for my church."

"Son, I think revival has come."

Tom recalls: *"Manley preached that night, didn't give an invitation, got sick after the service, and was gone Saturday morning. But the message remained; it was the message of faith. We had heard things that we had never heard before, and that message was sown so deeply into the hearts of the members of Eastwood Baptist Church that for years to come we had our compass set. Manley taught us in those few days the principle of getting a report, getting a word from God, then showing us that faith was simply cooperating with God in what He has said. Manley put it this way: 'God's will is revealed by the Holy Spirit, through the Word. He taught us that faith is not just believing God can do something, but faith is acting on the basis of what God has said."'*

That message revolutionized Eastwood Baptist Church. In a relatively brief time it went from 500 in attendance to 1,000 to 1,500 to 2,000 to 2,500. Before long Eastwood became known as *Exciting Eastwood.* The church started a summer youth camp in the Siloam Springs area of Arkansas, an annual event named *Faith Week,* in honor of Manley and his message. Church youth groups from all over that area of the United States began participating. The camp continues to this day, thirty-six years later. At the camp hundreds have been called to preach. Missionaries around the globe today first heard God's call during *Faith Week.* Manley ministered there every year but one—every year that is until the Lord took him home.

Manley's Message

The Bible declares: *"The just shall live by faith"* (Heb. 10:38). Though most Christians are familiar with this verse, it still remains one of the most misunderstood statements in Scripture. An understanding of what this means, however, is fundamental to everything else in the Christian's life because the Bible also says: *"Without faith it is impossible to please God"* (Heb. 11:6).

One of the reasons for misunderstanding this fundamental requirement to please God is the "easy believism" prevalent in today's churches. Many have the idea that mental assent to certain historical facts is all that is needed—therefore, the repeating of certain words, or the "signing of a commitment card," is all one has to do to begin the walk of faith. Others think that an emotional experience confirms they have begun this walk. These are not wrong in themselves, but ***genuine faith is more than mental assent or an emotional experience. It is the inward response to truth that has been revealed to the heart by the Holy Spirit who quickens and makes our spirit alive.***[12]

These are the three basic types of faith: the *grace of faith*; the *gift of faith* and the *impartation of faith*. Faith can never go beyond the revelation of truth to the heart. When the Holy Spirit illumines our minds and hearts regarding a particular matter, we are then given the ability to trust the Lord Jesus to the measure of light that has been revealed.

The Grace of Faith

The *grace of faith* is the God-given ability to convert truth into reality and receive a word from God for a particular need. This faith is first evidenced at new birth when, made aware of our need of salvation by the Holy Spirit, we are granted the faith to believe—the ability to exercise faith in proportion to the amount of light we have received. The Bible says that *"faith cometh by hearing and hearing by the word of God"* (Rom. 10:17).

This "new birth" faith, however, is just the beginning in practicing the *grace of faith* in our lives. As it is in salvation, so does it continue to be operative in the daily choices and circumstances of life from that point forward. We are faced with the choice to operate in this manner every time God permits a need in our lives for which we know He has the supply. When the Holy Spirit quickens our hearts to a promise from God's Word, a promise that relates to our need, God holds us responsible to exercise the *grace of faith*. In it all, however, we must never forget that all of this, ***every circumstance God takes us through, is designed to bring us into a deeper relationship with a "living person," the Lord Jesus Christ. A living person—not just an historical fact***.

We may believe the Bible is inerrant truth, but that does not mean it has become living truth to us. This chasm between belief and experience is bridged by the Holy Spirit when He reveals the truth of God's Word to us. For example—someone may believe everything they have heard about Jesus, but if the Holy Spirit does not show that person their need of a Savior, that person cannot be saved. A salvation "decision" based solely on a person's knowledge of God's Word, made in his own will-power, is a form of humanism and not real salvation. And so it is in our everyday walk with the Lord—the Holy Spirit must communicate to our hearts specific truths from God's Word for our particular set of circumstances in order for us to experience the reality of Christ's life at work in us.

In Psalm 81:10, God told Israel, *"I am the Lord thy God which brought thee out of the land of Egypt. Open thy mouth wide and I will fill it."* God revealed Himself to them and told them exactly what to do. Is God not just as ready to fill our mouths today as He was back in the times of the Old Testament? The more we open our mouths, the more He can fill them. We have all been given the same measure of the *"grace of faith."* How we respond to this is, in one sense, up to us. God wants us to make a practice of going to Him to receive illumination from Him concerning our daily needs. When we do, He will *"make all grace abound to (us) you, that always having all sufficiency in all things (we) you may abound to every good work"* (2 Cor. 9:8). Most of our needs are met by exercising the *grace of faith.*

The Gift of Faith

In the first epistle to the church in Corinth, the Apostle Paul lists the gifts of the Holy Spirit that are given to the Body of Christ. In 1 Corinthians 12:6 he says, *"There are a variety of gifts, but the same Spirit, and there are varieties of ministries and the same Lord. And there are varieties of effects, but the same God who works all things in all persons"* (NASB).

The three words to consider in these verses are *gifts, ministries,* and *effects.* The first word, translated *gifts* in verse 6, comes from the Greek word *charismata,* meaning supernatural endowment or motivation. Each believer has been given at least one major gift to equip him or her for a particular area of service in the body of Christ. In Romans 12:6-8, we find these major motivations or gifts listed as *prophesy, service, teaching, exhortation, giving, ruling,* and *mercy.* These gifts supernaturally equip a believer for service in the church.

The second gift listed is from the Greek word for *ministry.* It concerns the different places of service in which each believer may use his or her *charisma.* So we have different believers with different abilities, using them in different places and ways to serve the same Lord.

The last gift mentioned is taken from the Greek word meaning "effect," or "manifestation." These different manifestations take place when a child of God is ministering—as the Holy Spirit leads—for the good of the whole body. In Romans 12:9 we find the *gift of faith* listed as one of these manifestations that the Holy Spirit employs. ***The Bible is very consistent in the fact that God has a sovereign purpose for every situation and that we cannot isolate, restrict, or coerce Him into doing what we want.*** This has been the problem with the healing movement that has swept across the nation. Some people have taken Scriptures concerning healing and have tried to manipulate God with them. Beloved, God will do only one thing—He will act according to what He initiates. He will always be consistent with Himself. Our faith must rest on God's will that is revealed to us in His Word, not on what we'd personally like to do or see happen.

The *gift of faith* comes and goes according to the will of God. It manifests itself when and where God wishes it to, and when it does, no question exists as to what God's will is. We just know. We have the assurance and witness of the Holy Spirit. This assurance is so real that we have no problem in confessing what God has already accomplished.

In my ministry over the years, the Lord has from time to time given me this gift of faith. For example, I would know without a doubt that God was going to heal a certain person. I would pray the prayer of faith and without exception, when that gift was manifested, that person was healed. Now, that does not make me a *Faith Healer,* but I have been at times, an instrument through which the *gift of faith* has operated.

The Impartation of Faith

In Galatians 2:20 the Apostle Paul says that the life he lived was being lived by *"the faith of the Son of God."* Paul had arrived at the place where he knew that in his own strength he was absolutely helpless, and in that state of helplessness the Lord Jesus had become his very life and faith. This is God's desire for each of us—that we come to the point of recognizing our own inadequacy so that the life of the Lord Jesus can become the daily source and supply for our lives. This is the highest form of faith.

This *impartation of faith* became especially real to me in the midst of my sickness. I could not find a promise in the Bible that would allow me to use the *grace of faith*. I did not have the *gift of faith* operating in my life for that situation, so I asked God to grant me the kind of faith the Apostle Paul had. I prayed: *"Father, will you give me the faith of the Lord Jesus to be my very own faith?"* In a matter of days I received a measure of faith beyond anything I had ever experienced. I was given the full assurance that the life I was living was not my life but that of the Lord Jesus. I had been brought to the place of such inadequacy that all I could do was to cast myself on God for the faith I needed. He exchanged my helplessness and frail human strength for His faith and life.

When we get to the end of ourselves, then He takes over. When we recognize our weakness, then God will show Himself adequate for whatever the situation may be. As for me, I was dying. Everyone, except my wife Marthé, had given up. My doctors said that I was not going to make it. I had nowhere else to turn but to God for the faith I was going to need to hold on to the promise God had given me, the promise that I would live to see my children's children. ***I began to experience what it meant to live by the faith of the Son of God when everything else in my life was pointing to the very opposite of what God was telling me.***

Observation: Manley lived by what Dr. Stephen Olford used to call *"a new principle."* He was living by the life and faith of another, the Lord Jesus Christ. Though many would consider this to be life on a plane that is inaccessible to "ordinary" believers, is this not really what God desires for each of His children? Is this not closer to what Scripture teaches as being the "normal" Christian life?

11
Three Elements of Faith

"Faith enables the believing soul to treat the future as the present and the invisible as visible. Faith is dependence upon God and this God-dependence only begins when self-dependence ends."
— Manley Beasley

A Testimony

"Manley Beasley was one of the most dynamic preachers on faith I have ever met. I will never forget when I first heard him in Dothan, AL, where my uncle, Henry Johnson, was pastor for over 30 years. The city was experiencing an outbreak of revival in the Civic Center. Manley was staying in my uncle's home. As a young man, having just become pastor of the *Open Door Baptist Church* in Tuscaloosa, I had the privilege of spending four or five days with Bro. Beasley.

"I remember the little booklet on faith that he passed out. I'll never forget the Scripture he quoted from Hebrews 11:1, *"Faith is the substance of things hoped for, the evidence of things not seen."* Then, he made this statement, *"Faith is believing something is so when it is not so in order for it to be so because God says it is so."* From that time on Manley Beasley's teaching on faith and his Faith Workbooks have literally changed this preacher's life. Now, after twenty-five years of full-time ministry, after watching God grow one of the greatest churches in Alabama, after becoming the dean of the seminary and vice president of spiritual life at *Liberty University,* and now finding myself president of *Tennessee Temple University*, I can honestly say that it was the early teaching of Manley Beasley, and the example of the faith life that he lived, that has enabled me to accomplish whatever I have through the power of the Holy Spirit and the Word of God. I am deeply indebted to a man named Manley Beasley. "

—Dr. Danny Lovett, president
Tennessee Temple University

Another Testimony

"I will never forget a *Ten-Minute Preaching Moment* that Bro. Manley did one year at the Southern Baptist Convention. The building grew quiet; hallway conversations were suspended; a hush settled over the entire auditorium as we heard from God through a weak vessel. I saw Manley the next day and commented about the life that poured from him to those of us who listened. He said: *'Bill, I was at death's door last evening but God can resurrect life out of death.'*

"I asked him one time if he ever failed to determine God's will. He chuckled. *'I'm sure I have missed Him hundreds of times over the years.'* That was a comfort to a young preacher like me, to realize that every great man of God is just a man who, himself, had to learn to listen to God.

"*'What are you believing God for right now?'* is a question he asked me every time we met. After a while I would plan ahead so I would have something to say! At times he would add, *'that if He didn't come through you'd be sunk?'* I, and countless others, were privileged to come under the mantle of Manley Beasley. Rare are the opportunities to be mentored by a godly man."

—Bill Elliff, pastor
Summit Church, Little Rock, AR

Testimonies, such as these two, speak volumes about the influence Manley had, and to the ongoing impact he still has on countless numbers of people across America and beyond.

Manley's Message

Faith has such a unique place in the Bible, and is so tied to the whole economy of God, that until a person arrives at the place where he knows how to believe God actively, he will never become a mature Christian.

For you, a believer, everything you need must come in response to faith. If you want to be a "just person" the Bible says *"you must walk by faith"* (Rom. 1:17), as opposed to the world's philosophy of *"doing the best you can."* Sanctification is not only achieved by studying the Bible or praying many hours a day—it comes by faith. I've known people who read their Bibles diligently and pray regularly who are as mean as the devil. Prayer alone does not sanctify you. Reading the Bible alone does not sanctify you. Acts 26:18 says that you are *"sanctified by faith."* You can be a moral, upright person, but if you don't have faith, you have no access to God. 2 Thessalonians 1:3-4 says that you grow in "steadfastness" by faith. Paul said the only way he could live was by faith. The way Christ dwells in our hearts, in His fullness, is by faith.

Faith is the only law placed at our disposal that supersedes the laws of nature as we see in Matthew 17:20. *"If you have faith as a grain of mustard seed, ye shall say unto this mountain, Remove hence to yonder place and it shall remove."* Peter saw Jesus walking on the water and called out, *"Lord, if that is you, bid me come to you."* Peter walked by faith (Matt. 14:25-32). When Jesus cried out. *"Lazarus, come forth,"* he was speaking in faith, believing that His Father would raise Lazarus from the dead (John 11:40-44). When Jesus blessed and broke the five loaves and two fish, He did so in faith, knowing that the Father was going to feed all those thousands of hungry people (Mark 6:41-44). Everything God has for us has already been provided. The secret to tapping into His provision is using the key of faith.

I recall a time when God was showing me things about faith I'd never seen before, and I was having to learn them "the hard way." Sometimes, when I would return from being on the road in ministry, my wife, Marthé, would ask how the meetings had gone. I would usually say, *"Praise God, we had a wonderful time."* But then she would ask what I meant by "wonderful?" She wanted more detailed answers and there were times I had to admit that things had not gone all that well. I would quickly add, however, that it wasn't my fault. I would begin blaming it on the church that hadn't prepared well, or on a deacon who resisted everything I did, or on one thing or another. I found myself rationalizing, justifying, excusing, and blaming my failure on others.

At this point God in His mercy began to teach me things about faith that I really needed to learn. He had His messenger, Satan, deliver me a "material" problem. We found ourselves having to come up with $9,500.00 (closer to $20,000 in today's economy) in two weeks. *"Oh God,"* I prayed. *"If you will just miraculously provide this money, I will give you all the glory and never bother you again."* I was soon to discover that God is not always interested in having us experience an immediate, one-time, spectacular miracle that we can talk about for the rest of our lives. I learned that sometimes He stretches it out over a period of time to teach us how to trust Him from day to day.

Soon after being faced with this financial crisis, God engineered another series of circumstances that included our only car burning up in a rainstorm. In a rainstorm! Now here we were, not only owing money but needing to buy another car. I began realizing that it was one thing to talk to my wife and blame others for what was happening, but it was going to be a different matter when facing a banker. I knew that the bank was not going to accept any excuses.

When things did not improve, I cried out to the Lord. This time I asked what I had done wrong. As far as I knew I was trusting Him. I had faith, at least I thought I did. Then He showed me that I still didn't really know what faith was all about. He showed me that I had not yet learned that *"faith is substance,"* Obviously I didn't have any "substance." When I finally got honest with God and confessed my failure, He began to open my eyes to things I had never seen before. I began to see that faith has three elements. These three elements are *intellectual* faith, *emotional* faith, and *volitional* faith.

Intellectual Faith

It wasn't difficult to see that I had *intellectual faith*. This is the kind of faith that believes God can do anything and that He is the rewarder of those who diligently seek Him. I had that kind of faith. You have that kind of faith. We believe that God can do anything. The Bible says, *"According to thy faith be it unto you"* (Matt. 9:29). This can also be translated, *"According to your faith God is working."* But, isn't it true that you believe God can do a lot of things that He is not doing right now? ***If faith is just believing that God can do a particular thing, then why is He not doing what you believe He can do? Could it mean that your faith is incomplete?***

In my situation, I believed that God could solve my problem. But in searching the Scriptures I discovered that He not only could solve it but that He wanted to solve it. In fact He had already made provision for it. From His point of view my problem had already been solved. Now, I knew this intellectually, but *intellectual faith* is only one element of the faith life. After all, even the devil has that kind of faith. He and his demons know that God can do anything.

Emotional Faith

Not only did I believe that God could meet my need, I desperately wanted Him to meet it. I hoped, I planned, I prayed, and I fasted. In my mind I found myself telling God that if He didn't soon solve this problem, He was going to lose a good evangelist. I promised Him that if He got me out of this predicament I would never get into another one like it again. It is now obvious to me that at the time I didn't have the sense to know that God Himself had arranged the predicament I was in.

I tried bargaining with God. I even attempted to play on His sympathy—but God doesn't respond to either of those approaches. You can wish; you can desire; you can anticipate; you can do all kinds of things but still not have "substance." Sadly, that is about as far in the walk of faith that a lot of people go. *They know intellectually. Their emotions desperately desire. But neither of these in or of themselves move God into action.*

I told God that if He would just solve my problem, I would never doubt Him again. As I look back, I realize that I was getting it backwards; I was trying to get God to meet my need so that I could really believe. I did not realize that anyone can believe "after" they have received. That is not real faith.

Volitional Faith

I was finally beginning to see that faith was not only *intellectual* and *emotional* but also *volitional*. God has given us a *will*. With that *will* we make choices—choices to either accept something or reject it. When our *will* acts, our whole body reacts. When we choose to sit on a pew in church, our body responds to this decision of the *will*. The pew, however, cannot hold us up if we only believe it can. We have to place our body on the pew in order for it to perform the function for which it was built. We have to make a conscious choice to place ourselves at the disposal of that pew.

I began to realize that God was waiting on me to act on His revealed truth because faith is acting on the Word of God. I must not only believe He can meet a need; I must not only want Him to meet a need; I must begin to act as though the need has been met, even though I might not be able to see it, feel it, smell it, taste it, or hear it. I must begin acting as if it is so, when it is not so, in order for it to be so, because with God it already is so.

This now meant that I had to begin acting as though I had the $30,000 I needed to cover the note and the car. I said, *'Lord, I don't understand it."* He said, *"That's none of your business."* I said, *"How are you going to do it?"* He said, *"That's none of your business, either."* I said; *'But Lord, what if I fail?"* He said: *"Who said you were a success?"* I already knew that I was a failure, but that moment I decided that sink or swim, live or die, I was going to trust God.

I turned to the promise of Philippians 4:19 and read *"But my God shall supply all your need according to his riches in glory by Christ Jesus."* Over the verse I wrote, *"God HAS solved my problem."* I went and told a preacher friend that God was solving my problem right then. He said, *"How?"* I said, *"I don't know and that's not my business."* He said, *"How do you feel about it?"* I laughed and said, *"Like a fool, but I still know God has met the need."* Two hours later the problem was solved!

True belief is acting on God's revealed truth. In the Amplified Bible, Matthew 21:22 reads, *"And whatever you ask for in prayer, having faith and (really) believing, you will receive."* If you have been praying for something that you know is God's will, when are you going to believe that your prayers have been answered? You say, *"I'll believe they are answered when I see the answer."* That's not faith. You must act on the living Word of God as though it is already so. It's that act of faith that places you completely in the arms of Jesus. Did you not by faith put yourself in His arms when you got saved? Didn't He convert the truth you had received into reality in your life? What are you believing God for right now? What truth, what revealed word is He waiting for you to act on?

When the ten lepers came to Jesus and asked for healing, he gave them what might seem to be a strange answer. In Luke 17:14, He told them to go and show themselves to the priests. This was part of the Jewish law for lepers who had been healed, a part of the temple ritual they had to submit to before being permitted to return to normal life. When Jesus spoke those words, however, they had not yet been healed. They obviously believed that Jesus could perform miracles (intellectual faith) or they would not have asked for healing. They certainly wanted to be healed (emotional faith), but the Bible says that they were healed *"as they went."* They were healed when they acted as though they had been healed (volitional faith). They were healed as they were walking toward the Temple to present themselves to the priests. **The lesson here is that only when their will moved them to obedient and believing action God granted their request**.

What are you believing God for right now? Are you facing a crisis in which you desperately need God's intervention? Has God given you a promise that He will meet that need? Are you acting on that promise to the extent that He has to perform a miracle to keep His Word? When, on the basis of His revealed Word, you act as though a thing is so when it is not so, God will move into action to make it so. That's what faith is all about.

A Testimony

"When I knelt down on the sidewalk in front of the bar I ran in Houston, TX, to ask God for mercy and forgiveness, my life was instantly changed. Though my name, Iris Urrey, would always be on the record books of the *Goree Unit of the Texas Department of Corrections* in Huntsville, TX, in God's record book my past was wiped out the moment my name was entered into the *Lamb's Book of Life*. I had been made a new creation— I'd been born again. I had a new ID.

"With the 'new birth' came an immediate sense that not only was I headed for heaven, but that the way I would live from that moment on would be completely different, because I was a new person—well, I was soon to learn just how different it would be. I met Manley and Marthé Beasley.

"When I lived in the world, and worked for the world, I thought like the world and followed its way of operating. But when God moved me from the *Kingdom of Darkness* into the *Kingdom of Light* I didn't plan to live that way any more. I knew that I would no longer be trusting in the same things I had been depending on in the past. I knew that from that point on God was going to be my source of supply, not just for some things but for everything.

"So, I began to look at other believers to see how they lived this different kind of life. What I saw, however, more than anything else were people who claimed to be Christians but who still seemed to be depending on the same things the world depended on. I heard preachers on television begging for money. I saw churches planning budgets the same way the world did. I was confused. I didn't see anybody whose life could not be explained in human terms, then, in God's goodness, I ended up in a meeting where Manley Beasley was preaching.

"This man spoke about trusting God. He talked about faith. It thrilled me. Though I was still just a young believer, I recognized "truth." When he finished, I ran up to him and said, *"I'm an ex-con and a saved prostitute. I want to know more about what you said."* He laughed and told me that I needed to talk to his wife. When I met Marthé, she told me that in a few weeks they were going to have a "Deeper Life Conference" at First Baptist, Euless, TX. She invited me to go with them. She said that Manley, Ron Dunn, Jack Taylor, Miss Bertha Smith, and some others would be there. I had never heard of any of them, but I was excited.

"I stayed with the Beasleys that week. When we were at their house between services, Manley would tell me stories. I would sit on the floor. He would read the Bible to me and talk to me just like he would to a little child. I was hearing what I had thought being a Christian really was from the time I was saved, but this was the first time anyone explained it to me. I began to understand what walking by faith meant. I knew right then that this was the kind of life I wanted to live. I soon learned, however, that it was not going to be easy—but with God's help and the encouragement of Manley and Marthé I was determined to learn it and walk it.

"I admit times occurred when I would really get frustrated with Manley. He watched me struggle to believe God for certain things, such as wanting to go to the *International Congress on Revival* in Europe. He told me that I would have to trust God for the money. He would ask me, *"Iris, are you going to go with us?"* I would say, *"I hope so."* He would say. *"Well, you're not going, because it's going to take a lot more than hope."* I would get mad. He told me years later how in those early days of my learning the walk of faith that he wanted to help me out financially. But he said he knew that if I was going to grow, my faith had to be tried and tested. To the glory of God, I never missed any of those *Congresses on Revival.* I have seen God work miracles in so many other situations. And He is still doing it in our family and ministry as my husband, Blue, and our son, Denim, look to God as our Provider for everything we need."

—Iris Urrey Blue
Duane and Iris Blue Ministries, Lucas, TX

12
Getting a Report

*"Faith is the God-endowed ability given to every child of God
to convert divine truth into present reality."*
—Manley Beasley

A Testimony

"My coming to Christ created major difficulties in my life. I
had two scholarships to Louisiana State University. My mother
held high aspirations for me. When I told my family, however,
that I sensed God calling me into the ministry and that I wanted
to transfer to Louisiana College, a Baptist school, they made it
clear that they were not going to contribute a penny toward my
education. I didn't know how I was going to afford the tuition
of a private institution, but I felt I had to make the move.

"Not long after making the transfer, friends of mine invited
me to attend a "revival meeting" in a small rural church where
a man named Manley Beasley was preaching. That night I heard
things that would forever establish the foundation of my
Christian life and ministry. He spoke about the life of faith. As
I listened my heart began to race. I had no idea that such a life
was possible. I came under such deep conviction that I had to
get off by myself, even though it meant my getting up in the
middle of the message. Outside the church, I made an old tree
my altar. As I wept before the Lord, His Spirit began to minister to my heart and faith began to rise in my soul.

"The next morning I had to go to the administration office
to see what might be worked out for me to pay my bills. I asked

how much I owed for the remainder of the semester. The attendant pulled up my record and with a puzzled expression said: *"You don't owe anything."* I was shocked. He went on to say that the *Sammy Tippit Scholarship Fund* had taken care of it. I didn't have a clue what he was talking about. That was my name, but, *"what scholarship fund?" Who is paying for this fund?"* He replied, *"The source has asked that it remain anonymous."*

"I ran to my room, fell on my knees and poured my heart out to God. He had begun to teach me the walk of faith. This was the first step that has resulted in my traveling to more than eighty countries to preach the Gospel. I have watched God provide millions of dollars to bring the message of God's love to a lost and dying world. God has never let me ask for money but rather to trust Him to meet all my needs. It all began when I heard a man named Manley Beasley teach what it means to live by faith. Manley's message that night in a little country church taught me that I could actually trust God for anything—anything, when I knew I had heard His voice. This walk of faith has turned into an incredible adventure, the adventure of following Jesus."

Manley played another important role in Sammy Tippit's life some years later when God began convicting him that his ministry had grown beyond his character. In studying the life of Moses, he sensed that what he needed more than anything else was a "desert" experience in his own life, a place and time for God to develop his character, to humble him and teach him His ways—his own personal Midianite desert.

A Chance Encounter?

Sammy continues: "I was flying through Atlanta, GA, on my way to an engagement in Florida. I was standing at the departure gate when I heard someone say, *'Sammy, is that you?'* There stood Manley. I had not seen him in several years. *'Manley, how are you doing?'* His face looked as white as a sheet. *'Sammy, I have just returned from Europe where some missionaries shared with me a burden they have for you. They feel that you are to move your ministry to Europe. They asked me to contact you about it, but I told them that I would not play God. I told them that if He wanted me to talk with you He would have to supernaturally bring you across my path. The missionaries and I prayed together and asked God to do just that. We asked that it be in a manner that I would know for certain that it was the work of the Holy Spirit. And here we are . . . . Oh, my plane is about to leave. I have to get to my gate. Be sure to pray about this.'*

"I stood there with my mouth wide open. Two weeks later I received a letter from a church in a small mountain town in Germany asking me to be its pastor. I moved to Germany. As I look back, I believe I grew more in Christ-like character during those days than at any time in my life. And while God was working on me He was growing that little congregation into one of the fastest growing churches in Western Europe. How I thanked God for once again bringing Bro. Manley into my life."

—Sammy Tippit Ministries International
San Antonio, TX

Manley's Message

Many believers have difficulty in two areas of the walk of faith. First, discerning God's mind and will in a given situation. Second, fighting the fight of faith once God's will has been discerned. I can't overstress the significance of "getting a report" before we begin to believe God. Not until we have received a word, a confirmation of what His will is, can faith truly be exercised. What does it mean to get a report? What does it mean to get a word from God?

Getting a Report

Everything God did in creation was in accordance with His divine nature. Everything He does relating to His new creation is in accordance with who He is. We know that *God the Father* devised the plan for the old creation. He is the One who has devised the plan for the new. Everything that has come into existence first began in His heart and mind.

God the Son is the embodiment of the Father's thought and being. This is how He is described in the Gospel of John—the *Word of God made flesh.* Andrew Murray calls Jesus Christ the "Speaking Self" of the Father. Everything the Father is, in thought and invisible being, Jesus Christ became in His incarnation. When the Father determined it was time to create the world, the Son spoke it into being. This is consistent with Jesus' life and ministry when He lived among us. He was always checking with heaven to find out what was the Father's mind and will—then He performed it.

Jesus told the disciples that He would be departing. He said when He did, He would send them another Comforter who would guide them into all truth and who would be everything to them that Jesus was when He was with them and even more. The Comforter He spoke of was **God, the Holy Spirit,** the same Person of the Godhead who was active in creation. As the Father revealed His will to the Son, and the Son confessed it, the Holy Spirit went out and created the visible out of the invisible. Each Person of the Godhead performed His part, bringing that which "is" out of that which "was not." We find here the three elements of creation—*thought, word, and action.* The Father's thought is being spoken by the Son and is made visible by the operation of the Holy Spirit.

It is imperative that we see our part in this divine process of creation. *We receive the truth from the Father; we speak the word we have received with our mouths; and we hold fast the confession of our faith, even in the face of contradicting circumstances, while the Holy Spirit brings into visible being what was true all along in the invisible, spiritual world.* Do you see our part in this process? We could liken our position to that of Christ when He was here on earth. Our part—our job— is to confess on earth what is true in heaven.

When we became "new creations" in Christ, we were not made into a *co-Father* or a *co-Holy Spirit,* but we were made *joint-heirs,* co-heirs with Jesus our Savior. We have been given *co-rights* with the Son, the Lord Jesus, Himself. Now, as part of the Body of Christ, we have the responsibility, even as the Son had on earth, of speaking the thoughts of our Father. Now, do you see how important it is that we learn to hear God speak and to discern His will?

Only what originates in the Father's heart and mind can I speak with the authority of God behind it. In the Gospel of Mark we find this principle illustrated. The Lord Jesus was talking to the Centurion who came seeking healing for his servant. He recognized Jesus as "one under authority." He asked Jesus to simply "speak the word" and his servant would be healed. Jesus marveled at this man's insight into the creative process of the Godhead. He said: *"Truly I say to you, I have not found such great faith with anyone in Israel"* (Matt. 8:10, NASB).

Oh, how vital and necessary it is that we learn how to get a "report." But a word of caution is needed here: Getting the report is not the end; it is the beginning of faith. After receiving a word on a certain matter, we must not stop there. We must go on to believing, receiving, confessing, and standing, in order to make what we have heard a present reality.

During those periods when I was so very ill, when everyone

had given up on my recovery, it would have been easy for me to have gone through the Scriptures and have pulled out verses on healing and claimed them as my own. Somehow I knew this would not have worked. It also would have been easy for me to have gone the "positive thinking" route and call it God's will because I wanted it to be so. But I knew this would not work either. *Theological concepts that are created by mental gymnastics will not save you in the storm. If our theology will not work in the storm, it will not work anywhere else.*

Over the years I had studied the life of faith. I had become convinced in my heart that God would never call me to trust Him for something without my having first received a word from Him. I knew this because a genuine step of faith is never a leap into the dark. It is a step into the light. I may not always understand everything that is going on, but I have learned that often "understanding" comes after commitment.

One of the greatest lessons I learned regarding this matter of "getting a word" came as I was restudying a verse in the 11th chapter of Hebrews. In verse two it says, *"For by it (faith) the elders obtained a good report."* I had puzzled over this verse for some time as I felt it contained something that I was not seeing. I was asking the Lord to show me what was there, especially as it applied to my own situation. What I saw was amazing, and when I saw it, the answer seemed so obvious though I had never seen it before.

What I saw was that these great men and women of God mentioned in Hebrews 11 received a "good report" because of their faith. I had always thought that they had received a good grade from God because they had trusted Him. Then I realized so much more was in this record than that. The Greek text indicates a two-fold experience is involved. First, a testimony, or witness is given to their hearts. Second, a report is actually received. What we see here is that in addition to having the approval of God in their hearts, they have also received God's word as a report. It is one thing for God to speak to us, but it is another thing altogether to *receive* His word when it is spoken.

This brings us to the very heart of this walk of faith. The moment we are born again, God has given us the ability in our spirits to see and hear divine truth. This is an ability beyond our physical eyes and ears. One of the most important dimensions of the Christian life is the reality of a world beyond that which our senses can perceive and our reason can understand.

At new birth, we are given a new set of faculties that are capable of seeing and hearing what is going on in the spiritual world. This is something that the unregenerate person does not have. This faculty to live on a spiritual plain is one the greatest things that happens when we are born again—*we can know God.* Salvation is so much more than missing hell and going to heaven when we die. *The crowning glory of being saved is our being given the capacity to know God—to communicate with Him.* The moment we are born again, we take on the ability of living in two worlds at the same time. Our position in the spiritual world is described by Paul in Ephesians 2:6 where he pictures us seated in heavenly places in Christ Jesus. From this position we can see and hear things in the spiritual realm that only God can reveal.

This is what happens when a familiar passage of Scripture suddenly becomes alive to us. It is what the Apostle Paul is referring to when he talks about his looking at those things that are invisible rather than at the things that are seen. This was the experience of Job when he said, *"I have heard of thee by the hearing of the ear; but now mine eye seeth thee"* (Job 42:5). The end result of Job's great suffering was the ability to see God with spiritual eyes—with the eyes of his heart.

This was true for Elisha's servant, who reported with great fear that a large army was encamped around the city—that is, until Elisha asked the Lord to open his servant's eyes. When he looked a second time, God had pulled back the veil and Elisha's servant looked into another world. He saw a world filled with horses and flaming chariots. The first time he had seen only with his physical eyes, the second time he saw with the eyes of the spirit. He saw those things that were really happening. He saw what counted most. He saw what God was doing.

When the Apostle John was *"in the spirit on the Lord's Day"* he saw things with his spiritual eyes that theologians are still arguing over to this day. And in the prayer our Lord taught the disciples we find these words; *"Thy kingdom come, Thy will be done in earth as it is (being done) in heaven"* (Matt. 6:10). Jesus is telling us to pray that what is going on in heaven might be moved to earth—that it might become reality in our own lives.

God's perfect will has already been determined. He has made provision for its being carried out down here. *We participate in bringing God's will from heaven to earth by believing, trusting, obeying and cooperating with Him.* We are the instruments through which He fulfills His purposes. Regrettably at this point we so often fail.

Matthew 16:19 sheds further light on this. The NASB translation comes closest to the original language—it says: *"Whatever you shall bind on earth shall have been bound in heaven, and whatever you shall loose on earth shall have been loosed in heaven."* In other words, we do not tell heaven what to bind or loose, but rather, we bind and loose "only" those things that have already been bound and loosed in heaven. How often, however, do we tell heaven to do what we want. We find ourselves in difficulty and figure out what we think God should do. Or we make our plans and then ask heaven to bless them. When they don't work out, we wonder why. **If we expect God to be involved or bless what we do, we must operate by His rules. These rules begin with our finding out what is hap-**

pening in heaven; what God has to say about it—by getting a word from Him.

This was what our Lord did when He lived here on earth—He was continuously checking in to see what His Father was doing. That is to be, or should be, our normal practice, but how often do we spend our time being busy for God, doing things for Him, without consulting to see what is on His mind; what his plans might be.

Have you gotten a report from Him regarding what you are going through—the problem that you face? Why not take your Bible and get alone with God and ask Him to speak to your heart? You may have to change some attitudes and motives. You may be shown some sin that needs to be confessed and forsaken. Of this you can be sure, that when your heart has been prepared and God is ready, He will speak.

Two Testimonies

Among Manley's close friends were the Hall brothers, T. D. and Dudley. They spent a lot of time with him. Though Manley may not have always seen eye to eye with them on everything, he never did lose his love and affection for them. This was one of Manley's endearing characteristics.

"We joined Manley in ministry on numerous occasions in the United States and Europe over the years. We fondly recall the many precious times we had praying and discussing theology and family matters. Manley was a seeker of truth. He would ask difficult questions that demanded study and meditation. We would put him in the category of a mystic. His relationship with the Lord was so intimate that it was difficult to explain him. He was a good listener, always open to input from others, which made the long discussions we had with him so meaningful.

"In the late 1970's and early 1980's we spent a lot of time with Manley. He mentored us without ever setting up a formal structure for doing so. Under the guise of asking us to help him think through some concepts, he taught us many things that still guide our lives to this day. We can still remember the question he'd ask us so many times: *'What are you trusting God for today that if God doesn't answer, you are in a mess?'* We never felt condemned by this question as we knew Manley's desire was to have the Lord magnified in our lives as we learned to trust Him.

"It became difficult for Manley to accept our association with some who believed differently about cherished doctrines, though he was always open to discuss our differences. We regret that he did not feel that he could join us in what we considered to be a genuine move of God, as he would have been an immeasurable help in discerning the real from the false.

"One of the most precious moments we have ever had was when we stood by Manley's bed during one of his latter hospitalizations. He was so weak that we had to bend over to hear him whisper: *'Brother Dudley, T. D., I have been to death's door again. I have come back to tell you that the only things that matter are Jesus and your friends. You are my friends.'* That is gold that can never be stolen."

—T.D. Hall
Fellowship of Connected Churches, Euless, TX
—Dudley Hall
Successful Christian Living Ministries, Euless, TX

13
The Fight of Faith

"The final stage in the life of faith is attainment of character. The life of faith is not a life of mounting up with wings but a life of walking and not fainting."

—Oswald Chambers [13]

A Testimony

"Manley Beasley was the greatest man of faith I'd ever met. I had read about faith; I had preached on faith; but Manley was the walking personification of faith. In August 1988 he came for Sunday and Monday meetings at our church. I had spoken to him about concerns I had. Though we were making some progress, I felt at times that I was trying to roll a rock uphill. The congregation was showing little interest in going on spiritually.

"Just before he preached on Monday evening Manley said to me, *'You'll know when I am through tonight if your ministry is over here.'* He spoke out of Isaiah 6 on, *'Who Wants to See the Glory of God?'* It was one of those moments when the presence of God was so evident. Twenty years prior, this church had experienced a mighty movement of God. I longed for a rekindling of that fire. I was encouraged at how many had returned for the Monday evening service. I thought surely no one could stay in their seats when the invitation was extended. My wife and I immediately went to the altar and began to pray. A few minutes later Manley walked off the platform, placed his hand on my shoulder and said; *'Now you know.'*

"With 400 in attendance, the only people at the altar were

the staff and a few members of the congregation. When I faced the congregation I saw blank stares—I knew it was over. God had released me from that ministry. Less than a month later the search committee from Sherwood Baptist Church in Albany, GA, contacted me for the fourth time and immediately my heart began to turn toward them. I became their pastor in December."

—Michael Catt, pastor
Sherwood Baptist, Albany, GA

Manley would seldom if ever tell you what to do, but he would always direct you to the One who had the answer. Sometimes it was done in such a way that you would know where God was leading even before you went your way. At other times he would simply have helped you head in the right direction. He would often ask this simple question—*"Where do you see God blessing?"*

He was also careful not to get ahead of what God was doing in a person's life. This was at times obvious in dealing with someone who had come to kneel at the altar during a time of response, especially if that person seemed to be under conviction. He felt that too often a well-meaning counselor would interfere with the work the Holy Spirit was doing in a person's life by immediately interjecting themselves into the situation. He was also sensitive toward those he knew were not true believers but who thought they were. This was the case with J. L. (Skeet) May, who became one of Manley's closest friends and chairman of the board of *Gospel Harvesters*, Manley's ministry.

A Testimony

"I met Manley in 1974 soon after my wife and mother-in-law had heard him in a Myrtle, MS, Bible conference. They told me I really needed to hear this preacher who was very different.

My wife had just recently been saved after having been a Sunday School teacher, president of the Women's Missionary Union, and a host of other things in our church. I could tell that Manley's messages were really speaking to her, so, I went to hear him myself. The first time he looked at me, he knew I was lost, but he didn't push me.

"As I got to know him better I would drop in on some of his meetings. He would ask me to pray with him before the services. He could tell just by my praying that I was lost. I began to wonder about that myself. I recall how gentle he was with me. As time passed I became increasingly concerned about my relationship to God. Then one night, in a meeting where Manley was preaching from Romans 6:16, *'Don't you know that to whom you yield yourselves slaves to obey, you are that one's slaves whom you obey, whether of sin leading to death, or of obedience leading to righteousness?'* That night I switched loyalties and have never looked back. I became a *New Creation*.

"This confused many of my acquaintances because I had been a church member for years, I had taught Sunday School. I had been chairman of the deacon board at my church. Manley then began to nurture me in the faith life. He taught me what the Bible says about trusting God, how to yield to the Holy Spirit, and how to recognize the warfare that comes when you are obedient to the Lord.

"Meeting Manley redefined my whole life. I had gone into business on my own in 1969. When we met I was in the process of expanding it. Manley changed my whole outlook on how to run a business. Some of my peers couldn't figure it out. They thought that I was just lazy when I talked about trusting the Lord. They accused me of not being willing to get out there and do what it takes to be a success. All the time I was learning to lean on the Lord.

"Whenever Manley was in the Memphis area, he would stay

with us. On one of those occasions, two local pastors asked to spend a little time with him, so we invited them over for breakfast. They were both having struggles in their ministry. After some small-talk Manley asked; *'Brothers, what seems to be going on?'* They both began telling him about the problems they were facing in their churches. When they had finished, Manley said: *'Well, what do you think the Lord is saying?'*

"One of them replied: *'I think that maybe the Lord just wants me to get out of the ministry; what do you think, Bro. Manley?'* Very matter-of-factly, Manley replied: *'You know, that's exactly what I think you ought to do.'* The pastor, a little shocked at Manley's response, said: *'Do you really think so?'* *'Yes sir. If you feel that you can leave the ministry, that is exactly what you should do, because if God has called you, you would not be able to do it.'* This changed the whole atmosphere of the conversation.

"Manley then began ministering to that pastor, explaining that if God had called him, he needed to recognize where the warfare was coming from and resist the attempts of the devil to discourage and defeat him. He needed to start believing what God said and not what the devil was saying. To God's glory, those two pastors walked out of our home that morning with their batteries recharged. Manley hadn't tried to give either of them a particular answer to what they thought their problems were, he just pointed them to Jesus.

"I will never forget what Manley told me when my first wife, Jonelle, was dying. God had not given him any specific word regarding her situation. He did know that what I needed to do was to die to the issue of whether she would be healed. He knew I needed to get to the point that whatever happened—life or death—I would be content with what God's will would be. *'God can heal her,'* he said, *'but you have to die to the issue.'* That gave me the hope I needed to realize that it was all God's business. Living or dying is God's business. As best I knew how, I took my hands off the situation and gave her to the Lord. Manley had a way of getting you into the presence of the Lord. So many people want a concrete answer. Bro. Manley would lead you to Jesus, where you could begin seeing things as He sees them.

"In Manley's style of preaching he would either give you the answer or the question. Rarely did he give you both. He wanted you to get alone with God. He was either objective or subjective, but he seldom was both. He made you dig to find out what God's answers really were. Whether the issue was salvation, something having to do with the walk of faith, or whatever you might be facing, he wanted you to get the answer from God. Most preachers ask the question and then give you the answer. That was not Manley's way."

Manley's Message

Having embraced God's word to us, having confessed it with our mouths, the stage is set for what I call the *fight of faith*. We must continue in it if we are going to see the invisible become visible. At this point we can define faith's activity as *acting as if it is so, when it is not so, in order for it to be so*!

The Fight of Faith

We sometimes falter or give up in converting divine truth into present reality. The fight of faith and its activity are extremely important. This is where our faith is tested and tried; it is here that we prove whether it is real. It must be tested in order for us to grow in faith. We are strengthened when we stand firm on the word God has given us. We continue to stand when the enemy tells us how much we are going to be embarrassed if we fail. We look beyond the circumstances to God's promise. In it we rest, knowing that faith is the unseen substance that assures us that the invisible is true. It is the receipt for what is reserved for us in the heavenlies.

As my body wasted away, my only hope was in accepting what God had said, as truth. I continued to call my circumstances a lie in view of what God had spoken to my heart in Chattanooga, TN. He told me that I would live to see my children's children. And as I thought about the great men of old and their walk with God, I realized that they too were tested in order that endurance might be produced in their lives.

Remember Jehoshaphat, King of Judah? He received word one day that a vast army of Moabites was approaching Jerusalem to destroy it. His own army was no match for the enemy's forces, so he proclaimed a fast throughout the land and gathered the people to seek the Lord. God responded with a word spoken by one of His prophets: *"Be not afraid nor dismayed by reason of this great multitude, for the battle is not yours, but God's"* (2 Chronicles 20:15).

This was a wonderful, encouraging word to know that the battle was in God's hands. For it to become reality, for the Moabites to be defeated, Jehoshaphat had to engage the enemy with his forces. He had to go and fight. Jehoshaphat was now so sure of victory that he sent a men's choir to lead the troops into battle. They led the way singing praises to God. And we know what they found when they got to the battlefield: the enemy had fought among themselves and had killed each other off. All Jehoshaphat had to do was take home the spoils. God performed what He had promised. The king had to act on what God said, in the face of all odds being against them.

Another example of this *fight of faith* is found in Exodus 17. We find Joshua's army in battle with the forces of Amalek. As long as Moses' hands were lifted up toward heaven, Joshua's forces were winning. But when his hands were lowered, his troops were in retreat. I learned from this that faith is a continuous action, not a once-for-all act. This was especially true since an immediate victory (the healing of my body) was not God's plan for me. I had to continue to take a stand and act on God's word. Every day a fresh stand even as the devil was there — every day — suggesting an alternative to trusting God.

So many other examples in Scripture encourage us to persevere in the *battle of faith*. We could talk about Abraham; we could look at Daniel; or we could watch Peter who as long as his faith was focused on his Master and not on the waves even the laws of nature were subject to what he was doing. Now we know that none of these men were free from problems. In the midst of their troubles they saw God as their source and chose to get in on His provision. When they saw it, they became persuaded of it; they embraced it; and they confessed it. They fought the fight of faith. As sure as day followed night, God performed what He had promised!

As I held fast to the promise God had made, looking beyond the circumstances to Him, the "angel of the Lord" got through and my body began to heal. I remember the doctors examining me — one with tears in her eyes, unable to explain what was happening. But I knew! I had received the report from the Great Physician, I had stayed in the battle, fighting the *fight of faith,* holding on to the word I had received. Though I still carry all the diseases in my body, God has raised me up. I am today alive by His life.

14
A View from the Inside

*"A good name is rather to be chosen than great riches, and
loving favor rather than silver and gold"*
(Prov. 22:1).

No one knows a person better than family, friends, and
work-associates. The vast majority of us only see or know "public personalities" from a distance. We are disappointed when we
do get to see behind the scenes and discover that the private life
of someone in the ministry does not live up to the image portrayed in public. Mack and Dottie Kearney served Manley and
the Beasley family for five years. They had as close a relationship to the "running" of the ministry and to the family as anyone could have had. Mack was Manley's associate in charge of
advance-meeting preparation, radio programming, publishing,
and other day-to-day responsibilities. Dottie was Manley's secretary/administrator of the Euless office in addition to being
available to help the Beasley family in a myriad of personal
ways. If anyone would be aware of what happened behind-the-scenes, they would be.

Dottie's Testimony

"Working with Bro. Manley was an experience that changed
our lives forever. We learned what it was to trust God in so
many ways. We have often referred to him as our 'Father in the
Faith.'

"When we first met Manley, it seemed as though those piercing dark eyes were looking right through us and that he knew everything about us. We felt that we needed to repent! That was often the effect he had on people. As Manley's secretary for five years I spent many hours in the office, working closely with him on ministry matters as well as assisting with Beasley family items. Working with someone whom God was using so powerfully is serious business. We also experienced those lighter moments. A side to Manley that few people saw was his being a prankster.

"This 'lighter-side' was expressed at the most unexpected moments. If he had arrived at the office before I did, when he heard me coming he would sometimes hide behind the wall in the hallway and the moment I stepped off the elevator jump out and make some awful noise that would scare me half to death. At other times, having retrieved a soft-drink can from the vending machine, he would approach my desk, vigorously shake the can, tap the top of it several times, hold it toward my face, then pop it open. I never failed to respond as he knew I would. Of course, the tapping of the can stopped the carbonation from exploding. That always worked except one time when he went through the routine. For some reason the can exploded and the drink went all over my paperwork, his invitations, the checkbooks, and other important things including the wall and the new carpet that had just been installed. I would have paid anything to have immortalized on film the look on his face that day.

"When God led us to sell our business to go and work with Manley, we took a step of faith. We understood that Mack would not be put on Gospel Harvester's payroll and that I would receive a small maintenance salary. As time passed, however, and our savings and home equity were exhausted, we found ourselves pressed into a walk of faith that we had not known to that point. Manley would later tell us that there were times when he had pleaded with God to let him help us, but the answer was always, *"No."* What we did not realize at the time was that God had us in a school of faith that was preparing us for the international ministry we would one day have. As I reflect back, I am so grateful for a servant who put aside his natural desire to help alleviate our financial burden in order to let God go on teaching a young couple how to trust Him.

"Then there were those periods when I would be left by myself to keep things going back at headquarters, while the rest of the team were 'out there' ministering across the land. It would get lonely and I would find myself longing to be part of the action. I remember how sensitive Manley was to this. One day he said to me, *'Dottie, this ministry is eternal, and every time you lick a stamp in this office, whenever you do anything to keep us going, you are ministering.'* Those words were precious to me. They have stuck with me throughout life. Manley genuinely felt that way.

"Invitations to minister were constantly arriving. He could have preached in several different churches every week of the year if he had had the strength to do so. Rather, he would read and spend time praying over each letter, asking God to give him wisdom as to where he should go. It was an enormous task and never far from his mind. And he was never too proud to seek counsel. He loved to bounce things off of you and let God speak to him through others. He had great respect for other ministries and never displayed any spirit of competitiveness that seems to be so prevalent today."

Mack's Testimony

"My first encounter with Bro. Manley was in 1977 through some of his sermon tapes given to me by a friend. I began to hear things on those cassettes that challenged almost everything I had been taught or believed as a Southern Baptist. A year later

Dottie and I heard him preach in a town not too far from Memphis, TN, where we lived and where I owned a successful advertising business. Following the service we were invited to join him and several others for dessert and coffee at his hotel. Manley had never laid eyes on me and didn't know a thing about me, so you can imagine how shocked I was when suddenly he said: *'When are you moving to Texas?'* After I caught my breath, I replied, *'I don't have any plans to move. Why?'* *'Well,'* he said, *'if God hasn't spoken to you, don't worry about it.'* I was confused. On our way home I said to Dottie: *'Someone needs to hang a sign on him, 'Rooms for Rent.'*

"Three months later we met again, this time in the house of a mutual friend in Memphis. To my amazement, Manley repeated that same question. I gave the same answer. He replied, *'If the Lord hasn't spoken to you, don't worry about it.'* Well, I did begin to wonder about it. I was sensing that the Lord was calling me to surrender to some kind of ministry, but I did not know what. I began to ponder what Manley had asked. The Lord brought me to the point of willingness to do whatever He wanted of me. Not long after that as I was driving down the road listening to a Stephen Olford broadcast on the radio, God spoke to me as clearly as anything I had ever heard: *'I want you to put Manley's ministry on the radio.'*

"About a month later Manley was back in Memphis for a meeting. He happened to be staying in the home of our mutual friend, Skeet May. One evening after the service Dottie and I were invited to drop by for fellowship. We went in fear and trembling. I prayed for the courage to tell Manley what I felt God was saying to me. Finally I blurted out, *'Bro. Manley, God has told me that we are to move to Texas and put your ministry on radio.'* I remember watching him as he sat on the fireplace hearth. What would his response be? Suddenly he leaped to his feet and started shouting and walking around the room. When he calmed down, he turned toward me and said: *'I have been asking God for two years to send me someone to put the ministry on radio. The first time I saw you six months ago God told me that you were the one. That's why I've kept asking you when you were going to move to Texas.'* One year later we had sold our house and business, moved to Bedford, TX, and entered a school of faith with the Lord and Bro. Manley as our instructors.

"*'What has God been saying to you lately?'* Manley asked over and over again. This was Manley's way of introducing me to one of the laws of faith, that you cannot trust God for any more than He has initiated in your life. How often I have heard him say: *'Find out what God is up to and join Him. When you know that God has given you a word, then go act on it!'* This was sometimes demonstrated in Manley's life in the simplest of situations, such as the time he and a friend were leaving their motel room to eat. Suddenly Manley felt impressed that they were not to take their wallets with them. His friend recalls how his own faith was being tested during the meal but, just as they finished eating, and the bill had been handed to them, a man, who recognized Manley from the past, walked up to their table and picked up the check.

"*'What are you trusting God for right now?'* This was another question that he not only asked others but one that God was continuously asking him. Manley would never settle for a generic answer, such as, *'I'm trusting God for everything.'* He wanted to know something specific that I was trusting God for; anything else was a cop out. How often through the years I have recalled his taking the time to teach me the importance of being specific with God. *'He already knows your need but He still wants you to take a step of faith and say, 'God, I am trusting you for...' then begin expecting it, to the point of looking for it.'*

"I remember Manley telling me that God proves, or tests a man, in the area of his life's message. He was always concerned that his own faith become passive. He felt that this was the reason God kept so many faith issues going on in his life, not the least of them being his health. He knew that every day was a gift from God. One of the other specific faith issues that Manley faced for years was the annual funding and facilitating of the European *International Congresses on Revival* to which hundreds of missionaries, pastors and leaders from Western Europe and Soviet Bloc countries came, at no expense to them. Each year these funds were prayed in. I likened it to a woman bringing forth a child. No one knew the intensity of travail that Manley went through, fully believing that whatever God initiated would not lack for finances to see it through to its completion.

"When Dottie and I sensed the Lord leading us to pursue an overseas ministry, Manley wrote the following word to us. *'The establishing of a ministry does not happen overnight. It takes years, so don't be discouraged. The establishing of a God-initiated ministry usually follows this order: First comes the burden, then the vision, then the fears and desires (crisis of belief), then the work, then the results, and this may take a prolonged time. May the Lord keep you in His arms and safely guide you through the storms.'"

And so another of the many branches of Manley Beasley's ministry tree was set in motion—branches and influences that have touched the world.

Interlude
Manley the Mystic

"Son, are you ready to learn about faith?"
"Oh. I'm ready. Count me in!"
"OK," Manley said. *"Let's take something pretty simple . . ."*

During Manley's Memorial Service brother-in-law Mike Gilchrest referred to Manley's relationship with God as being "almost mystical." Though such a statement may conjure up thoughts of reclusive individuals who spend most of their time in meditation, we ought not to be surprised that Manley should be described in this way. After all every true Christian is to some degree a mystic. The Apostle Paul, in his Epistles, refers fifteen times to the "mystery" of the Gospel and the Christian walk. Some like Paul live in a spiritual dimension that sets them apart from the run-of-the-mill mystic. Others of us, however, though believing in the unseen, relate more to that which can be seen, touched, tasted, smelled, or heard with the physical senses than to those things that are unseen.

Every generation has had its notable mystics. Among those we could list from the past are Bernard of Clairvaux, St. Augustine, Brother Lawrence or Madame Guyon. In more recent generations some would include Watchman Nee, A.W. Tozer, and others who lived on a plain that not all their contemporaries understood or reached. In the historic sense, Manley Beasley was such a mystic. In his pursuit of God, in his walk of faith, and in his prayer life he set a standard that not only challenged but inspired his generation to higher heights and deeper depths in their walk with God. Some things in Manley's life and ministry can only be explained in terms of the *mystery of divine activity.*

Contrary to common belief, mysticism's primary focus is not on mystical "experiences," but rather on a lasting experience of God that leads to a consistent, gradual transformation of the life into the likeness of Christ. The Christian mystic aspires to understand spiritual truths that are inaccessible through intellectual means, as we find addressed in Scriptures such as 1 Corinthians 15:50-58, where the Apostle Paul says: *"Behold, I tell you a mystery . . .."* (vs. 51), or in Galatians 2:20 where he talks about his being crucified with Christ and that he was no longer alive but it was Christ living in him, or, Ephesians 6:19-20 where he asks for prayer that he might boldly make known the mystery of the Gospel. Other passages such as Colossians 4:2-4; 1 Timothy 3:16; II Peter 1:3-9; 1 John 3:1-3, all address the individual writer's desire for a complete identification with Christ, a unity of the human spirit with the Spirit of God. This is, of course, what all believers should be reaching for, but not too many attain, at least to the degree that God desires we should attain.

This zealous pursuit of God, however, has always had its dangers. Sometimes it has led to extremes, such as in the case of Madame Guyon, who ended up embracing the teachings of "Quietism," the doctrine of "sinless perfection," a falsehood that has raised its head in every generation under one disguise or another. Pushing the envelope too far was true during Manley's days of ministry. He saw this happen to several of his contemporary "mystics". In their pursuit of God, Manley felt they got caught up in "extra-scriptural" experiences. It needs to be said, however, that in spite of differences of convictions, these differences never did affect Manley's care for, and love toward those friends with whom he disagreed, or whose actions he might not have been able to endorse.

Reflecting on mysticism in his sermon, *"What Difference Does the Holy Spirit Make?"* A. W. Tozer made this observation: "Some of my friends good-humoredly—and some a bit severely—have called me a mystic. Well, I'd like to say this about any mysticism I am supposed to have. If an arch-angel from heaven were to come and were to start teaching me, giving me instruction, I'd ask him for the text. I'd say: *'Where does it say that in the Bible? I want to know.'* **I would insist that it was according to the Scriptures, because I do not believe in any extra-scriptural teachings nor any anti-scriptural teachings. I think we ought to put the emphasis where God puts it, and to continue to put it there, and to expound the Scriptures and stay by the Scriptures.** No matter if I saw a light above the sun, I'd keep my mouth shut about it. I'd check it out with Daniel and Revelation and the rest of Scripture to see if it had any basis in truth. And if it didn't, I'd think I had just eaten something I shouldn't have, and I wouldn't say anything about it."

If not continuously guided and guarded by the straight line of Scripture, anyone can be led into extremes or even error. Manley never strayed from what he considered to be the straight line of truth. The Bible was his plumb line for everything he believed. He then became an anchor to many who may have been tempted to take a detour.

In addressing in one of his sermons the issue of extremes, Manley said: *"All truth has a balance. To get out of balance is to be in error.* **Error is truth out of balance, and the confusing thing to 'onlookers' is that there often is some Scriptural basis for what they see happening, so they think that it must be authentic."** Dr. Stephen Olford used to explain it this way: *"Many 'extra-scriptural' experiences begin with the straight* *line of truth that is pushed a little bit for emphasis. But then, when you push it a bit more you get into extremism, and when you keep pushing it you end up in error."*

In the words of Ron Dunn: *"Manley never sounded an uncertain note in his preaching. People would ask me, 'Have you talked to Bro. Manley about this or that? What do you think he would say?' I'd reply, 'No, I haven't talked to him and I don't have to talk to him. He is at the same place he was last year; he's at the same place he was ten years ago; you don't have to keep updating your theology with Manley Beasley. The man has found the truth and he is safe in it.' I am eternally grateful that God raised up that man to preach. You never had to take a sur-veying apparatus to find out what he was believing."*

One of Manley's "behind the scenes" ministries that meant so much to him was pouring his life into young men who were in the early stages of their ministry. From time to time he would invite a "Timothy" to travel with him for up to a year at a time. Those who were given this opportunity would soon discover that this was not going to be any ordinary experience, but rather, an "on the road" seminary training in the life and walk of faith. One of these young men was Steve Graves. [14]

Traveling with a Mystic

"In the summer, between my freshman and sophomore years in college, I was invited to serve as interim youth director at a church in Memphis, TN, where Manley was scheduled to lead a fall 'revival.' When I arrived I discovered that the entire staff had resigned. I found myself with the responsibility of heading up the ministry of this church. In spite of the staff having resigned, however, Manley decided to keep his commitment to those people. I didn't know what to expect, though I had heard about him through several Mississippi College friends who had begun reading some of his writings.

"About the third night of the meeting, when we were in the elevator of his hotel, he turned to me and said: *'Son, what are you trusting God for, that if God doesn't come through your life would be sunk?'* I said, *'Excuse me?'* He repeated the question. As I had never been asked a question like that before, I needed a moment to think before replying. I finally said: *'In all candor, I'm not trusting God for anything like that.'* He said, *'I know. I just wanted to see whether you would own up to it. Few people are really trusting God for much of anything these days, but they won't admit it.'* I soon began to realize that I was with a man who was living on a spiritual plane that I knew nothing about.

"Right in the middle of his first message that week he stopped. *'Hold it. Hold it,'* he said. He then just stood there looking over the congregation. *'Two women in this church have been fighting with each other for years. You have been hurting this church. Before we can go on with this meeting you both need to repent and get right with each other. We are going to wait here until it happens.'*

'What on earth?' I thought. We waited for a few minutes, but nothing happened. So Manley sat down right in the middle of his sermon. I began looking around and thinking that this sure was not going to be your typical revival. I had already been made aware of this problem in the church but had not mentioned a word to Manley about it. He couldn't have known, other than the Lord's speaking to him about the situation. And so we waited, and waited, and waited.

"Finally I heard someone coming down the aisle. It was one of the church secretaries, the very one I knew was half of the problem. A few moments later the other woman walked to the front. There she and the secretary knelt at the altar. Many in the church knew how destructive their relationship had been. This was the beginning of a work of God that led to repentance and a spirit of brokenness throughout that congregation.

"At the end of the week Manley asked me what I was going to be doing for the next year. I told him of my plans to return to college. He said: *'Why don't you just take off and travel with me for a while?'* After some thought and prayer I felt that this was what I should do, little realizing how exciting and life-changing the next twelve months were going to be. It began on our very first trip as we were flying from Dallas to Colorado. Manley turned to me and said:

'Son, are you ready to learn about faith?'

'Oh, I'm ready. Count me in!'

'OK,' he said. *'Let's take something pretty simple. Why don't you sit there and talk to God while I sit here and talk to God, and we'll ask Him what the love-offering is going to be at the end of the week.'*

I said, *'What? What do you mean?'*

He said: *'Don't you think that God knows what the love-offering is going to be?'*

'Well, yeah.'

'God knows numbers, doesn't He?'

'Well . . .'

"He then went through a very elementary, remedial explanation of one aspect of faith that helped me understand what he was talking about. Then he said, *'Get a couple pieces of paper, give me one and you take one, and when you believe you know what God is going to provide for you this week, write it down, and I will do the same.'* Now, he's over there somewhere between, what looked like to me, sleeping and staring out the window, while I get out my calculator and began figuring the average giving of approximately 600 people a night over a six-day period. I was everywhere, all over the map in my figuring what I might receive in my personal love-offering envelopes. About ten minutes later he says: *"You got it?"* I said; *'I'm getting close.'* It was then that I began to learn that in the midst of his deep walk with God, he also had a sense of humor. I heard him chuckle as he took a pen and wrote a figure on his piece of paper. When I had written mine down, he said: *'Put these in an envelope, seal it, and at the end of the week, when we are on our way home, we will open it and see what God has done.'* I must admit that all week long I found myself continuing to calculate what I thought my offering was going to be.

"As the meetings were coming to an end, Manley asked the pastor to consider giving us the love-offering check before we left, though normally a church would wait a few days in order to include any late giving before sending the total amount on to Manley's office. Manley said: *'I'm trying to teach my boy here something about faith.'* The pastor said; *'No problem. We will go ahead and give you your checks.'* As the pastor was writing out the checks, after the final service, one of the deacons came in with an additional check for $100.00 which the pastor just signed over to Manley.

"To say that I was anxious to see what the love-offering was is putting it mildly. When we got back to the motel, we opened the envelope in which we had placed our figures, and then the envelope that contained the checks. My number was nowhere near what I had received, but Manley's check was to the penny, which included the last minute check for $100.00. There was no way that this could have been engineered. I learned that Manley knew what his needs were. He took them to God. He believed God was going to meet them even to the penny. This was my introduction to a level of faith that to this day—as I look back on that year—still is a part of the "mystery" of Manley's walk with God.

"Among the many other learning experiences I had during those twelve months was one that took place in his home where I would sometimes lay over between meetings. I was accustomed to hearing him pray (he usually prayed out loud) in the wee hours of the morning, but this particular night I was awakened by his talking on the phone. I looked at the clock. It was 2 AM. I slipped into the den to listen. I had learned that the Lord had lessons to teach me through Manley at the strangest of times.

"Though I could only hear one side of the conversation, I was beginning to pick up that the call was from a foreign country and that the caller had a significant financial need. I then heard Manley say: *'Give me a number where I can reach you and stay right there by the phone. I'll call you back within the hour.'*

"After he had hung up, he quickly briefed me on the situation. A young minister friend of his was in South America where crusade meetings were being set up, stadium contracts signed, and commitments made. At the last minute the party who had promised to underwrite most of the expenses had had to back out. This friend of Manley's was left holding the bag.

"Then I found myself listening in on a conversation between Manley Beasley and God. He talked out loud, he waited silently, he talked again, then he picked up the phone. As long as I live, I will never forget the next thing I heard Manley say: *'Son, you're not in any condition to be able to trust God to meet this need, so I want you to get on the bus with me and ride on my faith. Get on the bus and ride on my faith. God has shown me that He is going to provide everything you will need.'*"

Many observed the activity of God in Manley's life and ministry from a distance, as they watched him fight the battle of faith and overcome the many trials he faced through the years. The real *mystery of God's activity* in Manley's life and ministry, however, was only observed by those who were privileged to walk closely with him. Many of the things he did or experienced would not be known to us today if it were not for the testimonies of those who "were there" such as one of the battles of faith he waged one night when he received the news that on top of all his other physical challenges his kidneys were failing. This meant he would have to go on dialysis for the rest of his life.

Doubt Is not Sin

"Son, you got to see and hear something last night that folks don't get to see . . .."

Harry Layden was leading the music in a March 1987, "revival" at Immanuel Baptist Church in Enid, OK. Harry picks up the story:

"I had an adjoining room with Manley at the motel. I would leave the door open when we retired, just in case he would need me during the night. This particular night I observed something that really shook me. Manley had just received the news that his kidneys were only functioning at 9% and that he was going to have to go on dialysis. I saw it in his face; I heard it in the tone of his voice—he was questioning God. All night long he struggled with why God would allow this to happen to him. Here was this great man of faith doubting God.

He called me into his room early the next morning. He looked like he'd been through a battle, which in truth he had. He said: *"Son, you got to see and hear something last night that folks don't get to see—you watched me doubt God.'* I listened. *"I want this to be a lesson for you, that doubt is not a sin—it is a legitimate place where a believer may end up. It is a place where you are faced with having to either believe a lie about your circumstances or the truth of God's Word. Once God quickens the truth to your heart, you respond in faith; you turn from your doubt. **Doubt is not sin—staying there is sin."***

SECTION FOUR
Dealing with Adversity

The adversity that God chose to use primarily as a teaching tool in the life of Manley Beasley was physical sickness. For almost twenty years he lived with seven diseases, three of them terminal. The lessons God taught Manley during those years, and the scriptural truths that became a part of the very fiber of his life, are applicable not only to physical illnesses but to every kind of adversity a believer will ever face.

Other than at times he visited, Manley's stay at the Methodist Hospital in the Texas Medical Center in Houston in 1971 marked the first time he was in a hospital since his birth almost forty years earlier. Behind him were years of Kingdom service—years of faithfully preaching across the land, years of being mightily used of God, years that now seemed to be abruptly coming to an end due to physical diseases that initially no one could even diagnose. How would he manage it? What was he going to do?

At the time no one realized that this was not the beginning of the end for one of God's faithful servants. Instead it was the first piece of a mosaic that, when completed, would portray the picture of a life of faith lived in the presence of death. It depicted the glory of God pressing through a broken, yielded vessel.

This section, *Dealing with Adversity,* contains the heart of what Manley preached and taught during those years of testing. These were truths that deal with the reality of *affliction,* a reality that many of God's children are facing today.

> *Without the boiling process a teabag's of no use,*
> *But when immersed, its flavor is released.*
> *That's how it is with our lives, should God increase the heat,*
> *Our usefulness for Him will be increased.*[15]

15
Count It All Joy

(part one)

"Lord, thou dost show thy power by my frailty, so that the more feeble I am, the more fit to be used, for thou dost pitch a tent of grace in my weakness. Help me to rejoice in my infirmities and give thee praise, to acknowledge my deficiencies before others and not be discouraged by them, that they may see thy glory more clearly."

— A Puritan's prayer [16]

When Manley first became ill, God impressed on him that he would be given two options:

1. the miracle of physical healing, or
2. the miracle of being kept alive by the life of God.

Knowing his own heart and the danger of becoming prideful in what God would have done—or having the passage of time diminish the wonder of God's miracle of healing—he chose the second option. He chose to be kept alive by the life of his Creator. He knew that this would keep him constantly dependent on God for the very breath he breathed.

Manley knew that life's greatest lessons are learned in the school of adversity. So rather than asking God for deliverance from his affliction, he trusted God for the grace to live victoriously in his affliction. During those years of living in the presence of death, the resurrection life of his Lord was so manifested that it touched the lives of countless others. One of those was Ron Dunn, as we see in the following interview held in 1989, twelve months before Manley's home-going.

An Interview

Ron: "I first met you in 1972 at the Southern Baptist Convention in Philadelphia, PA. You had just been released from the hospital in Houston. When they wheeled you into the room where a number of us had gathered, my first thought was, *'this man is about to die, if he hasn't died already.'* You barely could raise your head. I shall never forget the very first thing you said to us: *'Folk, God won't hurt you.'* Do you remember that?"

Manley: "Yes I do."

Ron: "What I want to ask you now is; what did you mean by that? It sure looked as though you were hurting. Personally, I was going through a period when I thought God was killing me."

Manley: *"At the time of suffering it may seem that God is hurting you, but when you have passed through that valley of suffering and are able to look back, you see the benefits of it all. You literally forget the pain.* You realize that as you have been able to turn adverse situations over to Him you have learned the purposes He has in them for you.

Ron: "Are you saying that at the time of the trial there may not be anything but darkness and confusion, but once you are through it, you can see what God intended and that it was for your good? The reason I ask this is that many of us, when we are in the midst of suffering, feel such desolation and despair that we're not sure God is anywhere around."

Manley: "True. In spite of how we feel, we must hold on to some facts about God. One of these is that God is in charge. He is always aware of what we are going through. What is happening to us is limited by Him, according to His will and purpose. But even this may not always keep you from a point of despair. The last time I was hospitalized I hurt so badly that I would cry. That was when I found myself in a battle between the emotions of doubt and despair and the promise of God's Word. I had to hold on by faith in spite of my feelings."

Ron: "In other words, there is a deeper issue in this besides whether or not you feel good, or whether or not you even live."

Manley: "Yes. *The most unique point in this matter of suffering is that there is always the 'God-ultimate purpose,' which is to correct us and enlarge us and bring us through for His glory.* The Apostle Paul reached an understanding of the ultimate purpose of God, as did Job, and this happened as God enlarged their capacity through suffering to understand His purposes. Job was able to discover this as he went from the hearing of the ear to the seeing of the eye."

Ron: "You first began getting ill in 1970 and since then you have had many near-death experiences. I understand that this past year has been the worst ever. Has your attitude toward suffering changed from the first time you became ill? What about your attitude during what you have recently been through? What I am trying to say is that it is easy for us to form certain opinions about suffering if we haven't done much of it. After being in the crucible for some time, our beliefs change, our praying is different. Do you pray differently now than when you prayed the first time you got sick?"

Manley: 'Oh yes. I pray differently now because I am not ignorant of what God is up to. Now, I don't ask God what is going on, I just say, *'Lord, I know you are doing a work. I want to cooperate with you.'* Yes, I have changed somewhat, but I have not really changed in my views about God and healing, I just react differently. The first time I struggled with death both physically and spiritually. This time I struggled with death physically but not in my spirit. You have to realize that most people never face death but once. I have faced death every day for almost twenty years. My ideas about life and death have matured over the years. I am conscious that I am supposed to be dead. I could be dead. If it were not for the sustaining life of God, I would be dead today."

Ron: "Obviously, what you are saying is that the greater issue is the glory of God. So, tell me: do you think that God is glorified in a greater way than if He had instantly and totally healed you?"

Manley: "That is a good question, Ron. In the early days of my illness God spoke clearly to me that I could be healed if I asked Him to heal me, or that I could stay as I was and have to trust Him to keep me alive every day. I made a deliberate choice to trust Him to sustain me on a day-to-day basis because I knew that if He had healed me instantaneously, it would not be long before His miracle would be something in the past, something that would grow dimmer and dimmer. I chose to have to depend on Him every day rather than have an experience that ten years later I would forget. This way I can't forget because I have to depend on Him for a miracle today."

Ron: "So, when you preach today, you are not talking about something that happened years ago but something that happened this morning when you got up. In other words, you are not just proclaiming truth, you yourself are the proclamation. People like me are ministered to by you just as much by the miracle of your still being alive today as we are by what you say."

Manley: "I have come to the realization that my life is as much the message as what I say is. I am finding that sometimes when I am helped to the pulpit that people will stand and applaud. At times I have wanted to rebuke them. Then the Lord rebuked me by showing me that they were not clapping for me but they were clapping for what the Lord was doing in me by just keeping me alive. It is for Him.

Ron: "This brings me to a very important question; does God have to take us through suffering, of one degree or another, in order to really use us for His glory?"

Manley: "I don't find anything in the Bible that says a person must go through a time of brokenness and suffering in order to be used of the Lord. My conviction is that it is probable. The examples we have in Scripture of those who were greatly used of God were folk who went through some kind of breaking. I say some kind of breaking because it would be very foolish of me to suggest that the only suffering that God uses is physical, because for some, emotional trauma is as great a suffering as anyone would want to experience.

Then there is what I call the trauma of environmental activity such as finances or family. This kind of trauma can actually lead to emotional brokenness and even physical suffering. I also believe that suffering can be God's answer to a desire or prayer on the part of a Christian who wants, no matter what it will cost, to go deeper with God—to know Him more fully even though they do not know what valley they may have to go through. God sees the desire of that heart and allows certain things to happen that will conform that child more into the likeness of Christ than anything else could.

Ron: "When you were recently released from the hospital, I phoned you from Georgia. You told me a little bit about what was going on, then you made a statement that has intrigued me. You said: *'God has shown me some things that I don't think people are going to want to hear.'* Now I know that you get many calls from hurting people all across the country who want to talk with you because they know *'you have been there.'* Do you find, however, that many of these are really wanting a simplistic answer rather than the truth?"

Manley: "Ron, this is perhaps the most difficult thing for me to communicate at this time. I am still trying to put together the things that the Lord has shown me. Some things I know in my spirit that I do not yet understand in my mind. Until I do understand, I can't really pass on what I know. Months later, I am still in the process of understanding what I know. This last time in the hospital they tell me that I literally died six times. My heart stopped beating and I stopped breathing. When they told me this, I wondered why God did not show me heaven like I understand others have experienced when they were supposed to have died. I asked the Lord about that and three weeks ago He showed me that if I had seen heaven I would not have wanted to come back. That's a simple but factual answer.

"Sometimes, however, answers are not that simple. I sense that when some people call me, they either are looking for healing or an aspirin kind of answer—you take it and in a few minutes the headache is gone. That way the purpose God has for the suffering would be totally lost. You see, suffering is a vehicle that God uses to teach us. When God does show you some revelation of Himself, suffering keeps you from exalting yourself. It keeps you humble. I think that was at least part of the reason for Paul's suffering. Paul had received so many heavenly revelations from God that he could have become important in his own eyes, so God kept him humble through suffering.

"Some of what I believe the Lord has shown me is that what I have just been through has been a preparation for God to be seen more distinctly through my life and circumstances than ever before. He desires that people see the sufficiency of His provision both physically, in keeping me alive, and in other ways. Let me explain: My financial needs for this past year, including my hospital bill, were about $800,000. I would never have thought that I would be prepared to face such a difficult time financially. God's people gave in a proper way, I was able to trust Him, and the insurance policies stayed intact, which was in itself a miracle.

"Now let me come at this from another angle. I recently received a call regarding a young man who was about to have a tumor removed from his brain. They asked me to pray. After the surgery, which was not fully successful, they called again to ask if it would be alright for this person to talk to me himself. This young man was one of America's outstanding 'Revivalists.' Knowing that he was going to call and that he had now been given at the most only several months to live, I said: *'Lord, what am I going to say to this young man who is in the prime of life and at the height of his ministry?'* The Lord said: *'Son, I have been preparing you for years to talk to him. You don't have to come up with anything new. You have already experienced what you need to say.'*

"The phone rang. *'Bro. Manley, what do you do when you are told that you have only a few months to live?'* Though my answer may have sounded simplistic, at its heart is the very essence of what we are discussing. I said: *'What you do is simply trust Jesus to be your life.'* He said: *'I'm not sure I completely understand what you are saying. Will you explain?'* I said: *'When I and my family were faced with a doctor's report that I would not live past noon, we did the only thing that we knew to do. That was to place my life in God's hands; to trust Him. I didn't hear any bells ringing or experience anything unusual. I just trusted Him to do that which would bring Him the most glory. And that's what I am still doing every day.'*

"Ron, when you called me from Georgia and I said what I did, I was trying to understand to a higher level what God is saying in this matter of His glory. When you get to the place of being able to say, *'Lord, whichever it is, life or death, just as long as You get glory,'* then you have placed yourself totally at His disposal, and actually, whichever way it goes, for you it is life. There is a freedom here that only comes from trusting God that way—freedom from worry, freedom from care, freedom from substance, freedom from death.

"There is something that I have had to cope with over the years, however. Though I have never considered myself a spiri-

147

tual man, having to admit that God has had to give me the kind of *thorn in the flesh* that He has, to keep me down, to keep me humble, has been an issue with me. But God has been allowing me to see that He has had to do this in order that He might be glorified. This has given me great comfort. For instance, before you arrived today I was in such pain that I hardly knew how to deal with it, except to say, *'God, you deal with it.'* Now, as we sit here talking, I am totally unconscious of any pain whatsoever. So pain is not the issue. With many, however, if not with most, pain, suffering, adversity, finances, problems of all kinds, are still the issue. Thank God He has faithfully brought me to the point where I no longer see my problems that way. The issue is His glory. God's purpose in my adversity is using it to get glory to Himself.

"Ron, this is really not what most people want to hear, so I find it difficult to get this across. I am dealing with people who have very, very serious problems, but when I tell them that their suffering is their friend, they don't want to hear that. *Many see their adversity as the activity of the devil. They don't seem to understand that the only way the enemy can be involved is when God uses him as the messenger boy.* I find it hard to get this across to people these days. We have to believe that God is working things out for His purpose. We must let Him bring us to this point of trust so He can use our circumstances as opportunities to express His glory. I hope I have made myself plain."

Ron: "A little bit too plain, perhaps. Are you saying then, that as long as we believe it is the devil, we're not there yet, but when we accept the fact that God is in charge, this is what makes the difference? Am I hearing you say that, when we do ultimately come to that point of trust, our primary motive will not be to get rid of our problem, whereas, if we do not see the problem from God's perspective, our motive is going to be to get rid of it?"

16

Count It All Joy

(part two)

"God is not trying to take you out of your troubles,
He is trying to teach you how to act in them."

—F.J. Huegel [17]

A Testimony

"One of my best friends, Manley Beasley, died in 1990. I guess the only thing that surprised us is that he lived as long as he did. Stricken by numerous diseases in 1970, three of them terminal, Manley spent the next twenty years on life-support systems, both of the medical and spiritual kind. Jesus literally became his life. In Manley's words, he was alive by His life. There must have been a dozen or more times when Manley came to the brink of death only to come back, stronger than before. I remember going to the hospital at least six times to say goodbye to him because the doctors said he wouldn't make it through the night. I said to him once, *'You're the hardest man to say goodbye to I've ever known.'* Yet in spite of his physical condition he carried on a worldwide ministry and taught thousands what it means to walk by faith."

—Ron Dunn [18]

The Interview Continues

Manley: "Ron, the answer to the question you asked about the difference in seeing a problem from our personal perspective and seeing it from God's perspective is not easy for people to accept. Let me answer with an illustration. A lady with a termi-nal illness called one day to say that she and her husband would like to see me. They were a missionary couple. I knew they were wanting me to pray for her healing. We set an appointment for their visit. For the next several days I prayed, asking God what I was to do when we met. The first thing I was impressed to ask when they arrived was, *'Why do you think you are ill?'* She said, *'I really don't know.'* I said, *'Have you thought that if you did know why you are ill, that you might not want to be instant-ly healed?'* Now, this is a very hard matter to consider but it gets to the bottom of the issue of adversity in a believer's life.

"This is what I am trying to say: Even though the enemy may deliver the adversity to your door, whatever it may be, that is no sign that God is not involved. He is not only aware of it, but He has allowed it. His purpose for it is to display His glory. Now, if God chooses not to show me why He has sent it, He is saying, 'Child, just trust me.'"

Ron: "Someone asked me one time about Abraham's age when God tested him regarding his sacrificing Isaac. He was old and had already been through so much. I thought about that in relation to you, Manley; not particularly the age factor, but all that God has put you through since 1970. Some of us might say that surely you have suffered enough. Why doesn't God leave you alone for awhile? Do we tend to think in this way because we feel that we can finally get to the point where we have learned all there is to learn or that we have given all that we should have to give?"

Manley: "When we think that way, Ron, it shows a lack of understanding of Scripture. The word "temptation" is used many times in the Bible, but when people think of that word they see it only as it relates to an enticement to do evil. Hebrews 3 refers to the wanderings of God's children in the wilderness as being a time of "temptation." As you study Scripture, however, you discover that the three words temptation, trials, and testings, have a two-fold purpose and meaning. One reason for testings is for what they will do in and for us personally, as God uses them to expose our own wickedness and to correct us. *Another reason for testings is for what they will do in the lives of others, as they watch and learn from what God is allowing in our own lives.* The test that Abraham faced—and passed—was not just for him but others, including us today. It was the greatest test he would ever face, as it touched both the physical and spiritual realms. What he was called on to do contradicted the promises of God for both Abraham's physical and spiritual descendants, but he was able to see beyond the moment and look across time to see the *Lamb of God.* Jesus confirmed this in John 8 when He said, *'He rejoiced to see my day!'* It took serious adversity in Abraham's life to teach us the lessons we are still learning today.

Ron: "I guess what bothers me about all this is that I would like to reach that point of total abandoned trust, but the way there is not easy. In my own walk in this area I've sometimes found that the pain, or circumstances, make it difficult for me to get hold of God. I've even had the feeling of being abandoned. Did you ever feel that way, and if you did, at what point were you able to get beyond thinking primarily of the pain and the suffering.?"

Manley: "There were two hospitalizations during which I recall facing a crisis of belief similar to what you are talking about. The first one was when I was in a Houston hospital for four months, and the other happened in 1988 when I was in a hospital in Dallas for almost six months. In both cases I experienced periods when I felt God had forsaken me. I then remembered Jesus, how His Father turned His back on Him as He was bearing our sins in His body on the cross. This reminder of the struggle my Lord had was the help I needed. I believe the abandonment that Jesus felt was both physical and spiritual. In His humanity He was experiencing the excruciating pain of the cross. In His deity he was experiencing the forsaking of His Father who was having to turn His back on His Son due to the sin of the world He was bearing. This, of course, was on a God-level, but lessons still exist for us to learn from it.

"For us, I believe the sense of abandonment comes from two sources; from God withdrawing His conscious presence so that we have to learn to walk by faith, without any feeling. The other is because our spirit is like the sea. Let me explain. When our spirit—that I'm picturing as a sea—is calm, you can drop a hair on it and it will cause a tiny ripple. If our spirit, however, is disturbed; if our emotions or our environment is in turmoil, it is like a storm at sea in which you could drop a ship in it and it would not make a ripple that anyone would notice. When our spirit is not quiet, when we are not at rest, we cannot hear the voice of God. He has to get us to a point of stillness and calm before He can really speak to us. Then when He does, the victory is there, even though the suffering may get more intense."

Ron: "This brings a lot of thoughts and questions to mind. Though it is scary to think of God withdrawing His conscious presence from us, it helps to see it in the context of our Lord's own experience. So many of us have the attitude that if our lives are right with God, then we are always going to feel His presence. What you have said also helps me understand that perhaps the deepest part of pain is not so much the physical suffering but the sense of being separated and abandoned by God."

Manley: "That is definitely the most serious pain that we can suffer, yet this is all a part of God's teaching us how to walk by faith—faith, in the midst of adversity; faith, when the feeling is not there; faith, when everything looks as though God has forgotten you, even as Job and Joseph experienced."

Ron: "To know that you, Manley, have gone through what

many of us go through has been a great encouragement to me. It's an encouragement because, when we look at you, when we hear you preach and teach about faith, we think, *"Oh, how we wish we had the faith of Manley Beasley who never has to experience what we do."* Forgive me for referring again to the phone call I made to you from Georgia when you had just been dismissed from the hospital, but I need to tell you this. I have never felt the Spirit of God coming through a phone line like I did that day. When I hung up, I was in tears. Then after Kaye and I had talked about the things you had shared, I said to her: *'I'm so glad that I have not had to go through all the things that Manley has had to go through.'* And, no sooner had I spoken those words, I realized that, in essence, I had just said that I was so glad that I was not as close to God as Manley Beasley was."

Manley: "I prayed a prayer several years ago, Ron, that God is still answering. I asked Him to help me never to think of myself as a 'somebody,' because I never want to stop growing. I want to stay hungry, I want to keep walking with Him and be willing to let Him discipline me as He delights; to be ready to be taken through the measure of affliction that will most glorify Him. That way He will be able to keep using me, but the moment I begin thinking I have arrived, it will be over."

Ron: "It is a blessing and encouragement to those of us who have watched you over the years, to see how you have responded to adversity. We have seen that, rather than being limited by suffering, God has used it to expand your ministry beyond anything that you could have imagined."

Manley: "So many miss the truth that God wants us to complete, or as Paul puts it in Colossians 1:24, *'fill up that which is behind of the afflictions of Christ in my (our) flesh for his body's sake, which is the church.'* If the Father would have His Son learn obedience through the things that He suffered, how can we think that we should be immune from it?"

Ron: "Thank you, Manley, but I do have one more question to ask: *Has it been worth it?*

Manley: "If I had a thousand lives to live and I knew that I had to go through the suffering I have experienced with each of them, I would offer them all to my Lord to do with them as He would choose. To have the peace of God that comes from knowing that He already has provided the victory, no matter what may be delivered to our door is all the assurance we need. Yes, it has been worth it, Ron, and I do, *count it all joy!"*

17
Turning Adversity
into Blessing

*"Faith does not always take you out of the storm;
faith calms you in the storm."*
—Manley Beasley

Dear Manley,

As my wife and I visited with you in New Orleans at the Southern Baptist Convention last month, we knew in our spirits we would never see you again this side of heaven. We were saddened, yet envious of your home-going. *"And after you have suffered for a little while,"* as we read in 1 Peter 5:10, the God of all grace . . . called you to His eternal glory. What God began in grace, He has completed in glory.

You have taught so many, so much. You have shown us that merely coping with adversity simply is not enough. You taught us through your life how to live victoriously in our trials. You have reminded us that any religion will do in days of prosperity but only Jesus suffices in days of adversity. We have learned through your life that we walk by faith and not by sight. You have shown us literally how to live by faith. Thank you for being there to encourage my wife through her catastrophic illness. You taught us how to lay hold of the precious promises of God granted to us so that we can be full partakers of God's divine nature. Now you walk by sight and not by faith. Now you see face to face, whereas until recently you saw in a mirror dimly.

Most of all, thank you for speaking to so many of us through your life as you allowed Jesus to live in and through you in the midst of pain, inconvenience, and chronic illness. These liabilities became your assets and were channels through which the very life of Jesus flowed, for you always carried about in your body the dying of Jesus that the life of Jesus also might be manifested through you. Though death worked in you, life worked in us. We will miss you until we see you in heaven.

Dr. Bob Bender, [19] pastor,
First Baptist Church, Black Forest, CO

Every family has its challenges, whether they are financial, physical, or spiritual. The Beasley household was no exception. For close to twenty years, not only did Manley live with his "thorn in the flesh"—three terminal diseases plus an array of other complications due to his *Connective Tissue Disease* condition—but the whole family lived with it. It was always there. They never knew when the next hospitalization might be necessary, whether or not another spell in *Intensive Care* was just around the corner, how many meetings would have to be cancelled, or where the money would come from to meet their needs. All this was just a part of life—a part of the lives of a father, a mother, and four children; a part of the Beasley family.

How did they make it? By God's grace. Some days faith would be tested to what might seem the extreme. It was during these "battles of faith" that the roots of Manley's trust in God and His promises were growing deeper and deeper. And this was not lost on a watching family, as is witnessed by Manley Jr., the eldest son, who for several years worked alongside his father in the ministry.

A Testimony

"God privileged our family with the unique blessing of having unrestricted access to my Dad over the years. Though he was not physically well for much of that time, we knew we always had his ear. His counsel and life-lessons greatly influenced us children. Then eventually I had the added blessing of having a ministry relationship with him. During those days I recall my Dad returning over and over again to 2 Corinthians 4:7.

"*'We have this treasure in earthen vessels that the surpassing greatness of the power may be of God and not from ourselves'* (NASB). In a day when the emphasis seems so often to be on polishing vessels, on how we appear, on charisma and human ability, he constantly reminded me that the issue is the *treasure within the vessel.* Dad was always very gracious to fellow ministers of the Gospel, but he did not have a lot of regard for men who stooped to the world's methods. He believed that the vessel was designed to contain a treasure and that treasure was the Lord Jesus. *'Son,'* he would say. *'You are not what this world needs. The treasure in you is what it needs.'* My dad never compromised the truth of this principle.

"In verse 8 we read, *'We are afflicted in every way but not crushed, perplexed but not despairing; persecuted but not forsaken; struck down but not destroyed, always carrying about in the body the dying of Jesus that the life of Jesus may also be manifested in our body. For we who live are constantly being delivered over to death for Jesus' sake, that the life of Jesus also may be manifested in our mortal flesh. So death works in us, but life in you...knowing that he who raised the Lord Jesus will raise us also with Jesus and will present us with you . . ..'* (NASB)

"Dad taught me that trials are a necessary part of the life of a Christian if God's glory is going to be revealed. He taught me that the only way the treasure is going to be exposed is when the

157

vessel is broken. This is not a popular teaching in our day when so much of today's church demonstrates an unwillingness to be broken. Among the last messages my father preached was one from Revelation 3 that talks about the gold being refined by fire. In his last days he expressed to me his concern that most people are just not willing to pay that kind of price.

"In verse 16 of the fourth chapter of 2 Corinthians, Paul goes on to say: '*Therefore, do not lose heart, and though our outer man is decaying yet our inner man is being renewed day by day. For the momentary light affliction is producing for us an eternal weight of glory, far beyond all comparison. While we look not at the things which are seen but at the things that are not seen, for the things that are seen are temporal but the things that are not seen are eternal*' (NASB). My Dad taught me that keeping the eyes of faith on things that are unseen is the key to victory. During the last few weeks of his life, I observed him looking at those things that are unseen more than he ever had. He began talking more and more of where he was going than where he was. His momentary light affliction was producing in him an eternal weight of glory."

Manley's Message

As I talk with people across the country I find that most of the adversity they face is centered in three areas: health, money and family. That is where most problems seem to surface, because these are the areas of life in which we are most involved. Several ways exist in which you can deal with each of them. You can stick your head in the sand and try to deny that they are there. You can try positive thinking and refuse to accept them. Or, you can try alcohol or other mind-altering drugs, whether prescription or non, that will help you temporarily forget that you even have a problem. None of these, of course, is going to provide the answer. They certainly are not the approach the Bible takes, which is what we will be considering now. Though I may not get to all the Scriptures I'm going to give you, you'll at least have them for your own personal meditation. Romans 11:36; Colossians 1:13-25; Hebrews 12:5-11; Proverbs 16:4; Deuteronomy 8:1-13; Judges 2:22-23 and 3:1-2.

A matter needs to be settled before we go on. It is this. Whether we like it or not, everyone is going to face some kind of adversity in life, be it something that touches them personally or affects someone they know and love. As we have all experienced, this last one is often as difficult to deal with as the personal ones are. Another matter we need to correct is the teaching that if you are a righteous person, you are not going to have problems, that everything is going to go right. This is a myth. Often the righteous have more problems than the unrighteous have. *People interpret some Old Testament Scriptures as saying that those who are right with God are going to have everything go right for them. This belief is a result of a misunderstanding of what "right" is in God's sight. Things "going right" in God's eyes are not always what "going right" is in man's eyes.* This false teaching is also due to a misunderstanding of what "blessings" are. The blessings that Scripture often talks about are blessings that arise *only through adversity.* That's the difference in how God looks at things and how man looks at things. The important issue is not how you look at it but how God looks at it. Everything went right for Job, didn't it? That is true if you look at it as God looked at it—everything went right. For forty chapters, however, if you looked at it from a 'human only' perspective, everything was going wrong for him.

The most important thing in this matter of adversity is that we understand how God looks at it. Put another way it's the relationship between God and adversity. This is the key, because nothing happens in my life or your life that God does not permit and limit. You say: *'Bro. Manley, I have a difficult time accepting that.'* Well, it was no small matter for me. It has taken me years to fully understand this myself. The God I know today, the One we find in Psalm 139:16, has no difficulty in knowing, permitting, and limiting everything that touches one of His children in an adverse way. Here's how the Psalmist described it: *'Thine eyes have seen my unformed substance; And in Thy book they were all written, the days that were ordained for me, when as yet there was not one of them'* (NASB). Before you became a being, God knew you. Before you were substance, God knew you. He even wrote down in a book what you would become. This kind of God has no problem in being aware of your adversity. He not only is aware of it, but He permits it—not only permits it but limits it.

In Colossians 1:16-17, we read: *'For by Him were all things created that are in heaven, and that are in earth, visible and invisible, whether they be thrones or dominions or principalities or powers; all things were created by Him and for Him. And He is before all things, and by Him all things consist.'* These passages show us there is not a thing in this world that exists that is not in accordance with His will. In Paul's epistle to the church in Rome he says; *'For of Him and through Him and to Him are all things, to whom be glory forever'* (Rom. 11:36). Nothing is beyond God's knowing, even the adverse things in our lives, because He permits and limits them. So, even Satan is limited in His activity toward us, because in these matters he is a servant to God. You might say that in God's scheme of things Satan is a necessary evil. That's right.

We see here that *in the economy of God, a negative has to have a positive*. If there were not Satan's negative to God's positive, the positive could not function. Now God could have set it up any way He wanted back there in the Garden of Eden when Adam and Eve disobeyed Him. He could have destroyed them and Satan. Instead He chose not to destroy them. At that point He set in motion what we are talking about. Now, let's go a step further. If a negative and a positive did not exist, we would not be people who have a will. We would not have the power of choice. We would be robots.

We face this issue every day. We know this is true, but some folk still don't understand how this negative-to-a-positive works. Many believe—at least they live as though they believe—that one day God is in charge and on another day the devil is in charge. In fact, if we were to take a survey, that is how most people in our churches believe. We don't even have to teach this. It is a normal conclusion that we come to by watching world events and sometimes home events! You can take that anywhere you want. I've even heard mature Christians talk as though the devil was in charge of a certain situation. You can pretty well tell how much people really understand about how God operates by who they blame for what is happening.

That's how I thought for years—or at least that's how I lived. On those days when things were going well, God must have been in charge, but when life was being turned upside down the devil must have been in charge. That's all I understood about God at that time. But I moved on. Now listen carefully because this is fundamental to any understanding of God and how He works. God knew you before you were. He knew what you were going to do before you did what you did. He was aware of it, whether you were acting wrong and letting the devil have his way or whether you were acting right. He knew because He is the Lord of the living and the dead.

You say: '*Well, if the Lord is that much in charge of things, it sounds as though you might as well do away with the devil.*' Absolutely not! But that does not mean that we won't take advantage of what the devil is doing, because God has shown us how we can turn everything the devil is doing into our good. Knowing how to respond to what the devil does is the key to victory. What he means for evil, what he uses to try to destroy us, can be turned into good when we understand what is really happening. Amen? Everything that touches your life has been permitted by God and is limited by Him. The devil cannot go any further than God allows, because in every adversity you face God is right there on the scene.

For a long time I only saw God as the God of the mountain-top. When I saw that He was also God of the valley, and every-thing in between, it changed my life. I saw that everything that happens is done according to the counsel of His will. You ask: *'Everything?'* Yes sir. Even to the horrible things that happened to our Savior. Everything! There is nothing more hideous than what He went through. Everything! God permitted it and God limited it, according to His divine will and plan, and don't ever forget—when adversity arrives at your door, it has been passed through the divine will of our Lord.

I had enjoyed at least fifteen years of what people would call a very successful ministry before I began to understand what we are talking about. For all those years I struggled with this mat-ter of God permitting everything that touched my life. Then I began to get ill in 1970. At that time, as far as I knew, I was as right with God as I could be, but I did not yet understand God's two-fold purpose in adversity. Now listen closely. You need to get hold of this. If the adversity is due to a sin problem, God will shut everything off, because sin separates you from His fellow-ship. But if it is adversity for the purpose of enlargement, you will find that your problems will run parallel with His blessings. It took me a while to understand this. I saw the problem of my sickness on one side, while God was still blessing on the other. There I was dying physically, yet God was supernaturally meet-ing every financial need I had in a way I had never experienced before. This initially confused me until I began to see that my adversity itself was part of God's blessing. I realized what God was allowing was not due to a sin problem but rather to a part of His enlargement process.

Let's go back to the matter of the negative and the positive for a moment. *Though God was totally in charge of my being sick, the devil was the one who made me sick, not God. The devil was allowed to attack my body, but he could go no further than God would let him go.* Now I want to insert something here before we go on. I think it will bless you, but you will need to understand the significance of numbers in the Bible to get the full force of what I am about to say.

We all know that the number "7" represents perfection. It is the perfect number. Now watch this. *I was taken to the hospital in the 7th month, carried to the 7th floor where the 7th doctor diagnosed me as having 7 diseases, and this doctor served as my primary physician for 7 years, then in the 7th month of the 7th year he dismissed me.* This, of course, was not anything that could have been planned. Nor did we realize what had happened until my prayer-warrior sister, Henry Mae, noticed this pattern when she was going back over the notes that she always kept so meticulously. It was just another confirmation to us that God had been in charge all along.

Now back to my adversity. During a brief time when my seventh doctor had gone on vacation, my family got permission to take me to see a man of God from Europe who had been like a spiritual father to me. He had moved to America, so we were able to drive to where he lived. When we arrived, they carried me into his home and stretched me out on the sofa. Because my tongue had collapsed, as had most of the other muscles in my body, I could barely make myself understood. I was able to at least articulate one question; *"How far can the devil go?"* Now, though I was beginning to understand that the devil was the "delivery boy," I was still young in understanding what it all meant, and like many people I was so caught up in the "delivery boy" aspect that I was not getting the message that he was delivering.

This man of God[20] replied to my question with his own

question. He said; *"Have you considered the story of Joseph?"* I said, *"Yes I have, until that story has lost its cutting edge."* He went on to recount the story of Joseph's brothers selling him into slavery and how God used a famine to bring them back together. Then when Joseph revealed to them who he was, we hear him explaining the ways of God to them. He reminded them of the evil act that they had done, an act that the devil himself was a part of. Then he showed them how God was in it from the beginning, that what was meant for evil was used of God for the good of them all.

This man of God then asked me another question. *"Bro. Manley, who brought Job's name up first; God or the devil?"* I almost said, *"the devil."* Then as I thought about it for a moment, I realized that it was God who first brought up Job's name during that council of heavenly beings to which Satan had been invited. God turned Satan's attention toward Job. We all know the conditions and limits that God placed on the devil's activity. God placed a hedge around his servant through which the devil could not pass.

When I saw that the testing of Job had been God's idea, the scales began to fall from my eyes. That day I had a personal revival on that couch. Though I couldn't physically raise my hands or shout *Hallelujah,* I could cry tears of praise. That day my life was changed as I saw how God had initiated, permitted, and limited all that Job went through. And I believe in some sense, it was a compliment to Job that God would trust him with that adversity.

This is not the end of the story. It is just the beginning. It is the foundation upon which dealing with adversity is built. It is truth that has to be digested and settled in our hearts if we are going to be able to turn adversity into blessing, if we are going to be able to turn adversity into good.

18
So as by Fire

*"Let sight give us discouraging reports as it may, but pay
no attention to these. The Living God is still in the heavens
and even to delay is part of His goodness."*

—selected [21]

A Testimony

"A *Winter Bible Conference* was scheduled at Applewood
Baptist Church in Denver (Wheatwood), CO, where I was on
the ministry staff. We had a strong lineup of speakers. I was
given the assignment of selecting a topic for each one, a topic
that would be complimentary to their particular ministry emphasis. The overall theme of the conference was, *'The Life of the
Pastor,'* so I thought it would be appropriate to assign Manley
the subject, *'Dealing with Setbacks in the Life of the Pastor.'*

"I was beginning to feel good about this choice when
Manley opened his remarks with, *'I would like to know who
came up with this topic.'* He continued: *'He apparently doesn't
know his Bible.'* I was ready to crawl under the pew.'
'Setbacks?' Manley said, *'There are no setbacks for the person
who is walking with God. What we view as setbacks are simply
situations permitted by God for our good.'* I learned a lesson that
day that I have never forgotten. It has been a major source of
encouragement to my wife and me countless times over the
years."

—Dr. Ralph Speas, president, Meridian University
Tulsa and Oklahoma City, OK

During Manley's first hospitalization in Houston the Lord raised up several special prayer warriors, among whom were his three sisters, Henry Mae, Joyce, and Pat. He would contact them with specific requests, whether it was a financial need due to his not being able to hold meetings; whether it had to do with his physical condition, or whether it was for a particular doctor or nurse to whom he was witnessing. These requests changed the lives of these prayer warriors as they saw the power of God miraculously answer prayers as He worked in and through their brother.

On days when Manley was strong enough to talk, Dr. Cooper, a Jewish physician from South Africa, and head of the Neurological Section at Methodist Hospital, would bring by his "doctors in training" to see the "Reverend Beasley," as he always called him. One thing in particular amazed Dr. Cooper — how Manley was able to meet his financial needs without any "visible" income. Dr. Cooper would say: *"Reverend Beasley, tell these doctors about your unusual banker."* Manley would then take the opportunity to not only talk about his financial needs being met, but he would share about Jesus.

During his first hospitalization, Manley was so very ill that a special messenger from the Lord walked into his room. Manley describes it like this: *"I looked up and there stood this lady wearing a print dress just like my mother used to wear. As she began talking to me I noticed that she was also talking to someone else in the room—someone I could not see. I finally realized that the "someone" she was talking to was Jesus. She would speak to me and in the same sentence she would be talking to the Lord, just as though she was carrying on a three-way conversation. I had never seen anything like this before. She would lean over to me and pray, then step back and talk to her Lord. Heaven had come down. Whew! I've never experienced anything like it since."* That "special messenger" was Corrie Ten Boom.

God used Corrie's visit, and her intimate fellowship with her Savior, to help Manley make it through some very difficult days—days that lengthened into months. It helped transform that hospital room from a place of gloom into a place of glory. It helped him keep his focus, to stay the course in spite of the excruciating pain for which the doctors were unable to provide any relief. It helped him hold on when all the muscles in his neck collapsed and he was not able to move his head nor take care of any of his personal needs. It helped him cling to the promise God would give him from Psalm 128:6, *"Thou shalt see thy children's children."* At that moment Manley knew he would live to see his grandchildren.

This was the promise that Manley would recite to himself when the medical profession had given up all hope for his survival. It was the promise he held on to as his loved ones watched him waste away, as his flesh and muscles shriveled up, when only skin was hanging from his bones. This was the promise he clung to when Dr. Cooper gathered the family together to tell them that he could not live. What Dr. Cooper did not know at the time was that his prognosis would be but the first of many such medical predictions over the years, as time after time Manley's faith would be tested, *so as by fire,* and time after time he would walk out of the furnace, holding on to God's promise, to travel on to yet another preaching engagement.

Manley's Message

When things are going well, it is not difficult to believe that God is in control of everything that pertains to us. It is when life takes a turn for the worse that we begin to question His sovereignty. When we do get to the point of accepting the fact that He not only allows adversity in the life of the believer, but also limits it, we must then seek to understand why He has allowed it in the first place. God has a purpose in everything that touches our lives. He has lessons for us to learn, and these lessons are often taught in the furnace of adversity.

Often when something negative happens, our tendency is to blame it on something or someone. We may blame ourselves or our spouse, which often is the easiest thing to do. Or we may blame the pet or an inanimate object like the car. As long as we play the blame game, however, the less likely we are going to find the real reason behind what is happening to us.

We are all aware that we are daily dealing with the world, the flesh, and the devil. God may use any of these to deliver a message to us. You could say that since the devil is involved in all three, he ultimately is the "delivery-boy." His goal, of course, is to destroy, while God's goal is to teach, to correct, to redeem, to restore, to enlarge our capacity to know Him. That is why it is so important that we understand what God has in mind in permitting the adversity in the first place—what his purpose is for it. We can be sure one of the main objectives is to have us turn toward Him, to seek Him. This has always been true. Remember what the Psalmist said? *"In the day of my trouble, I will call upon Thee"* (Ps. 86:7).

You would be shocked at how often God uses adversity to speak to us—how often He uses it to get our attention. We have examples of this all through the Old Testament. God led the Children of Israel from one adversity to the other, beginning at the Red Sea. God had a unique purpose for every trial they faced, a specific lesson for them to learn. And so it is for each one of us. For every adversity our goal ought to be to see what lesson God has to teach us because, if we don't learn it the first time we are going to be given "another opportunity" to learn it in the midst of another trial.

In the case of God's dealing with Israel, the adversities the people faced were part of His preparing them to enter the land of Canaan, the land of plenty, the land of blessing. God knew what they would face and the temptations that lay ahead. He used adversity to prepare them, to get their attention, and to bring them to the end of themselves so they would turn to Him. I recall an experience in my own life when God taught me a much-needed lesson in this area, something that I had never considered before. He taught me how significant adversity is in God's economy—how important it is in His dealing with His children.

I was on the road in a meeting when Marthé phoned me to say that one of our sons, Stephen, who was then just a baby, had suddenly become very ill. She said the doctor was not sure he would live. It shocked me to the point that I fell on my face on the carpet of that hotel room and began crying out to God. I prayed and I prayed and I prayed. I was wanting some word from the Lord, but I heard nothing. I kept on praying, but I heard nothing. I finally got to the place that I was prayed out, and I said, *"God, there is nothing else for me to say. I've been calling on you all this time. Isn't there something You have to say to me?"*

It was almost as if I heard an audible voice: *"Who placed this call?"* I thought about that for a moment before answering: *"Lord, I called You."* It was then that the Lord began to impress on me a truth I had never seen before. I began to realize who had actually placed the call. In my spirit I heard the Lord say: *"That's the problem. You thought you were placing a call to me, when I had called you. When I let your son get ill, I placed the call. All you had to do was pick up the receiver and say, 'Yes Lord, what is it You have to say to me in this situation?' but you just started to talk and talk."*

I then realized what God was saying. I had acted as if, when someone called me on the phone, instead of asking the person who had called me how I might help them or what they wanted to say, I just took off on a one-way conversation. I said, *"Lord, forgive me. What is it You're wanting to tell me?"* The moment I asked that question He put His finger on a problem in my life. *"That's what I want."* I quickly got it right with Him and the moment I did, I knew in my heart that my son would not only live but would fulfill the purposes of God.

The lesson for us all here is that there was a purpose for that adversity, but I was not listening to God to find out what it was. When this happens we miss out on God's two fundamental reasons or goals in allowing us to go through adversity. These goals are to correct us or to enlarge us. Sometimes the adversity accomplishes both.

❧

19

The Hospital, Our Second Home

"Unbelief says, 'How can such be?' But faith has one answer to the ten thousand 'hows'—GOD!"

—Unknown[22]

A Testimony

"From the first time I met Manley I was attracted to the living faith I saw in his life. Though I did not continue in some of the more mystical aspects of his faith walk, his boldness to say what was on his mind, and his desire to experience the reality of God remain most important contributions to my life. His input into my own walk of faith was unforgettable. I am deeply thankful to Manley for his care during those formative years. I owe much to him.

"His devotedness to those he taught was a most notable characteristic. He genuinely loved those who followed him. He made exceptional efforts to be involved in their lives. My own commitment and desire to trust God for all my finances, without asking anyone but God for money, is largely due to my early association with this man of God. I saw firsthand that God was able and willing to support those who trusted Him."

—Jim Elliff
President, Christian Communicators Worldwide
Kansas City, MO

Most people seldom, if ever, see the inside of a hospital, other than to visit a patient. For the Beasley family, however, hospitals were almost like second homes. For Marthé especially, when she was not walking the halls getting to know, and witnessing to, the occupants of every room on the floor, she was keeping an eagle eye on what the nurses were doing with Manley. She constantly watched the medications they were administering to Manley. She acted as a general monitor of what was happening relative to her husband.

The better part of 1971 was spent in the Methodist Hospital, in the Texas Medical Center in Houston, where Manley was diagnosed as having what is now called *Connective Tissue Disease*. The connective tissues are the structural portions of our body that essentially hold the cells of the body together and directly affect the immune system. CTD is described as an overlap of three diseases: *systemic lupus erythematosus, scleroderma, and polymyositis*. In addition to these three basic diseases, Manley's body was also infected with numerous other ailments that, back then, were difficult to diagnose.

These hospitalizations were challenging days for the family, especially since everyone had pretty much given up. Manley's friends were out spreading the word of his impending death. His doctors were not able to give any hope that he would leave the hospital alive. In the midst of times such as these God would use Marthé to stimulate Manley's faith. On one such occasion, when he was in *Intensive Care* hooked up to all kinds of medical paraphernalia—with tubes everywhere and all visible signs pointing toward his pending demise—Marthé looked at him and said: *"Well, Poor God. Poor God. I guess He's not going to be able to pull you through this time. I remember once hearing an evangelist say that . . . .."* She then quoted something that Manley had preached in a sermon on faith. Manley began to stir and not long afterward was once again behind a pulpit preaching.

The waiting and the watching, the praying, and the holding on to God's promises were punctuated with kingdom business as Manley took every opportunity to share his faith with the medical personnel who attended him. And then there were those divine appointments that Marthé regularly had, such as the encounter in an elevator with a lady in her late eighties.

"She looked so cute with those little 'foo-foo slippers,'" Marthé said. "I leaned over, tweaked her toe and said. *'You look so pretty.'* To my horror, she burst out crying. I thought I had hurt her. The nurse who was pushing the wheelchair said, *'Oh, don't get her started.'*" Later that day Marthé found out where the lady's room was and paid her a visit. After another crying spell, Marthé was shocked to hear what came next: *'Would you believe that these legs once danced in the Ziegfeld Follies?'* Sure enough, Miss Gertrude, or Miss Gertie as she preferred to be called, had once been a Follies dancer. She went on to tell her story.

Miss Gertie's late husband had advised her to put the bulk of her inheritance into diamonds, which she had done. A niece, however, had ended up taking off with most of them. Gertie was now left with very little. But almost as important to her at this point in life was her little doggie, which she was not able to have with her. Marthé quickly took things in hand, assuring her that her husband, Manley, who had many friends, would know what to do. So down to his room they went.

When he was well enough, Manley was accustomed to Marthé's bringing him visitors to talk to, but never had he met one like Miss Gertie. After hearing her story, Manley began to share with her about the Lord Jesus and how her meeting Marthé was surely part of God's plan to draw her to Himself. Before long she repented and confessed Jesus as Lord. Shortly after that God began to meet her other needs. Manley contacted a Christian lawyer friend in Houston, who took up her cause. He not only succeeded in getting her diamonds returned but he arranged for her to be put in a Baptist nursing home where she was reunited with her puppy. Upon her home-going she left her "diamond estate" to the nursing home.

Only eternity will reveal how God used those hospitalizations to draw souls to Himself. Among them was Dr. Cooper, chief of the Neurological Division of Methodist Hospital with whom Manley stayed in touch over the years. Dr. Cooper's two sons also put their faith in Christ. Our understanding is that one of them is now in the ministry.

Manley had an intentional agenda for physicians. When traveling in meetings he'd invariably set up an appointment to meet with doctors along the way. It was not uncommon for him to get a check-up whether he needed it or not in order to interact with physicians who, when they would check him out, could not understand how he was still alive. His condition was much more significant to those in medicine than to lay people because they knew how *out-of-the-ordinary* it was that someone like Manley was even alive. Many times, what he did amounted to his leveraging what was going on in his world in order to get to talk to the medical world. He always had a kingdom intentionality in his relationship with doctors. A physician who recognized that his being alive was a miracle would sometimes be ready to meet him for a meal to talk about "who" was behind it all. Manley would cut to the chase and give an incarnational witness about the faith life and how he was kept alive.

Manley's Message

Let me enlarge on the two fundamental purposes or goals God has in allowing adversity in our lives. These are to correct us or to enlarge us. Often we find that the adversity does both. Now it is one thing to know this; it is another matter to understand it. You "know" what I am saying, but do you "understand" what I am saying? Let's work on that.

In addition to understanding the two basic purposes or goals God has for adversity, we need to understand the four basic reasons God needs to use adversity in our lives. The Scripture background for this is found in Deuteronomy 28:1-13: Judges 2:22-23 and Judges 3:1-2. Let's take these one at a time:

God allows adversity in our lives to expose the wickedness of our hearts—to show us what is in us. When squeezed by adversity, sometimes we see, for the first time, what is really there. In leading the Children of Israel out of Egypt God could have avoided the Red Sea and the "bitter water" experience at Marah. Instead He chose to use these experiences to expose what was in their hearts. And so it is in His dealing with us. When we see what is in us, when we "blow our stack," when we act in an unChristlike manner when the pressure is applied, if we repent, if we turn to God, He uses it to grow us in grace, to correct us and enlarge us. If we don't, our communication with God is affected. Instead of our lives being an expression of the nature of our Lord, the life of Christ in us, all that the people around us see is the wickedness of our hearts as it is exposed.

God allows adversity in our lives to reduce us to weakness. This is a very significant issue in our day because a whole system of teaching has emerged and is probably one of the largest businesses in the world. It is the business of motivation. This industry teaches that we have the ability in ourselves to accomplish anything we want, if we just think right, believe in ourselves, and keep a positive mental attitude. Though to some extent these may be valuable when they pertain to the world, when they pertain to the Kingdom of God, they are some of the biggest hindrances to the Lord's work.

I find it interesting to note how some of this teaching is actually based on Scriptural principles. However, when these principles are not kept under the Lordship of Christ, we end up trying to do the Lord's work in the flesh. All we will ever accomplish is what man can do. When the motivation is to better yourself, you have slipped from the teaching of God's Word into teaching that man has the ability within himself to accomplish these goals. When you do that, you have made a god of yourself.

When your motivation, however, is founded in God's Word and His will and when the objective of your life is to become more like Christ, you then place yourself in the position of being blessable and usable by God for His glory, not yours. God allows adversity in our lives to reduce us to weakness, to reduce us to the cross. The cross is where God takes over. In 2 Corinthians 12, Paul talks about his *thorn in the flesh* which God used to keep him humble and dependent. Jesus taught that we are to take up our cross daily. ***The cross is an instrument to die on, an instrument to bring us to the end of ourselves so the Lord can express Himself through us.*** Man, motivated to succeed in his own strength, will do everything he can to avoid the cross because the cross will make him less dependent on himself and more dependent on God. In my own life, God has used adversity to make me so weak that I have to depend on Him.

God allows adversity to shut us up to faith. In Deuteronomy 8 we read that man shall not live by bread alone but by every word that proceeds out of the mouth of God. Jesus in the wilderness temptation used this passage in responding to the devil's temptation. What these passages are saying is that we are not to live by what we can see, taste, smell, feel, or hear, but by the truth of God's Word. In other words, we are to live by faith. No faith apart from truth exists. We know where truth is found.

When our living is based on what the Word of God says, even though our circumstances contradict our understanding or our feelings, we have the Word to hang on to. The Word will renew our minds and transform us in the midst of confusing circumstances or feelings. God takes adversity and uses it to shut us up to His Word. Jesus often led the disciples into adverse circumstances to teach them this truth. When He turned to Phillip in John 6 and asked him how he was going to feed that crowd, Jesus was shutting his disciples up to faith. Jesus' invitation to Peter to walk on the water was shutting him up to faith.

God allows adversity to fulfill the law of antagonism (Judg. 2:22-23; 3:1-2) The Israelites were in the land of Canaan. The old warriors that God had used to get these people into the land were dying off. The young men who were coming along did not know how to be warriors and overcomers. So the Lord said that He was going to leave the enemy in the land to come out against them and make war against them, because He had to teach their young men how to be warriors and how to overcome. It was *"only in order that the generations of the sons of Israel might be taught war, those who had not experienced it formerly"* (Judg. 3:2). The fact is this: if nothing is available to battle against, you are not going to be a warrior. You certainly aren't going to be an overcomer if there's nothing to overcome. I call this *the law of antagonism.*

This law is very vital for the spiritual health of God's children. This is of such importance that we see in some measure why God allows the devil, even though he is defeated, the freedom he has. A teaching going around says that if you just turn everything over to God, life is going to be fine and everything will work out just like you want it to. But that is not always true. *One of the reasons the devil is alive and active is for the battles we need to be fighting to keep us strong. The blows he wields are to stimulate us, to arouse us to take our stand with God's Word in hand, to resist him, and to defeat him.*

The story is told of a Texas catfish farmer who used to stock his fish pond with catfish he'd catch in a nearby river. People would come to his place to look at the fish. Sometimes they would select one to take home to eat. Occasionally one of the "spectators" who didn't know much about catfish would express his or her concern that some of the fish looked as though they were dead. The person did not know that catfish that are hand-fed over a period of time—catfish that don't have to work for their meals—get very lazy and just sit there getting fat. The farmer had to agree that some of them sure did look as though they were dead, so he came up with a plan. He purchased a small barracuda and dropped it in that catfish tank. When the barracuda hit the water, those catfish came alive.

In order to awaken us, God has to sometimes put a barracuda in our tank to arouse us, to stimulate us, and to antagonize us. God may have put a barracuda in your life. All you can think of is how to get rid of it, while God's purpose is to wake you up—to spiritually exercise you until you become a healthier, stronger child of His.

A Testimony

"Manley was the kind of friend I could call with my questions or problems day or night. He was the only preacher I have known who did not have to preach a sermon; his life was a sermon. I visited him in the Houston hospital the first time he was diagnosed with all those diseases. He was so sick that I never thought he could live. When I left his hospital, I phoned preachers and friends all across the country to tell them that Manley was going to die. I went back to the hospital a few weeks later and he rebuked me. He said: *"Freddie, why are you telling everyone I am going to die?"* Over the years I visited him many times when he was in the hospital. Each time I would predict his death. Every time he would rebuke me. Even at his lowest, Manley never lost his humor. One time when he was very sick he told someone: *"Tell Freddie that I'm back in the hospital.*

That way I'll know for sure that I'll be getting out of here."

"Manley loved preachers and their families. Preachers from all over would call Manley to seek his counsel. He has had an incredible influence on our four sons who are all ordained preachers. Proverbs 17:17 says that a friend loves at all times. Manley told me one time that a real friend is one who walks in when everyone else is walking out.

"Thank you Manley for being my friend. Our loss is heaven's gain. I still want to pick up the phone to call you."

—Freddie Gage, evangelist
Euless, TX

20
Heavenly Sandpaper

"Many Christians stop short of experiencing all that God has for them because they have never understood that there is such a thing as perseverance in faith."

—Manley Beasley

A Testimony

"I'll never forget what Manley said when we reached the car: *'Blue, there's one thing that you are going to have to learn about marriage, and that is that your mate is your heavenly sandpaper, but son, in your case, you married a grinder.'* I got really mad at him. I thought he was being ugly toward Iris. I thought he was insulting her, that is, until he hit me with: *'Blue, with you, sandpaper would never do the job. You need a grinder.'* With that, he got in the car and drove off. I stood there, trying to figure out what I had just heard. Finally, I walked back to the trailer."

Iris and Duane Blue, better known to the church at large as Iris and Blue, had a rough time in the early days of their marriage. Both with such strong personalities, and both bringing so much past baggage into the relationship on more than one occasion were ready to call it quits. Iris, whose checkered past included grand theft, years in prison, drugs, running topless bars, and everything that went with that kind of world, had brought her share of baggage. And Blue, who at sixteen had walked in on his mother's suicide; who had spent years living with two German shepherds in a school bus; who could barely read or write, and who only worked when he had to in order to pay for his drug habit, had brought his share of baggage into the marriage, too. Now, here they were, joined together, in the providence of God, as man and wife.

"We were living in a trailer in Magnolia, TX," recalls Blue, "and we were going through another difficult time in our marriage. We had just had a big fight so I called Bro. Manley, who was in a meeting about 45 minutes away. I told him that we were probably going to get a divorce. He said that he would come over after his meeting that night. When I told Iris that I had phoned him, she hit the ceiling. She got madder than ever because she respected Manley so much that she did not want to disappoint him. She was still mad when he arrived, so when he walked through the door, she said: *'Well, have you come to referee?'* *'No. sister,'* he said, *'I've come to take over. Sit down.'* I thought, *'Oh, oh, we're in trouble now.'*

"I'll never forget what he said. It was short and to the point. *'You two can just pull those shades down and live for Satan and be of no value to each other or to the Kingdom. Or you can get right with God and with each another and go on to be of some value to Him. Blue, walk me to the car. I'm going back to the hotel.'*

"I thought, *'Is that all he is going to do? That ain't going to help.'* But the counsel we got that night from Bro. Manley, and the lesson I learned about heavenly sandpaper, has seen us through many rough waters since then. And God is still grinding away on me to make me more like Jesus."

—Duane Blue, *Duane and Iris Blue Ministries*
Lucas, TX

Manley's Message

A daily, never-ending work of the Lord is to conform us to His image. It is not just to get us to heaven by and by, but to cause us to act like and look like Jesus on the way there—whether in the home, in school, on the job, whether we're up or whether we're down. God's purpose is to have the character and life of Jesus press through our lives. To accomplish this He is going to use everything He needs to work on you, to make you more like Himself. This is what I call divine chastisement. This is the process He uses to correct you and enlarge you—His positive and negative at work.

I used to think I had backslidden if people could be around me and not be aware that something was different about me—not be aware of the presence of Jesus in my life. My desire is that I live so close to my Lord that this is what people sense when they are with me. Christianity is a lifestyle. Christianity is not just a profession of faith. It is a life that reveals the nature of the Lord Jesus every day. This is God's objective for us whether we are 9 or 90.

Here's a question for you. I want an "absolute" answer. What do you get when you squeeze a lemon? If your answer is lemon juice, you could be right, but also you could be wrong. Did you know that you can be right but not right enough? In this case the correct answer is, when you squeeze a lemon, you get out of it what is in it. That is an "absolute." You see, what God is watching for is what comes out of us when we are put in a squeeze by our mate (they can usually do it better than anyone else), our children, our friends, our pets, or sometimes even an inanimate object like a car. This is where it gets funny. You go to get in your car in the morning, only to discover that one of the tires is flat. The squeezing begins. You get mad and start talking to that tire as if it had sense enough to plan what happened to it. Now, if you are regularly in the habit of reacting this way to situations like that, you have a problem. You have a spiritual problem. You would be shocked to know, however, how many people actually do act that way when they are squeezed. But when you think about it, though it doesn't make sense to react that way, it sure does reveal what is inside of us. This is getting right down to where we live. Amen?

I want now to focus in a little closer on what this is all about. *The Lord wants to bring us to the point that whenever we are squeezed, what comes out will be the nature and fragrance of Jesus.* Do you think that Jesus ever acted unlike Jesus? You say, *"But He was the Son of God."* The Bible says, however, that He did what He did as the *Son of Man*, because no one saw God at any time, so the God-side of Jesus was not seen. What was seen was Jesus, full of God. When people saw Jesus, they saw the expression of His Father. He never acted unlike Jesus even though He was acting as the *Son of Man*.

The point to all this is to say that God is constantly putting you in situations that will expose you to what is in you. *When you are squeezed by life's circumstances, you are being squeezed by basically two things: temptation and trial.* This may surprise you, but these are the two things that God uses. Now here is the difference between the two. *Temptations are redemptive to you while trials are redemptive to others.* This really helped when I saw this truth, that God uses circumstances to show us what is in us. He already knows how we are going to act, but He has to show us so we can make the adjustments that will make us more like Jesus. God will constantly chip away at us to make us more like His Son.

A good illustration of what we are talking about is the story of the man who was invited to the studio of a sculptor who was going to sculpt a horse from a large piece of rock. The man asked how the sculptor was going to make that hunk of rock look like a horse. The answer he got is a wonderful picture of how God is working on us; *"I am going to knock everything off of that piece of rock that does not look like a horse,"* replied the sculptor. Yes sir, that is God's purpose for the temptations and trials that we all face—to make us more and more like Jesus on the inside and outside, to chip everything away that is not like Him.

Here's another question; *"How does God do this? How does He accomplish what we are talking about?"* In John 15:1 we read about God being the vinedresser, the husbandman, and the caretaker. In other words, He oversees what goes on in the vineyard. *God is in charge of the condition of the vines under His care. God is in charge of our lives. Everything that comes to us, everything that happens to us has to go through His hands. What a picture of the sovereignty of God when it comes to His children.* He is the God of the living and the dead. Whatever may happen to us has been allowed by God to bring about change—first of all in us personally. We sometimes talk about a church that has a problem, but when we boil it down, individual church members have the problem. When the individual members get right, the church will be right. God is the caretaker. He is the vinedresser. Your part in the process is to respond in a positive way to what He is doing, to cooperate with Him.

Years ago I was in a church meeting in the Rio Grande Valley of Texas. The pastor and his wife were in their mid-forties. Soon I discovered that they were going through one of those mid-life testing times. One day when I was talking with the pastor, his delightful, vivacious wife walked in. No sooner had she sat down when he said something that shocked me; something that I had never heard before. *"You know, Bro. Manley, my wife is my heavenly sandpaper."* *"Well,"* she immediately snapped back, *"I may be his, but I want you to know that he is mine."* They noticed that I looked puzzled, so they asked; *"Don't you know what heavenly sandpaper is?"* I said that I was not sure as I had never heard the term before.

It was really precious as both of them went on to explain what they meant—how God is working to make us vessels for His honor, vessels that will reveal the nature of Jesus wherever we go. What He will do is put people together for the purpose of sandpapering. The pastor said: *"There is no one in the world who can upset me as quickly as my wife. God keeps using her on me to smooth me down. She is my heavenly sandpaper."* By that time I was getting the picture. I said: *"Friend, I know exactly what heavenly sandpaper is. I've been living with her for years."* Sometimes now, my wife, Marthé, introduces herself as *"Manley's heavenly sandpaper!"*

Out of that experience with that dear pastor and wife I began to see something I had never seen before. God sends sandpapering people, or circumstances, into our lives for the purpose of making us more like Jesus. And do you know how long the sandpapering experiences will be around? Until we are like Him. One of the uses I have learned that God has for heavenly sandpaper is to teach us to be thankful in all situations — in all things. You say, *"Bro. Manley, do you mean I am to get to the place where I can actually praise God for my heavenly sandpaper?"* Yes, that is exactly what I said. This is what God is out to accomplish. Amen?

Real genuine thanksgiving and praise acknowledges God for what He is doing. He is going to keep working on you until you can praise Him for whatever problem you may face. And you can be sure of this: heavenly sandpaper in some form is going to stay with you until you are ready to act like God wants you to act. Then when you start acting like God wants you to act, something interesting begins to occur. You become less and less aware of the sandpaper's work, because you are allowing the life of Jesus in you to respond to the circumstance. The more you are like Him, the less irritated or frustrated you will be with the sandpaper.

In closing, Manley referred to the Apostle Paul who admonished the church in Thessalonica to be thankful in everything. He went on to say that the way God gets us to that point of thanksgiving is by the use of some kind of sandpaper in our lives, whether it be people, or trials and circumstances of many different kinds. It is all a part of His redemptive work to bring us into conformity to His Son. Manley went on to say a time may arise when God actually chooses to remove some form of sandpaper. If He doesn't, He will so work in us that we will not want the sandpaper to be removed because we see how much we need it. Then we will praise Him for it.

When the Apostle Paul admonished the church in Thessalonica to be thankful in everything (1 Thess. 5:18), he was not writing from an ivory tower but right out of personal experience. He may have even been thinking of the time he and Silas had been flogged, chained, and thrown into an inner cell in the prison at Philippi. His ability to respond the way he did to that situation derived from lessons learned at other times when God had sandpapered him, had tested him, and when God was shaping his character through persecution and illness. I'm not sure what happened that night in the Philippian jail, but it may have gone something like this:

"Silas, wake up. It's time to sing. We need to praise God."

"What are you saying, Paul? It's midnight, and our backs are still bleeding from the beating they gave us last night. These chains are tearing the skin off my ankles. You must be kidding. Did I hear you say that you want me to sing with you?"

And sing they did! And praise God they did! We all know what happened. An earthquake occurred; the prison doors were flung open; and a jailer and his whole family were converted. Paul's response to that prison experience is the same response God is looking for from all of us. May we be as sensitive and ready to cooperate with God in whatever He is doing, whatever the circumstances may be, whatever form His heavenly sandpaper may take, and from whatever direction the testing may come.

SECTION FIVE
Instrument of Revival

Beginning in the mid-1960s the conviction that the church in America was in major need of revival began to grow. By the early 1970s this hunger for God to do something had taken on major proportions as more and more ministries began emphasizing the message of 2 Chronicles 7:14, *"If my people who are called by my name will humble themselves and pray and seek My face, and turn from their wicked ways, then I will hear from heaven, and will forgive their sin, and heal their land"*(NASB).

Though the theme of *Revival and Spiritual Awakening* was always a passion of Manley's, not until Manley became ill in 1970 did this dimension of his ministry begin to expand beyond anything he could have ever imagined. God used his infirmity as a platform to impact countless thousands of souls as his life became a living example of God's strength being made perfect in weakness.

These were the days, as Manley was in and out of the hospital, that Jack Taylor was finishing his book, *The Key to Triumphant Living,* that Keith Miller was promoting *A Taste of New Wine,* that Reid Hardin was opening the *Department of Lay Renewal* at the Southern Baptist Home Mission Board, and that Bill Hogue, the SBC's director of evangelism, was creating the *Office of Prayer and Spiritual Awakening. These were the days* when Ben Johnson was establishing the *Lay Renewal Movement* among the Methodists and when revival was breaking out on the campus of Asbury College in Wilmore, KY. This revival soon was spreading to countless campuses across the land, including Southwestern Baptist Theological Seminary in Fort Worth, TX.

These were the days when hundreds of Presbyterian churches would leave the liberal *Presbyterian Church in the United States* (PCUS) to form the *Presbyterian Church in America* (PCA). *These were the days* when God would come in revival to Ebenezer Baptist Church in Saskatoon, Saskatchewan, Canada, and in that same city, at the same time, Henry Blackaby would be living out the principles of what would one day impact millions of people around the world through what we now know as the study course, *Experiencing God*.

These were also the days when, not coincidently, God was painting outside the lines of the traditional church—days when out of the hippie subculture of Southern California emerged what would be called, *The Jesus Movement*. This was a psyche-delic brand of Christianity made up of ex-drug addicts and other young people who felt disenfranchised—who had dropped out of society in protest over what was happening in the nation, including the Vietnam War. **These were days** of an unquestion-able moving of the Spirit of God across cultural, societal, and denominational lines—a time of spiritual awakening in America that we, who were privileged to be witnesses, did not, at the time, fully understand what was happening. And these were the days when a weak, broken vessel would be used to touch so many of us. *These were the days* of Manley Beasley.

21
Manley and
the Milldale Years

"Revival is that strange and sovereign work of God in which He visits His own people, restoring, reanimating and releasing them into the fullness of His blessing. It is a work of God in the church and among individual believers. True revival always results in an unusual harvest of souls."

—J. Edwin Orr[23]

Milldale Bible Conference and Campground in Zachary, LA, was birthed in the heart of Jimmy Robertson in 1963. From its inception, Manley was a part of that dream—a dream to develop a place where people would come for a fresh encounter with God.

Jimmy and Sonny Holland had met Manley for the first time in 1961 at Camp Zion, in Myrtle, MS. Their hearts were instantly bonded in their longing and desire to see a mighty outpouring of God's Spirit in revival and spiritual awakening across America and beyond. Jimmy was pastor of Bluff Creek Baptist Church in Clinton, LA, when he invited Manley to lead a series of meetings. While there, Jimmy told Manley of the great Methodist revivals that had taken place years before, right where they were. They could see what was left of the tracks of a railway spur that had been laid specifically by the Louisiana Railroad system to accommodate the crowds, numbering in the thousands, who were attending these camp meetings in the

Louisiana countryside. Manley and Jimmy could almost hear the sound of singing as redeemed souls, riding those trains, sang the songs of Zion on their way back to their homes. They began to envision people again arriving from across America—no more on railroad tracks but by the busload, in automobiles, on planes, just to be where God was working.

They prayed; Jimmy began looking. In 1963 he took a step of faith and purchased a piece of land fifteen miles north of Baton Rouge, in the community of Zachary. Before long Manley's heart would begin turning toward Milldale. In the summer of 1965, six months after the birth of their youngest son, Jonathan, the Beasleys made their move from Myrtle, MS, to what was now the Milldale Bible Conference and Camp Grounds.

Manley, Marthé, and the four children initially moved into a trailer until a rental home became available six months later. Eventually Manley would buy a small acreage of land where he and Marthé built a house, where the children also were able to have horses. Truthfully, the horses were not only for the children; they were for Manley. He loved horses. He loved to ride. Nothing was quite as relaxing for him than to dress up like a cowboy—from the boots to the hat—and go riding. He often said that the best deterrent to kids getting into trouble was occupying them with the care and enjoyment of farm animals. Horses became particularly important to their eldest child, Debbie. During her high school years she began competing in barrel-racing events and eventually got into horse breeding.

Those were "glory years" for the entire Beasley family. Those were years when 25 acres of Louisiana moss-laden cypress became a spiritual oasis, a place of changed lives, of miraculous answers to prayer, a place where God was pleased to visit as thousands came from the north, south, east, and west; cars, buses and vans with license plates from states near and far filled the parking lots. No tuition or fees of any kind were ever charged. People slept free in the dorms and ate free in the dining room. And God never failed to meet every need.

In the early days, prior to the building of the 1,000-seat auditorium, the people met in a big tent. Jimmy Robertson recalls the very first conference and the very first meeting, when God used a severe storm for His glory. *"The thunder and lightning were intensifying and things were beginning to look dangerous for a tent full of people. We could hear the rain approaching. I decided that we had better cancel the meeting and let the people go home. Manley, however, thought differently. He said we should continue. He then went to the pulpit and prayed that God would direct that storm away from us. No sooner had he finished praying than that storm turned, went around the tent, and headed off. We actually could see it and hear it leaving. Not a drop of rain touched the tent. Not a drop. It was so dramatic that people went back to their homes, as far away as Baton Rouge, telling what had happened. The next day people began coming in droves to see where God had performed the miracle. The winds still obey His voice."*

God brought some very special servants of His to minister in this land of Cajun Culture and Crawfish Bisque. Both American and internationally renowned preachers stood behind the Milldale pulpit. A tent-packed congregation would hear the Scottish accents of a James Alexander Stewart, the Scottish evangelist/revivalist, or a Duncan Campbell who was so mightily used of God in the Hebrides Revival of the late 1940s and early 1950s. Stepping to the podium one night might be Roy Hession, British author and revivalist, or Dr. Oswald J. Smith, pastor of the famous People's Church in Toronto, Canada, known worldwide as one of history's greatest missionary statesman, yet whose heartbeat was for revival.

Another night, following exciting "camp-meeting" singing and prayer, a white-haired man, dressed in a white suit, stepped to the podium. Dr. R.G. Lee, pastor of Bellevue Baptist Church in Memphis, TN, was about to speak. At other times the crowds would be moved by the first-hand accounts of Dr. C. L. Culpepper and Miss Bertha Smith, as they bore witness to the mighty visitation of the Holy Spirit during the Shantung Revival in China. Also used of the Lord in those days were Leonard Ravenhill, who lived at Milldale for several years, or J. Harold Smith, Jesse Norris, Hyman Appelman. Of course at every one of the four annual meetings the crowds were challenged and fed by Manley Beasley, Jimmy Robertson, and Sonny Holland.

These gatherings in June, August, November, and February were not the normal, run-of-the-mill church conferences. They were more like conventions where business is transacted and where decisions are made that determine eternal destinies. These were days of God's calling His people back to Himself, days of repentance and days of glorious victory. From that piece of land, hallowed by the presence of God, transformed lives returned to their homes and their churches, renewed and revived, carrying with them the sweet aroma of worshipers who have had an audience with the King of Kings.

Manley would sometimes point out how unusual it was that such large crowds would assemble to hear preaching on sin and repentance. What took place during those years cannot be described in words. *"It was almost as though we were just standing back, watching the Spirit of God at work,"* says Jimmy Robertson. *"There was nothing spectacular—no worked up excitement in the flesh—just a genuine face-to-face meeting with a Holy God. Manley was a major stabilizing force during those years. Getting off track would have been so easy. We always felt secure when Manley was around."*

The ministry of those living at Milldale extended well

beyond the borders of those grounds. Among them was Sonny Holland, whose life and ministry was profoundly affected by Manley. Sonny, who became one of Manley's closest friends, recalls those days.

A Testimony

"Over the years Manley taught me three major life and ministry principles. He helped me to understand how to *live by faith*; he helped me understand how *to give,* and he helped me understand how to *die.*

"**What does it mean to live by faith?** Manley believed and lived the truth of two Scriptures found in the book of Hebrews; *'The just shall live by faith'* (Heb. 10:38), and, *'But without faith it is impossible to please him: for he that cometh to God must believe that he is, and that he is a rewarder of them that diligently seek him'* (Heb. 11:6). People not only heard Manley preach these principles, they saw them lived out in his personal life. That is why he had such a profound influence on people. He lived by faith!

"**What does it mean to give?** My wife, Dorothy, and I were attending a meeting at Camp Zion in Myrtle, MS, where we first met and heard Bro. Manley. We were a thousand miles from our home in Florida where I was a pastor at the time. Manley was preaching from one of his favorite Scriptures: "*Give, and it shall be given unto you; good measure, pressed down, and shaken together, and running over, shall men give into your bosom. For with the measure that ye mete withal it shall be measured to you again*" (Luke 6:38).

"Dorothy and I had just enough money to drive our Volkswagen back home. On Saturday morning while Manley preached, God spoke to my heart. He said: *'Give what you have.'* I took all the money I had to the altar and placed it in the plate. When the meeting was dismissed and we were getting ready to leave, I said to Dorothy, *'I am going to need the money that you have to buy gas. We only have half a tank left.'* 'What money?' she replied. *'The preacher said to give and it shall be given to you,* so *I put everything I had in the offering.'* We were still a thousand miles from home with a half-tank of gas.

"I decided that we would drive as far as we could and see how the Lord was going to provide. Fifty miles down the road we stopped to briefly say hello to a couple we had known for some time. We decided, however, that we would say nothing about our need. As we were leaving, the husband said: *'Sonny, I believe God wants me to give you this.'* He handed me a $100 bill. What a lesson in faith God was beginning to teach me. I had known the Scriptures, but through Bro. Manley God was now confirming to me that He meant what He said.

"Not long afterwards I sensed the Lord calling me into full-time evangelism. I resigned from the pastorate and moved to Milldale. In those days I had very few meetings scheduled, so Manley asked if I would help him set up an areawide crusade in Greenville, MS. He told me about a man in Greenville who had an inflatable tent that operated with blowers. Manley didn't have any money. I didn't have a dime. But Manley had a credit card that would get us started.

"I drove to Greenville and met Lawrence Bryant, the tent owner. Everything seemed to be in order, so I checked into the motel and started making preparations. I contacted Dr. James Stewart, the Scottish evangelist, who happened to be in the country at the time. He said he would be able to join us. I then took out a full page add in the local newspaper:

PORTABLE ASTRODOME COMING TO GREENVILLE
Speakers: Manley Beasley, Sonny Holland
and Dr. James Alexander Stewart.

"Everything was set. I calculated that the total cost for the meeting would be around $3,000.00. I got the phone book and started calling all the pastors in town, asking them to encourage their people to participate. *'You've got to hear Manley Beasley. You've got to hear James Stewart from Scotland.'* It took me about four days to get it all lined up before Manley arrived. The motel owner had agreed for me to put all the expenses on my motel bill.

"When Manley walked into my motel room, I was lying on the bed laughing. *'What's the matter with you?'* he asked. *'Well, Manley, they have just called from the newspaper to say that we are being sued for using the word* Astrodome *in our ad. It seems that it is a registered name and cannot be used without permission. I told them that I didn't have a dime and neither did the other man who was in charge of the meeting. I told them that they would be wasting their time and money suing us.'* We never heard another word from them.

"About 3 that afternoon Manley and I went out to check on how things were going with the tent preparations. When we arrived, the police were there along with the three men who were helping us get the tent ready. The police had stopped them because the tent did not meet city code. The tent entrance had revolving doors while the city's code required that the entrance have two double-acting doors. We finally found some carpenters who could hastily build us a little vestibule with double-acting doors. This met the city's building code and became the entrance to the 'Astrodome'!

"That night people were arriving in droves. Every so often the ushers had to stop the people from entering in order for the blowers to keep the tent inflated. The place was packed. In the middle of his sermon, Manley called me to the podium. He was sweating profusely. *'Sonny, go check the blowers. The tent is losing air.'* I went outside to discover that the owner of the closed service station next door, where we had plugged in our electric cord, had pulled the plug on us. I found him and said: *'Sir, you are fixing to kill all those people in that tent.' ' You didn't get permission to use my station's electricity,'* he said. *'I know. We couldn't find you.'* I said: *'Believe me, we will pay you. Just please don't kill all those people.'* The meeting went on.

"One night during the meeting Manley said to me, *'Sonny, we're really going to have to pray. We don't have enough to pay for all this and these people don't have much money. We're going to have to trust God for a miracle.'* Back at the motel, about 11 p.m. a knock on the door occurred. There stood Lawrence Bryant, the tent owner. He said, *'I couldn't get to sleep tonight. God told me to come and give this to you.'* He handed us a $1,000.00 check. We started shouting.

"The next day, when we were at the tent praying, a man named Big Six Ellington wanted to see us. He told us that a man in a big black limousine had visited him at his farm that morning wanting to buy some rice. Big Six told the man that he only had one silo left, but that the rice was full of worms. *'That's OK,'* said the man. *'I have a pig farm and I need the rice for them. The worms won't matter. I'll pay you $1,600.00 for the wormy rice.'* Big Six Wellington said that he had been on his way to the bank, all excited about the $1,600.00 check he was going to deposit, when God interrupted him and said, *'Don't you dare deposit that money to your account. Take it to those men down at the tent.'*

"Praise God, by the time that meeting finished we had enough money to pay all the bills, including Dr. Stewart's plane fare, the motel, the Astrodome advertising, the service station electricity, and the building of the vestibule. But God did not stop there; on top of it all, a love offering was enough for each of us to receive $500.00, which, in today's economy, would be equivalent to a total of almost $5,000.00.

"**Manley taught me how to die.** I never once heard him complain about his illnesses, which were many. Repeatedly, he would tell me. *'Bubba, if it wasn't for God, I wouldn't have gotten up this morning.'* In spite of the years of living so close to death, he pressed on. I watched him. He taught me. He called me two weeks before he went home to be with his Lord. *'Bubba, it looks like I'm gonna be leaving ya'll.'* I said, *'What do you mean, Manley?'* He said, *'God hasn't spoken to me about staying any longer . . ..'* We reminisced about the many cherished moments we had shared together. We cried, and we laughed. *'Goodbye, Manley. I'll see you in heaven.'*"

22
In Search of a Ranch

"Times of refreshing from the presence of the Lord' well describes true revival. We know that God is quite willing to visit us in the power of His own presence. When that time comes there will be revival—a revival which will magnify the name of Christ Jesus our Lord."

—J. Edwin Orr [24]

In 1970 while he was at Milldale, Manley's health began to take a turn for the worse. That, coupled with a changing school situation for the children, led him to begin considering a move west, preferably to Texas. He hoped to find a small ranch that would accommodate both family and horses. Nothing opened up, so he settled for some acreage in Sulphur, LA, a town named for the sulphur mines discovered in the 1870s. This area was also known as the gateway to the *Creole Nature Trail*. Though not quite to Texas, the new home was just twenty-five miles from the *Lone Star State* line. Here they would have the advantages of country living, be just a few miles off of Interstate 10, and have a place where they could still enjoy their horses.

By now Debbie, who was into breeding and rodeo competition, had a small herd of twenty horses. Marthé laughs as she recalls: *"What sold Daddy on this piece of Louisiana countryside as much as anything was the beautiful barn, not the house. We had to work a good bit on getting the family living quarters in shape, but the animals enjoyed their first-class living accommodations from the start!"*

During what proved to be a two-year "layover" in Sulphur, LA, in spite of his failing health Manley continued traveling to meetings. At home Marthé was overseeing household matters and twisting cow's tails, Jonathan was beginning kindergarten, Debbie was finishing high school, and Bubba (Manley Jr.) and Stephen were continuing their education in the Sulphur school system. As planned and predictable as these family developments were, something was about to happen that could not have been more unplanned or unexpected.

The Beasley family would soon be turned upside down. They were about to face a crisis for which no one would ever volunteer. This crisis would not only reshape their lives but the lives of countless thousands of others in the years ahead. Manley, who had never been hospitalized a day since his birth and who until recently had been the picture of health for almost twenty years of ministry, soon began to face the reality of death—in and out of hospitals, intensive care units, carrying in his body three terminal diseases, plus an assortment of four other illnesses for the rest of his life.

Every member of the family was impacted. Five-year-old Jonathan would never again have a daddy who could toss a ball with him. Stephen was called on to make adjustments that he found difficult, while Bubba (Manley Jr.) was perhaps the least affected—at least initially—because he would soon be going off to Liberty University, in Virginia, to complete his high school studies and go on to do his undergraduate work at Howard Payne and Dallas Baptist universities.

Debbie, on the other hand, would begin selling off her horses that had become so much a part of her life of barrel racing and rodeos. The first horse to go was her prize, *Jim Dandy*. With the proceeds, she purchased a car for her college commute. This was the beginning of a pilgrimage of faith that would take the Beasley family through the deepest of valleys, the roughest of seas, and to the highest peaks of victory. Ahead were years of learning how faithful God would be in preparing the way before them — a road He had providentially already begun to lay before they knew what they would be facing.

Part of this preparing for the road ahead was Manley's encounter with Jack Taylor seven years earlier. Little did Manley know how significantly God was going to use Jack and the members of Castle Hills First Baptist Church, San Antonio, to minister to him and to his family.

A Testimony

"Manley was nothing but a name to me when one of my deacons recommended that I invite him to preach a series of meetings at *Castle Hills First Baptist Church,* in 1965. This deacon had encountered Manley in Harlingen, TX. He had been profoundly impacted by Manley's message. Based on my deacon's recommendation, I decided to invite Manley to visit, little knowing what I was getting into. I had never before met anyone like him. He was somber and austere, with an aura of authority about him. His preaching style was void of fancy phraseology; he just simply talked; and the power of God flowed.

"I will never forget the first service. He just preached on *How Do You Know You Are Saved?* He hadn't been into the message more than 15 minutes when I began to wonder if half my membership was saved. He preached another 15 minutes and I wondered if any of my members were saved. He preached a bit more and I began to wonder if anybody was saved, including me. It shook up the place, because everybody was faced with checking up on his or her own salvation. Not many returned that evening, but the few who did heard what Manley had to say and would never forget it. At the end of that meeting Manley himself was not sure why he had accepted our invitation, but I sure did know why. God began to show him a picture of many little puddles that God was going to create, puddles that would grow and eventually merge to form one great river of revival.

"Manley had two men with him who, along with himself, presented a totally different brand of believer than I had ever known. I was impressed—in fact I was shocked. I knew at the time, however, that this was but the beginning of a special relationship I would have with Manley. My life was forever marked by that brief encounter of less than a week. Over the next few years our friendship developed and then, in the latter part of 1969 and early 1970, I personally met God in a life-changing way.

"When Manley became ill, we encouraged him to move to San Antonio from Sulphur, LA, to be nearer hospitals and to be helped by several doctors in my congregation. I became his pastor and our friendship deepened. As God began to miraculously raise him from his deathbed I was able to introduce him to churches across the Southern Baptist Convention. Before long he would join Ron Dunn, Bill Stafford, Miss Bertha Smith, myself and others, as an integral part of the *Conferences on Revival* that were being held across the United States. Noteworthy during this period Manley began developing his material on faith—material that would profoundly impact the lives of Christians all across the land.

"Manley and I eventually would begin to move away from each other. He felt I was going in a direction with which he could not agree. Though for a number of years we did not communicate, I recall visiting him in a Dallas hospital when he was in ICU. He couldn't talk. I took his hand and he began to weep. He motioned to the nurse who brought him a pencil and pad. In barely legible writing he scribbled, '*I'm sorry.*' I read into it that he was sorry, as I was sorry, that we had been separated. We then had a sweet time of prayer in which I verbalized what was on our hearts. I visited him again, this time in his home, not very many months before he died. We talked about where we were in our ministries, about the different directions in which we had gone. He said he had watched me over the years go right up to the edge and come back, but this time he felt I had not come back. I said. *'Manley, I can't go back.'* I wasn't talking about going back to where he was, but going back to where I had been. He was concerned that I was getting into an extreme position in the area of the Holy Spirit's fullness. I knew what he was talking about and though we were aware of our differences, no rancor occurred.

"Manley played a major role in my life. Though we did have our disagreements, I never lost my profound respect and appreciation of him. Manley was a prophet before any of us were talking about prophets. He was a prophet to his generation."

—Jack Taylor, Dimensions Ministries
Melbourne, FL

Another Move

Though moving to Texas had been Manley's ultimate goal when his family had left their friends in Milldale, LA, two years before, little did he realize that when his desire eventually would be fulfilled, the move would not be to a ranch but to a Houston hospital. Doctors gave little hope for Manley's survival. With Marthé's needing to be at Manley's side and the children living 150 miles away in Sulphur, before long they knew they were going to have to make another move. At this point, as Jack Taylor shared in his testimony, he and *Castle Hills, First Baptist Church* stepped in to help the family resettle—this time in San Antonio, 330 miles west on Interstate 10.

23
What Is Victory?

"I have written one of Manley's quotes in my Bible: 'Victory is having said of you what is written of you.' Manley also taught me that if God was going to use me there must be balance in my life and ministry."

—Johnny Hunt [25]

A Testimony

"Our church in Tacoma, WA, was strapped financially and in much need of revival. Knowing this, you can understand how excited I was that Manley had agreed to spend a Monday evening through Sunday morning with us. I was concerned about beginning on a Monday night so I did everything but threaten my people to be there for that first service. I even told them that if they had to miss Sunday, be sure to attend the first service of the 'revival.'

"Monday dawned an unusually beautiful day in the Northwest—that is until 7:50 a.m. when my phone rang. The voice on the other end was Manley's. He was in a clinic, sick, but felt he could get to us by Tuesday night. I came up with some warmed-over hash for Monday. Manley arrived in time for the Tuesday meeting and began grinding away. Not a lot was happening in the services. I began questioning my plan to turn the next Sunday evening service into a testimony time. Then Sunday morning arrived. Manley preached a message on *Soulish Conversion.* An invitation was extended, but no one responded. No one. Not one! I motioned to the pianist to stop playing. I asked the congregation to take their seats. As I was about to speak, a 9-year old boy with half his shirt-tail hanging out started down the aisle. The moment was awkward. As the pianist began playing again, I stepped down to talk with the young lad. I looked up to see a man, who had been a real problem to me from the day of my arrival at that church, coming down the aisle. Then suddenly many others began moving forward. Eight or more were saved that morning and forty or more got their hearts right with God. This became the turning point for our church.

"It was mid afternoon by the time we left the building. As we were walking toward the car, Manley spoke up:

'You know, Ruff, God didn't get into that meeting until the two of us got out of the way.'
'I believe you're right, Manley.'
'It's something when God uses a little boy to do what grown men can't do.'
'You're right, Bro. Manley.'"

—Ruffin Snow, pastor
TriCities Baptist Church
Conover, NC

Manley liked to pose questions that would stimulate people to consider things to which they had perhaps previously given little attention. These questions came out of his own walk with the Lord. These were often questions he was asking of himself. More often than not the answers would become sermons.

Manley's Message

Let's start with a question: *"What is victory?"* The Bible teaches that our Lord was victorious on the cross. Because of that victory we are more than conquerors. We all acknowledge that God's Word clearly states that we are to be victorious, but how many of us are really experiencing the reality of what Christ accomplished for us in our daily living? Now, in order to help us understand what I'm saying, let's look at Jesus as the *Son of Man*.

When I was a boy, I remember hearing preachers say that Jesus Christ was all man. I could live with that until in the same breath they would go on to say that Jesus Christ was all God. Now, I didn't have a problem accepting either fact by itself, but I just could not understand how He could be all man and all God at the same time. Well, I now have been a Christian for a long time, and I still can't really understand it. ***I am comforted, however, that the Bible says that it is by faith that we understand. It does not say that by understanding we have faith. Most of us are trying to understand so we can believe, but we must accept that we believe because the Word of God says it is so.*** Amen? Jesus is the perfect example of what we are talking about.

John 19 is a remarkable chapter. We may sometimes have difficulty dealing with it because of the anguish and suffering that Jesus was going through. Here in His last moments as the Son of Man we see one of the clearest pictures of victory. When he cried, *"It is finished,"* He was fulfilling what had been written of Him. In His fulfilling of this, He was paying the debt of our sin so that we today might have eternal life. That's victory: having accomplished what had been written of Him.

Now, let's turn this on ourselves. Jesus accomplished what He did for our redemption. Because, as the Apostle Paul says in Romans, we are more than conquerors through Christ who loved us (Rom. 8:37), victory is basically living up to what is written about us. Anything else is defeat. We cannot claim to have any kind of positive testimony to the world if it cannot be said of us what is written about us. This is what convinces the world that what we profess is real. Anything less is just words.

Victory is having said of you what is written of you

We desperately need revival in our churches today if for no other reason than the restoration of Christians to a lifestyle consistent with what is written about us in the Bible—a lifestyle consistent with our position in Christ. Let me say it again; *Victory is having said of you what is written about you in God's Word.*

There are many things written about us in the Bible that become reality only when we appropriate them by faith and obey what the Scriptures tell us to do. The Bible says that we are to work out our salvation with fear and trembling (Phil. 2:12). This does not mean that we are to *work for* our salvation, because we have already been saved by the grace of God. It means, having been saved, we are to *work out* our own salvation. In Christ Jesus we have certain privileges and responsibilities. These are to be *worked out* so that our experience in life will be consistent with our position in Christ—when it can actually be said of us what is written of us. That is victory!

We Are Saints

The Bible says that we are "saints!" What does that mean? *Saint* basically means, "holy one;" a person who is holy. Can people say that about you? I was recently in a church in Missouri where I specifically recall noticing a young lady at the Tuesday noon meeting. I thought she must have been a model by the way she looked and carried herself, but something beyond her outward appearance seemed to set her apart. I figured that she must have been reared in a very fine family, been taught the Scriptures from a young age, and had probably received the best of educations. She was so very polite and dignified, she simply stood out in the crowd. I couldn't help but wonder what her husband and family looked like because she seemed to be so full of the love of Jesus. After the service I asked the pastor about her. What he said, shocked me. I could hardly believe my ears.

"*Bro. Manley, seven years ago that girl was the most wicked woman in town. She was shooting dope and along with her husband was involved in every sin imaginable. Then they met Jesus. Their lives have been totally changed.*" I was amazed. The grace of God had made her so beautiful that I couldn't even see any marks of sin on her. The pastor went on to say: "*You can ask anyone in town who knows her to tell you what they think of her now. They would say, 'She may be only 27-years-old, but listen, she is a saint. She is a saint.*" This, my friend, is the true test of whether we are living in victory. Is it being said of us what is written of us? What do your family, your friends, your workmates say about you?

We Are Priests
The Bible says that we are "priests." You and I are called priests. When I was a little boy, I thought that priests were men who wore their collar backwards. Well, that may be true, but it means a lot more than that. A simple definition of a priest is someone who is a "go-between." A priest is someone who with one hand knows how to reach up to God and all His supply. With the other hand he reaches out to man and all his need. He then brings the two together. Oh, my friend, it is something when people know how to touch God on your behalf. Yes sir! Right now I am at a place where nothing in this world except God can take care of my situation. You can be sure that I am not looking for the crowd that says, "*I'll be praying for you,*" and then forgets what they said. I'm looking for folk who know how to reach up and get hold of God with one hand and me with the other and bring the two together. Do those who know you think of you as that kind of person? Are you one people know they can go to when they need someone to fulfill the duty of a

"priest?" Is what is written of you being said of you? That is victory!

A Life of Submission

Now let's look again at the life of Jesus, as the Son of Man, and how He was able to have said of Him what was written of Him. How did He accomplish this? The answer is: **He lived a life of** *submission.*

In the story of Jesus talking to the Samaritan woman near the village of Sychar, he tells the disciples, who had just been in town buying food, that his food was to do the will of His Father and that he had food they knew nothing about (John 4:32-34). Jesus' life was lived in submission to His Father. His motivation was to do the Father's will. In submitting His will to the will of His Father He was spiritually sustained. Revival will never occur until our motive is pure. We must desire it not for ourselves, but because it will bring glory to God, We desire it because He desires it. Jesus was so submitted to the Father's will that He never initiated anything on His own. What He did He only did after He saw the Father doing it (John 5:17). Now that's amazing!

Going to conferences and getting all fired up, inspired, and emotionally motivated is easy. Going back home and starting to implement things in your church is the difficult part. The problem is that your motivation may not have occurred by way of a word from God. You end up initiating things on your own. You start getting off track, find yourself running out of steam, and try to keep a program going in your own strength. A lot of church leaders today live as though God needs all the help He can get from them. Rather than waiting on God to see what He is doing, they grab the ball and hope God will bless their efforts. That's what Abraham did; we are still paying the consequences.

A Life of Renunciation

Not only did Jesus live a life of submission, **He lived a life of renunciation.** All power in heaven and on earth had been given to Jesus, yet He was brought to the end of Himself. He said: *"I can of my own self do nothing"* (John 5:30). You could rightfully say that Jesus Himself never performed a miracle. Yes, He turned water into wine, He fed the 5,000, and He raised Lazarus from the dead. Yet in reality the Father performed these miracles through Him. *"What is the difference? you ask."* For us the difference is having at our disposal the resources that we ourselves can come up with, or having available to us the infinite supply of heaven's storehouse. That is the difference in doing it our way versus doing it God's way. If we are going to have said of us what is written of us, we're going to have to live a life of submission and renunciation—submission to our Father's will while renouncing our own rights to ourselves and turning those rights over to another. And this all takes place at the cross.

We have a great deal of "soul-power" in the world today. A lot of it is in the church. Soul-power is power that has never been to the cross. This soul-power is operating under the name of the Lord Jesus Christ and is causing a great deal of confusion among God's people. The reason for this confusion is that most people cannot discern between God-power and soul-power. Soul-power is of such a deceptive nature that people think it is a work of God. In reality He is nowhere near it. The only answer to soul-power is the cross—man being exposed to his nothingness and weakness. Don't misunderstand me. God uses humanity, but the humanity that God uses has been to the cross and has come to grips with its inability. Then what is expressed through our lives is the life of God not our soulishness. No wonder we are told to deny ourselves, to take up our cross and follow Him (Luke 9:23).

A lot of the phenomena attributed to God we see happening today is nothing more than man's soulishness that has never been to the cross. Many think that if something is not evil, it must be of God. I'm not sure that we are ready for God to do a mighty work in our day if we think like that. We have yet to learn the difference between God's work and man's capacity, man's work and the work of Satan. If we are going to have said of us what is written of us, we are going to have to pass by the way of the cross; we are going to have to deny ourselves and let Christ be all in all.

A Life of Faith

Finally, for Jesus to have said of Him what had been written of Him, not only did He have to live a life of submission and renunciation, **He had to live a life of faith** — faith in His Father. He lived in such obedience and faith that if the Father had not worked supernaturally on His behalf, He would have been sunk. When He acted in obedience to His Father, He was trusting His Father to act in accordance with what His Son saw Him doing. And Jesus so often used these situations to teach the walk of faith to His disciples.

How did He handle the feeding of the 5,000 in John 6? He first asked Phillip how he would do it, just as He so often puts us in an impossible situation to see what our response will be. There are really only two ways that such problems can be managed: God's way or man's way. Phillip dealt with it man's way. He said, *"I've got about $40.00 but that's not going to do it."* Andrew did not do much better, but at least he brought the lad with the five loaves and two fish to Jesus. Then what did the Lord do? Well, He didn't ask God to send ten tons of fish and five tons of bread, he simply took the bread and fish and thanked His Father. He then acted like *it was so when it was not so, in order for it to be so, because He had seen what the Father* *was doing and He knew that it already was so.* He wasn't acting presumptuously because He had not initiated the situation and neither was He working in His own ability.

Now listen: You can't go out there and say that you have faith and make God your slave. Faith is acting in belief on what God Himself has initiated. You must be careful, because what God initiates is not always what you are seeing and hearing around you. People are building whole systems of faith on the basis of signs and wonders. Beware, because a faith built solely on this is humanistic and is not born of the Spirit. True faith is a work of the Holy Spirit based on getting a word from God. God's Word is made alive by the Spirit of God and applied to a certain situation.

An example of this in Jesus' life is found in John 11 when He raises Lazarus from the grave. When Jesus arrived at the tomb, He already knew what the Father was going to do. In fact He already knew what the Father was planning when he first heard that Lazarus was sick. When we hear Him pray at the tomb, we get a glimpse of the relationship between the Son and the Father. Let me paraphrase what Jesus prayed in John 11:43. *"Father, I am praying for their benefit because you and I already know what your desire is and what you are going to do."* It is clear that Jesus had not initiated this situation on His own, nor was He working in His own power. He was cooperating with the Father and acting in faith on what the Father was going to do. If we are going to have said of us what is written of us, we are going to have to learn to hear from God and act in faith. It does take courage to believe in God this way, but remember—faith is never a leap into the dark. Let me repeat: faith is never a leap into the dark. It is a step into God's light.

I was in a series of meetings in Mississippi when one night a man introduced himself as being one of my cousins. He said that another of my cousins would be attending the following night and that she would be bringing me some information about a great-grandmother of mine on my father's side of the family. I had thought all my Christian heritage was on my mother's side. The next night I was handed an obituary and an article that had been written generations before in the Mississippi Baptist state newspaper. I was moved to tears as I read about the deep faith of this ancestor of mine and how her husband had died, leaving her with eight boys and three girls. She reared those children herself to love the Lord. The three girls married preachers. All eight boys put their faith in Jesus. The Baptist newspaper article said that Mrs. Beasley prayed every night for her children, her grandchildren, and though she would never meet them, for her great-grandchildren. When I read that, I realized that I was cashing in on the prayers of my great-grandmother and that what I was reading was a testimony to her having said of her what was written of her.

Since learning about my great-grandmother, I have found myself praying that in another hundred years—if Jesus does not return—my great-grandchildren will look at my picture, read a story about me, wipe the dust off of some old portrait and be able to say, *"I didn't know him, but they say he was a saint. They say that he knew how to get hold of God and pray until heaven and earth came together, and we are reaping the benefits of his prayers."* God grant that it will be said of me what is written of me. If it is, that will be victory.

When Jesus cried out, *"It is finished,"* it could be said of Him what was written of Him. When it is your time to finish, will your testimony be one of victory? Will it be said of you what is written of you?

24
Turning toward Europe

*"We must differentiate between revival itself and the spiritual
state resulting from revival. Revival is NOT God's standard
for the church but is the process through which the Church is
restored to its splendor and glory. 'Wilt Thou not revive us
again that Thy people may rejoice in Thee'"* (Ps. 85:6).

—James Alexander Stewart [26]

Gruyère cheese and Nestlé chocolate; watches and cows;
skiing and ski-bobbing; David Niven and William F. Buckley
Jr.; fondue and a village hockey team. What do these have in
common, or perhaps the better question to ask, what do these
have to do with Manley Beasley and revival?

As great a surprise to the Beasleys, as it was to any of us,
was that the little Swiss mountain village of *Château d'Oex*
(pronounced "day"), nestled in the Alps halfway between the
eastern end of Lake Geneva and Interlaken, would end up having such a special place in the heart of the Beasley family.

This corner of Switzerland, known as the *Pays d'Enhaut*
(high country), was both residence and vacation spot for many
famous people. More importantly to our story, it was where the
International Christian Center, housed in Hotel Rosat, was sit-
uated. From the time it was given in 1953 to my father, John
Owens, it served the church in Europe, from Scandanavia to
Greece. Housed on this property over the years was a Bible
School, a church, the Evangelical Braille Work for Europe, and
a printing and literature distribution ministry that included *La*

Manne Cachée (The Hidden Manna), a periodical on revival that was sent out every month in seven languages to both Western and Eastern European readers. And while all these ministries were functioning, it also served as a hotel and conference center.

In 1973, three years after my wife Patricia and I had inherited the ministry leadership responsibility, another group from the States would arrive for the second annual *Swiss Conference on Revival.* The Chabloz busses from Château d'Oex were sitting in the Geneva airport parking lot. We were waiting. The flight was on time. Soon through the arrival gate appeared the Americans: Ralph Jr. and Ruthie Neighbor, Jack and Barbara Taylor, Ron and Kaye Dunn, Peter and Johnnie Lord, Tom and Jeannie Elliff, Bailey and Sandi Smith, and a host of others. Finally, slowly bringing up the rear came Manley and Marthé Beasley and their seven-year-old son, Jonathan.

Any flight from your home city in the U.S., through the *John F. Kennedy Airport* in New York, and on to Switzerland, is never easy for the hardiest of travelers. For Manley, who had spent the better part of the last two years in and out of hospitals, it had been very tiring. The anticipation, however, of spending the next ten days in the Swiss Alps with so many of his friends and fellow ministers helped outweigh the fatigue. Just two hours by bus and we would be there.

We would be there! But what they did not know was how much I was dreading "getting there," especially as I listened in on conversations of those who were so excited about seeing snow for the first time. No snow was in *Château d'Oex*! Two days earlier what all Swiss ski resorts dread the most—the warm southern wind known as the "föhn—had blown up the Sarine valley, melting all the snow. No snow! I had to tell them.

Outwardly they took it well, but inwardly, I had no idea. I tried to convince myself that their main reason for making the trip was to pray, to sit at the feet of godly teachers, to fellow-ship, and to wait on the Lord. But snow would have made it bet-ter. People travel to Switzerland in the winter for the snow. Some of them were already dressed for the slopes.

After the evening meal we met for our first meeting. In spite of their having to fight jetlag, our guests spent a precious time in the Lord. Now, before they retired, I was to lay out for them the next day's schedule, which included two morning ses-sions, lunch, then transportation to the cable cars and ski lifts for those who would like to ski, or just ride high into the Alps to enjoy the beautiful winter scenery. I was trying to figure out what alternative afternoon schedule I might offer when Marthé Beasley spoke up for all to hear. *"Don't worry. The Lord is going to send snow tonight. There will be lots of it in the morn-ing."* Manley told her to sit down. I did not tell her that I'd just checked the forecast and it called for more warm weather. I was going to have to ride on her faith.

You guessed it — the next morning two feet of snow covered the ground! I must admit that I had checked in the middle of the night. What a sight to see! By the light of the La Frasse street lamp below, I saw those beautiful, fluffy white flakes softly floating to the ground. Snow had never looked so good.

Excitement filled the dining room at breakfast that morn-ing. It was a challenge getting the group to focus on spiritual matters while surrounded by the beautiful, pristine, white blan-ket of snow beckoning to them through the windows. And it was especially so for two little boys — our son, Jeff, and for Jonathan Beasley, who had been promised by his mother, before leaving the States, there would be lots of snow. He may, in fact, have been the only one who believed his mother's forecast, for he had already seen God perform a miracle for him. And after all, he did have a ski-suit.

The Faith of a Little Child

"Daddy, God wants me to go to Switzerland with you."

"Son, there will not be any other children going. This is a conference for adults."

"That's alright, I love being with you and Mama."

"Jonathan, your mother has taken such good care of me while I have been so sick that I really want her to go with me, but I don't have enough to take you also, and we can't use Gospel Harvester money for your trip."

"That's alright. I'll believe God for my own money."

And so it went on. Every day Jonathan would talk about his going to Switzerland and every day his parents would remind him that they did not have the money. Then one day to their surprise he announced that he was also praying for a ski-suit because he would need one in Switzerland. By now, Manley was beginning to sense that more was happening than what appeared on the surface. He called Jack Taylor, who was putting the tour together, to see what it would actually cost for Jonathan to go. Jack calculated that if he were to sleep on a cot in the parents room, that it could be kept to half the amount of the adult cost; that would be $650.00.

"Ski suit?" Marthé thought. *"I've never seen a ski-suit in any store in Louisiana. Where would we even find a ski-suit?"* But God was tuned to the prayers of a little seven-year-old boy. He knew where the ski-suit was.

Marthé and her sister, Donnie, sometimes went shopping at the *Bargain Barn,* an outlet store in the Lake Charles area. This particular day, as they walked in, they saw at the end of the first rack of clothes a little boy's ski-suit. Marthé couldn't believe her eyes. She commented on it to the store owner, a Jewish lady. The owner said that she didn't know how the ski-suit happened to be included in their merchandise. It had arrived somehow from somewhere. Marthé began to tell her the story about Jonathan praying that he would be able to go to Switzerland and how he would need a ski-suit. The woman was so moved that she said: *"The ski suit is his. You don't have to pay for it. That story is the most precious thing I have ever heard."*

Now that Jonathan had the ski-suit, he knew for sure that God was going to provide the money for the trip. Every day he would run down the lane to the mailbox to check if the money had arrived. *"I would stand at the window and watch him,"* Marthé recalls. *"Down the lane he'd run as soon as he saw the mail carrier. Back he'd come to the house, looking through the mail. One day, as he was sorting through the letters, he started shouting, 'Mama, I think this is it. I think this is it.'"* He was holding an AIRMAIL envelope with a German stamp. Marthé opened it to find a letter from a private in the US Army:

Dear Bro. Manley,
I am writing you to say that several years ago you were preaching in a church in my town. You will not remember, but I and my whole family were saved that week and everything has been different since then. For a long time I have wanted to do something for you but I have not had much money. Just recently, however, I received a small inheritance from an aunt. I am dividing it up to send to several preachers who have been used by the Lord in my life. Enclosed is a check for $650 for you to use any way you want. "

Use it any way you want? Jonathan already had the check in his hand. *"I believe this is it, Mama. This is it, isn't it Mama?"* Yes, that was it. Jonathan would celebrate his eighth birthday in the Switzerland snow.

Being so weak, Manley was not able to participate in many of the scheduled activities, so he spent a good bit of his time in Room #19, meditating. Here he was in Europe; in the very hotel where James Alexander Stewart and his wife Ruth had spent some of their vacations over the years. It was here that Dr. Stewart had written several of his books. Here he was where Duncan Campbell had spent a week with a group from the British Isles, not long after seeing God work so mightily in the Hebrides Revival. Here Manley was where Billy Graham had stayed, following the first *Lausanne International Congress on Evangelism.* Here he was, not far away from l'Abri and the work of Francis and Edith Schaeffer.

During those quiet hours, looking out at God's magnificent creation, Manley was beginning to visualize the answer to prayers he had prayed and heart desires he had held for years—desires to one day be a part of a spiritual awakening among God's children in this part of the world. He recalled how twenty-five years had passed since he had first set foot on European soil in the Port of Hannover, Germany, during his rebellious *Merchant Marine* days. Now here he was wondering just what God had in store for him in Europe?

25
The Vision Takes Shape

"We pray, Lord, light the flame once more of Holy Ghost revival
fire. Come now as in the days of yore; for You we wait
with great desire. Come suddenly upon Your own
and make Your holy presence known."

—Wesley Duewel [27]

The vision God was giving Manley continued to take shape as he returned to *Château d'Oex* year after year until, in 1977, in the providence of God, the ministry of the *International Christian Center* was drawn to a close. Little did anyone realize at the time what the real significance of the *Château d'Oex* closing would be. Rather than being the end of something that God had begun years earlier, the closing was the beginning of a new chapter during which God would use Manley to touch not only the countries of Western Europe but eventually the lands behind the Iron Curtain.

The closing of the *Château d'Oex* ministry had not been easy. It represented years of labor by my parents, and to a lesser degree their children. I had spent my teenage years there. All my siblings went to school there. My youngest brother, David, was born there. When the final papers were signed in early 1977, we thought it was the end of what had been a very important part of our lives and ministry. It was time for closure. What lay ahead of ministry in Europe was in God's hands.

The Beginning of a New Day

The phone rang. It was Manley. He wanted to talk. More than two years had passed since the last *Swiss Conference on Revival* in *Château d'Oex*. Though Patricia and I had been ministering in Europe during that time, we were not giving any thought to resuming a conference ministry—that is, until Manley's phone call. We met at the *Lotus Flower,* his favorite Chinese restaurant in Euless, TX.

Before long he began sharing the burden he had been carrying since the closure of the *International Christian Center.* His burden was to bring the message of revival to Christian leaders in both Western and Eastern Europe. He felt that restoring the conference ministry would be the primary instrument God would use. The more I listened to Manley the more excited I got as he unfolded the vision God had given him. *"We will invite pastors and their wives, denominational leaders, missionaries. We will cover the expenses of everyone who cannot afford to pay. You find the place, get the word out, and God will provide."* By the time our meeting was over, plans were in the making for the first *International Congress on Revival.*

A Long Time in the Making

In retrospect what God was about to do through Manley was not so much a new thing as it was the fruit of seeds planted years before at Milldale where his life had been so deeply impacted by James Alexander Stewart. Here an unexpected turn of events would get Manley indirectly involved with God's activity in Eastern Europe. It all began with Dr. Stewart's travail in prayer one day for countries in which he had ministered over the years—countries that were now behind the Iron Curtain. Jimmy Robertson, Milldale's director, observing the burden Dr. Stewart was carrying, asked if any particular way existed that the folk at Milldale might help. Little did he realize what was about to happen.

"We have ways of getting Bibles and other literature into Soviet bloc countries, but we have run out of supplies. We don't have anything to take," responded Dr. Stewart. *"We don't have the resources."* At that moment, as though he had heard a voice from heaven, Jimmy knew that Milldale was about to enter into an entirely new ministry that would stretch their faith beyond anything they had previously experienced. At that evening's service Jimmy Robertson announced to the congregation that Milldale had launched—not was going to launch, but *had launched*—a new literature outreach to the countries behind the Iron Curtain. The first step of faith had been made.

Manley contacted a friend in Florida who had an engineering background and who was sensing that the Lord wanted him to be involved in some type of full-time ministry. Though he had never worked in, nor even been near a print shop, he accepted the challenge to become Milldale's "printer-in-residence." Ivan Carlson and his family were on their way to Louisiana where they would spend the next 34 years!

Now that they had a printer, they needed equipment. Jimmy told Ivan that they were not going to tell people what they were planning to do about a printer, or what they hoped to do, but what they were in the process of doing. They announced that they had placed an order for a *Five-Unit Web Press*. Just as they had expected, God miraculously provided the funds and before the press had even been installed requests for materials began to arrive. Can you provide 50,000 copies of the Gospel of John in Polish? Can you send us 25,000 Bibles in the Russian language? Bulgaria needs hymnals; Czechoslovakia needs . . . and so the requests flowed in. And the literature flowed out: Bibles, Halley's Bible Handbook, Gospels, tracts—in most of the East European languages.

Then in 1980 the grandfather of all orders arrived. This was the year the summer Olympics were held in Moscow, Russia, A need for 500,000 Russian-language New Testaments existed.

Not too big for God! Ivan and everyone on the Milldale grounds went to work and before long produced a half million Russian New Testaments—printed and delivered to countries bordering the USSR. Requests for Spanish language materials also began to arrive from Central and South America as well as inquiries for literature from the Ivory Coast of Africa. Millions of pieces of Christian literature would be printed and shipped out of that little corner of Louisiana—representing miracle after financial miracle.

Then there were those times when their faith was stretched, such as the Saturday that Ivan told Jimmy he was running out of paper and that he had just received an invoice for $50,000 that had to be paid in ten days.

"Jimmy, I suggest that we shut down for a few weeks to regroup. After we get the bill paid, we can order more paper and start up again.

"Is the literature we printed with the paper we still owe for already on the mission field?"

"It is."

"In that case, Ivan, order more paper immediately. God is going to provide everything we need. Keep the presses running."

The next morning, Sunday, Jimmy told his congregation at Milldale Baptist Church about the $50,000 invoice due in ten days and that he didn't have a dime. He told them that he knew they were already stretched and did not have the money, so he was not even going to bother to take up an offering. He went on to preach. After the service someone took him aside and said, *"I know you did not take up an offering, but you can't stop me from obeying God."* He handed Jimmy a check. Others came by with checks, too. By the time he walked out of the church that morning God already had provided $40,000 from just a handful of people.

Jimmy knew it was going to be an exciting week because God would be sending in another $10,000. He didn't have a clue from where it would come. Every time the phone rang, every time someone drove up, every time he went to the mail box, he was expecting it to be there. And it was! By the end of the week, every penny they needed had been provided. Miracle after miracle, illustration after illustration flood the memories of those days when what was happening could only be explained as the activity of God. At the height of this printing ministry they were using two tons of paper a day, printing 30,000 Gospels of John an hour, and by the time the Iron Curtain fell, the printing presses at Milldale had printed over *one billion* pieces of literature. And just as Manley shared his vision in that Euless Chinese restaurant, the presses were running and running and running.

26
International Congress on Revival

"Revival is God revealing Himself to man in awe-full holiness and irresistible power. It is such a manifest working of God that human personalities are overshadowed and human programs abandoned. It is man retiring into the background because God has taken the field. It is the Lord making bare His holy arm and working in extraordinary power on saint and sinner."

—Arthur Wallis [28]

An undertaking such as the *International Congresses on Revival* takes much prayer, legwork, and faith. God began to add facilitators on both sides of the ocean. Among those who are too many to mention, was Robert (Bob) Ferguson, pastor of *Faith Baptist Church* in Kaiserslautern, Germany. At the time, Faith was the largest church in the *European Baptist Convention.* Bob was convention president. Bob was invaluable in helping with land arrangements and getting the invitations into the hands of pastors and missionaries across the continent. He, along with John Wilkes, press secretary of the *Baptist World Alliance,* was key in making arrangements for church leaders from the Iron Curtain countries to travel to the free West, most of them for the first time.

Conference Ministry Revived
1980: *Thyon 2000:* High, high in the Canton de Valais Alps,

this ski resort offered an unparalleled panoramic view of the Matterhorn, Les Dents du Midi, and Europe's tallest mountain, Mont Blanc. But the greater beauty was what happened in the lives of hungry souls from America and Europe. Among these was Iris Urrey, who had recently been saved and who would soon be returning to Europe as, we could say, ICR's first missionary to NATO.

Testimony

"It was a divine appointment for me. That week was one of the most outstanding experiences of my life as a doctor. I no longer see my profession as a job, but as a ministry. Meeting brothers and sisters from so many other countries has helped me understand that my identity is not only with Christ but also with a family that is made up of so many different kinds of people and languages." — a Little Rock, Arkansas, doctor.

1981 and 1982

Interlaken (between the lakes) is one of Switzerland's oldest resorts, the home of the Swiss folklore hero William Tell. It lies just ninety minutes, through the Bernese Oberland by train from *Château d'Oex*. It sits at the foot of the magnificent Yungfrau. This was the breathtaking location of the next two Congresses. Manley, Jack Taylor, Ron Dunn, T.D. and Dudley Hall, and Lewis Drummond were the scheduled speakers, with Pat and me leading the music worship portion of each session.

Meeting in Interlaken's world-renowned *Grand Hotel Victoria Yungfrau* was a miracle in itself but not nearly as great a miracle as the changed lives, especially of the Europeans who were guests of the ICR. More responded to the invitations to attend than was expected. This meant additional funds would be needed. This in turn required an extra portion of faith on the part of Manley and those who had joined him in trusting God for the finances. Miraculously, the supply was there, right on time as was the blessing. This would be true for each subsequent ICR as the numbers grew. Those coming from afar, such as the brethren from the USSR, also needed their travel costs covered. Over the years, Congress after Congress, God provided the hundreds of thousands of dollars needed. Year after year, God's people returned to their homes and ministries, revived and renewed.

A special memory for those who were ICR speakers was Manley's approach to the preaching assignments for each service. Seldom were they pre-scheduled for any particular meeting, so all those who were "officially" listed in the brochure as part of the ministry team, plus occasionally several other ministers who were attending the Congress, would meet before the service for a season of prayer. After prayer, Manley would ask: *"Who among us has been given a word from the Lord for the people tonight?"* With few exceptions one or two among us had a message burning in their hearts. Sometimes Manley would have already asked one of the speakers to be ready. Occasionally he would call out someone in the prayer circle to bring a word. Manley would minister from time to time himself, though he seemed to prefer staying in the background. Those who experienced this unique "selection" approach knew the importance of staying "prayed up" and what it meant to be instant in season and out of season.

1983: Innsbruck, Austria

The Congress was held in the Innsbruck Baptist Church. In addition to Manley, this year God spoke through Bill Stafford, R.T. Kendall, pastor of Westminster Chapel, London, and Roy Hession, author of many books including *The Calvary Road*.

Testimony

"We cannot tell you what blessings we have from being here.

Thank God and thank you for possibility of our being with so many believers together." —Pastor from Croatia

1984: Salzburg, Austria

The birthplace of Mozart and famous for being one of the settings for the *Sound of Music* film was ICR's next home. Each Congress had its special moments that participants would never forget. The year 1984 was just a bit extra special. This was the year when Baptist leaders from the Soviet Union were allowed to attend for the first time, culminating several years of trying to arrange their participation. Among the four who attended were Alexei Bishkov, executive secretary of UECB (Union of Evangelical Christians, Baptists), and Michael Zitkov, pastor of Central Baptist, Moscow, the only Protestant church permitted in the city at that time. This was also the year that Ruth Stewart Fajfr, widow of James Alexander Stewart, and her husband, Vlado, who lived in Czechoslovakia, were able to attend. Ruth was asked to share a word of testimony. She chose to simply read the *Song of Solomon,* briefly commenting on the passage from time to time as she read. To this day, those who were there, still remember her words.

Testimony

"How we thank God for the ICR. Two things have happened; our marriage has been changed and we have gained a fresh insight into God's activity around the world. Thank you" — Couple from Texas.

1985: Salzburg

This year, in addition to the gracious moving of the Spirit of God in the Congress services—and the unique fellowship that came from Western Christians meeting Eastern believers—what followed the Congress was an experience never to be repeated.

An American contingent went behind the Iron Curtain into East Germany. This was more than a sightseeing trip. We were able to rendezvous with some Baptist leaders in order to give them money to make badly needed repairs on one of their churches. The trip combined tense, exhilarating and very humorous moments especially when attempting to outmaneuver the East German guide who had been assigned to keep an eye on us night and day. With God's help, the mission was accomplished, even to joining East German believers in a worship service. God used those days to encourage His children who were living under severe persecution. It was also an example and witness to us that God's grace is sufficient even in the most difficult of times.

Doors Open to the USSR

The year 1985 was a milestone in the history of the Congress. This was the year the ICR received its first invitation to minister behind the Iron Curtain. On May 10, R.T. and Louise Kendall from London; John and Doylene Wilkes, headquartered with the BWA in Switzerland; Bob Ferguson from Germany; and Patricia and I arrived in Moscow to be met by a delegation of Baptist leaders. We were relieved to finally see friendly faces, after having been through the most scrutinizing immigration experiences one could imagine. The officials seemed to take delight in making us feel uncomfortable for a couple hours.

Though the Russian Baptist Union would have loved to have had Manley and Marthé participate, for health reasons they were not able to go. After a day in Moscow, meeting with the Baptist Union (UECB) and going through an orientation, we divided up, ministering in Leningrad, Karkov, Poltava, Kiev, Minsk, and points in between. Many of these Russian/Ukranian brothers and sisters were seeing "free-world" Christians for the first time, even as we were meeting the persecuted church for the first time. And what a blessing it was to discover no "wall of partition" dividing us. We were never so hugged and kissed in our lives. Though we were a blessing to them, we really were the recipients of the greater blessing as we looked into those faces that shone with the joy of the Lord in spite of who knows how many having been imprisoned for their faith.

USSR invitations to the ICR followed in 1986 and 1987 as well as opportunities for ministry in Poland and Czechoslovakia. Though Patricia and I continued to minister in these lands over the years, whatever fruit was realized by any of us goes back to seeds sown at the *International Congress on Revival* and the fulfilling of Manley's dream.

1986 and 1987

Les Diablerets, Switzerland, is not exactly an appropriate name (little devils) for a *Congress on Revival,* but nevertheless it was a place where many met the Lord in life-transforming ways. More delegates, from more Iron Curtain countries (12), were able to attend. We were hearing names like Wiazowski, Kondac, Gospodinov, Nikolaev, Goncharenko, Sârbuirimia and Dajludzionek, along with the more common names of European pastors and missionaries. We were inspired by the reports of what God was doing in their respective lands and fields of ministry, though those from the Soviet Union had to be careful what they said as every delegation from each of the communist lands was accompanied by a KGB agent masquerading as a pastor. This was serious, while also humorous. We knew who these agents were, and they knew we knew who they were. They were the ones who when asked to pray always deferred to one of the "other brothers."

An encouraging note must be added here for those who attended the ICR over the years and remember Alexei Stoyan, the KGB agent who always traveled with the Russian pastors. We received word that in his latter years and severely ill Alexei was led to the Lord by the grandfather of one of our closest Russian friends. This believer reached out to KGB agent Stoyan when all his "government" acquaintances and family had forsaken him. Brother Stoyan? Nothing is impossible with God!

For many, the ICR was not only an annual "spiritual oasis," it was the only time some couples were able to "get away" and experience a week with their spouses in beautiful surroundings. These were times of physical and emotional restoration as well as spiritual renewal. We heard this expressed so often over the years.

Testimony

"We were worn out when we arrived. It has been a hard year. Just being able to get off by ourselves has meant more than you could know. And then to hear from the Lord as we have . . .. Thank you for making this possible." —Pastor and wife from Germany

1988

Back again to **Les Diablerets,** but this time it was different because Manley was not able to attend. Though he was not physically present, he was there in spirit. His influence through prayer and finances was everywhere evident. Dr. Stephen Olford, Ron Dunn, and others were used of the Lord to lead us into God's throne room. The Congress culminated with a Lord's Supper service where believers from twenty-four countries met at the foot of the cross. It was a moment in time that none of us will ever forget. It was an appropriate and timely high point to revival conferences that began in 1971. This was the last time Manley's *Gospel Harvesters Foundation,* the umbrella under which the ICR had flourished, was able to be directly involved other than through prayer. This was the year that the Congress needed to be officially incorporated as an entity of its own. And this we did, with Manley's blessing and prayers.

1989 and 1990: Chelm, Poland

At the invitation of the *Baptist Union of Poland* we ventured for the first time behind the Iron Curtain in 1989 for the first of two Congresses held in that part of the world. Since Manley's dream had been so focused on Iron Curtain countries, we felt it appropriate as the doors opened to begin turning toward Eastern Europe. We met at the *Baptist Union Retreat Center* in Chelm, a city not too far from the Russian border, and Krakow, the Polish capital. This proved to be of the Lord as expressed in the following letter from the President of the Baptist Union of Poland, Konstanty Wiazowski.

Dear Leaders of the International Congress on Revival:

On behalf of the Baptist Union of Poland I want to thank you for having the ICR in Poland. It was the most spiritually important meeting we've ever had in the Polish Baptist Union. Concentrating on the Word of God and revival is what we need. The Congress was a real encouragement to the people of God in this part of the world.

It will be memorable for us because it was the first time we have ever been able to have our wives with us in such a meeting. Thank you for having sessions for them to help them with their specific needs.

Pastors of other denominations were very glad that you invited them to attend also. They continue to talk about this when I see them. Also, I have just returned from the Soviet Union where I met many participants from the Congress. They are saying that this kind of meeting about revival for pastors and their churches is what they need most and it must be very often repeated . . . They join me in thanking you.

Though not as many Americans were now attending, we were able to invite three times as many pastors and wives from the Soviet bloc nations as we had in previous years— 270 in all, with many of them being young couples. The powerful preaching of Drs. Stephen and David Olford, Jim Elliff, and others; the spirit of repentance; the worship in foreign languages; and the breaking of bread together, would have brought so much joy to Manley's heart. And how we wish he could have gone with us to Bielsko-Biawa to see the house that ICR purchased for Gregory and Eva Bednarzyk to use to plant the first evangelical church in that city of over 100,000.

Dear Ron and brothers and sisters of the International Congress on Revival.

I greet you in the precious name of the Lord Jesus Christ. Our God is so good and gracious. Last Friday the deed, relative to the house in Bielsko-Biawa, was signed. That means that we can now officially start our ministry.

Our Lord overcame so many difficulties which seemed impossible to resolve. Just like it says in Psalm 111:3, "Splendid and majestic is His work." I am sure that what has happened is not an accident, but it is His mighty work. I want to thank you and all the other people who have had a part in it. Please share our gratitude with them.

Now I prepare for our first year of ministry. I expect great blessing as many come to meet our Savior and dedicate themselves to Him and the ministry of sharing the gospel in this city. Please abide with us in faith and prayer that God will manifest His glory and power.

Yours in Christ,
Gregory Bednarzyk

The one regret we have is that Manley could not be there to see what God was doing from seed sown in his heart many years before by James Alexander Stewart, who had himself planted so many churches in this part of the world. How he would have rejoiced to know how that seed was continuing to grow.

Little did we know at the time, however, that in just a few months our own lives (Patricia's and mine) would take an unexpected turn when Dr. Henry Blackaby would ask me to pray about becoming his associate in the *Office of Prayer and Spiritual Awakening* at the Home Mission Board of the Southern Baptist Convention. This invitation arrived almost at the moment when Manley was preaching his last message to Southern Baptists at the New Orleans Convention Pastor's Conference on June 10, 1990—one month to the day before God would call him home. We told Henry that we would pray and seek God's direction, even though it did not seem to make sense in light of the focus of our lives and ministry having been on Europe and the lands of the Iron Curtain for so many years. We were soon to discover that God has His surprises. Though we did not fully understand, we knew we were to change course and link our lives with Dr. Blackaby.

Now, what was to happen with the *International Congress on Revival?* This question would soon be answered in a phone call from Bill Stafford, one of Manley's dearest friends, and one who had been a part of so many of the Congresses over the years.

"Ron, what are your plans for ICR?"

"I'm not sure, Bill. Is God telling you that you are to pick up Manley's burden?

And so the fulfilling of the vision continued, even as it does to this day.

SECTION SIX
Heading for the Summit

When Pat Pylate finished teaching on Friday, she and her sisters, Joyce and Aunt Sister (Henry Mae) drove from Nederland to Grapevine to be with their brother. They spent all day Saturday with Manley and Marthé. Then on Sunday Henry Mae, who had gone prepared to stay longer if necessary, decided that was what she should do, so Pat and Joyce began driving back to south Texas.

It had been a good visit with their brother. He did not seem to be doing too badly in light of the recent hospitalization, the finger amputations, and the preaching appointments he insisted on keeping that summer. They were glad to have seen Jonathan before he left for Albany, GA, where he would begin his ministry as youth director at Sherwood Baptist Church. He was looking forward to his dad being there in a few weeks to speak at his ordination service.

After dropping Joyce off at her house in Jasper, Pat drove on to Nederland. Just a few blocks from her own home she began to weep. Pat suddenly knew that she would never see Manley again. Her husband, James, met her at the door with the news— *"Aunt Sister just called to say that they have taken Manley to the hospital."*

When my life's work is ended and I cross the swelling tide,
When that bright and glorious morning I shall see.
I shall know my Redeemer when I reach the other side,
And His smile will be the first to welcome me.[29]

27
A One-Day Pass to Preach

"I charge you in the presence of God and of Christ Jesus, who is to judge the living and the dead, and by his appearing and his kingdom: preach the word; be instant in season and out of season; reprove, rebuke, and exhort, with complete patience and teaching"
(2 Tim. 3:8).

The summer season of 1990 began with yet another hospitalization and surgery. Doctors amputated another finger, this time on his right hand. Manley's greater concern, however, seemed to be a preaching engagement he had scheduled at Bellevue Baptist Church in Memphis. He had been looking forward so much to sharing the ministry times with three of his favorite people; Stephen Olford, Ron Dunn, and Bellevue's pastor, Adrian Rogers. If this was going to become a reality, however, God would have to perform yet another miracle. Persuaded that it was God's will for him to fulfill his commitment to preach, Manley began the process of obedience.

Tuesday Afternoon
Manley: *"Doctor, I am going to have to fly to Memphis tomorrow to speak at a Bible Conference."*
Doctor: *"Manley, I'm sorry, but that is impossible. You have to stay in the hospital through the weekend. With the finger amputation you've just had there is serious danger of your getting an infection in the wound."*
Manley: *"Doctor, I must go."*

Doctor: *"If you insist on going you may end up not only getting an infection but needing to find another doctor because I can't authorize your release."*
Manley: *"I understand. But I have to go."*

The next day, Wednesday, Manley and Marthé were on a plane headed for Memphis. Thursday morning he was being helped to the pulpit at Bellevue Baptist Church.

Manley's Message[30]

I am so grateful that the grace of God can handle any problem. He has. He is. He will. Hallelujah! I'm not discouraged, disappointed, or disillusioned. I know that my Redeemer liveth. He is not only the God of the "was and the will be" but He is God of the "now". I like to stay in the "now" with Him. God says that we must believe that He is. Whew . . .. Yes sir, He is, right now. I'm not waiting on any tomorrows. I'm going to enjoy God's "now." Amen? I love 2 Corinthians 9:8 where Paul talks about all sufficiency in all things, always, everywhere. I'm counting on those alls and always. By the way (Manley points to a chair that had been placed next to the pulpit for him to sit in), these boys brought this chair up here on the platform for me to sit on. I want you to know it's their lack of faith, not mine.

In light of the physical difficulties I have faced in recent years I know you would expect me to take seriously the numbering of my days and not waste my time. I have done that to the best of my ability. I have asked God to sharpen my mind and make me sensitive that I might know what we are facing in these last days—that I might be able to address the issues surrounding us and that my time not be wasted. So I am here with a message that I believe addresses what we are really facing today.

Not knowing that the Lord would be calling him home in

less than two months, Manley went on to say:

In that it is so late for me, I am not worried about offending people. I'm not worried about being run off. I am not worried about being paid, because it is too late to consider such mundane things. Only God knows if this might not be my last time to preach. If it is, I want it to be the time that rings the bell.

Now, most of you will expect me to speak on some aspect of faith. So I'm going to give you something on faith while you are turning to the third chapter of Revelation. *The faith life is a life that is initiated by God, sustained by God, maintained by God; a life where God gets all the glory and you get the benefit.* There is a great deal of mystery about faith. I would love to take the time to talk about it, but God has put another message on my heart that I must share with you.

After reading verses 14 to 22 of Revelation 3, the letter written to the church in Laodicea, Manley continued:

What is the Laodicean condition? I believe it is a condition that is very applicable to the hour in which we live. The Laodicean condition basically means, 'the rule of the people,' and the Lord makes it clear to them that He knows exactly what they are doing. He says: *"I know your works."* There is not one thing that is hidden from God. He knows our works. He knows us better than we know ourselves. From this passage we see that the Laodicean condition is when a person is naked, wretched, miserable, broke, defeated, while thinking that he is fully clothed, rich, and successful. If you were to ask a Laodicean man, *"How are you doing?* he would answer, *"Great!"* The tragedy is that while he stands there wretched and naked, he thinks he is fully clothed and has it all together.

In light of this, what do you think Jesus meant when He said that he wished they were either hot or cold rather than lukewarm? I have asked God many times what this really means. I think I have been given some insight. When you are lukewarm, you are living in deception. You are saying that you have it when you don't. You are telling everybody, *"This is it."* In response to this kind of thinking the Lord says that he would rather have us dead. You know why? Because you are not going to deceive anyone when you are dead, but when you are lukewarm you are a deceiver. Your whole life is one of deception. You have a form of godliness that fools people while denying the power of God in your life; while the real you is spiritually naked.

For a long time we have judged ourselves by ourselves until we really believe that we are successful, while God says that we are naked, poor, and blind and do not know it. *The need of the hour is that we see ourselves as we really are. For no man will ever change until he sees what he really is. No sinner is ever saved until he sees himself a sinner. No saint ever goes from victory to victory until he sees himself in light of God's glory.*

Buy Gold

But Jesus does not leave them there. He says: *"I want to tell you how to solve your problem. I want you to go and buy gold, tried in the fire."* That's what He is saying to the churches today, *"I want you to buy gold that has been tried in the fire."* The church is so full of poverty that when the world comes looking for reality, for something lasting, for spiritual wealth, it finds poverty. The world finds a form of godliness that has no power. Anyone reading the New Testament picture of what God intended the church to be would be hard pressed to find one to join today. Some may be kin in doctrine, but they are not kin in glory. The picture of gold tried by fire is a picture of the church being purified.

Dear friend, the church today needs to experience the kind of purging by fire that brings her to the point of brokenness and submissiveness before the Lord so that when people see her, the only explanation for her is God. Gold has had all the impurities burned out. Buy gold so that when people come to your door, they will find the wealth that will meet their need. They'll find a flexible, submissive saint of God so yielded to the living Lord that nothing gets in the way of their being touched by the Master's hand. Oh that people might say of us that there is no explanation for our lives, there is no explanation for our ministries, our churches, other than the presence, the power and the glory of God.

At this point in the message, Manley directs his attention to a man in the audience who but a few months before had been as good as dead for three days. His brother, Jimmy Robertson, had called Manley from the hospital to tell him that the doctor had just advised the family that medical personnel had given him up, that he could not live. Manley asked, *"Why are you calling me?"* Jimmy answered, *"Bro. Manley, you've been there. It may be that you have a little gold that we can get."* Manley continues:

I was sitting on the end of the couch with the telephone in my hand, listening to the words, *"he's dead, he's dead."* I told my friend Jimmy that I would pray. I hung up the phone. And honestly, my friends, it was this casual. I said, *"Lord, do you have anything in me and in your Word for this man?"* I opened the Bible that was on the end table next to me. Now, I want you to know that I am not one of those who just drops a finger on a verse and claims it as a word from God for a situation. But in this case I tell you my Bible opened to 2 Corinthians 1:9. This is where Paul said that he and his companions thought they had received the sentence of death, but that it was to make them rely not on themselves but on the God who raises the dead! When I read that passage, I knew that I had something in the bank. It was that gold! And I can verify it this morning, because he is here with his wife and nephews (Manley then had Ray

Robertson and his family stand up).

I did not need to pray for ten hours, because the gold was already there. I called Brother Jimmy back and said: *"The reason your brother has had the sentence of death on him, the reason he has been clinically dead for three days, is to bring you to the point of not relying on yourselves but that you will totally rely on God. When you see that this is God's purpose for it all and respond to this reason, God will raise him up."*

I am not trying to magnify Manley Beasley, but all I want to say is that when that family had need of gold there was some in the bank for them. How many times people have come to our doors, to our churches, looking for gold, and there wasn't any. Oh God, bring us to the point that when people are looking for help, they will find the gold that they need. When Ray walked out of that hospital, the doctors didn't know what to say. We do. There was gold in the bank for him.

Buy a White Robe

God told the Laodicean church to buy a white robe; a robe of righteousness. When we are saved by the grace of God, judicially and positionally we become righteous. But in a practical sense we have to keep ourselves holy and righteous before God by repentance and faith. We have to keep our sins confessed up to date in order to keep that robe pure and clean. How quickly our robes become dirty. Don't forget, we never get so spiritually mature that we no longer have to confess our sins and make restitution. Do you know how you can tell a person whose robe is white? A spiritual twin to righteousness is "glory." When you see a holy man, you see the glory of God. Dear friends, what we need is for the people of God to buy that white robe so that the glory of God may again rest on us. Holiness and glory are the inseparable twins we need today, for without holiness there is no glory, no presence of God that causes lives to be forever changed.

So much of the church today can be defined by two words—money and numbers. One hundred years ago, the word that described the church of God was "change." *We used to preach until people were changed. Now we preach until we get people added to our number. Hear me! When the glory of God touches a life, that life will be changed, forever changed.* Then why are we satisfied with anything less? I believe it is because gold and a white robe come only at the cost of some things that have become so important to us that we are not ready to give them up. Oh for the day when sinners would walk into our churches and so encounter the glory of God that they would be overwhelmed with their need to repent of their sin.

I was never privileged to get the education that many preachers have these days. And I'm not against getting as much of that as you can. I can't tell you about the Hebrew and the Greek. I can't tell you about all the ramifications of the verbs and adverbs and all those things. But I'll tell you what I can do. I can tell you about the Author of all that. I can tell you how far I can walk with Him. I can walk right on in. Yes sir! Right into His presence and see His glory. Buy that robe and the glory will be there!

Buy Eye Salve

Jesus told the Laodiceans to buy one more thing; *eye salve.* I believe He is talking about having the Holy Spirit anoint our eyes so that we might see as the Lord sees. This is one of the great needs of the hour: that we might see sinners as Jesus sees them; that we might have eyes to see the will of God as it is happening in heaven; that we might embrace it and move heaven into earth. So let us pray for *eye salve* that we might see as God sees.

In the following story that Manley tells of his mother, we find her, for a third and final time, playing a significant part in his life. This, of course, is when he is at the point of death. [31]

Manley: The Christmas after we buried my mother the family was together. We were looking through some of her things. Though I already had a couple of my mother's Bibles, my siblings insisted that I have this particular one. They told me that I would know why I should have it when I turned to a certain page and read what she had written in the margin. I turned to that page and I read this in my mother's handwriting: *"I visited Manley today and everybody, including the doctors, say that he is going to die and it is over. But Lord, I thank you that you have let me see what you see and it's not over. Manley is going to make it."* Folk, that was a year before anyone knew that I was going to live. My mother was able to look on through and see what the Savior saw. She was able to hinge her faith upon what God said. She declared it in the margin of her Bible. Amen?

Think now about the difficulties you face in life. If you learn to truly worship, God will pull you aside and let you see what He sees. You will be able to walk up the side of a mountain, as Abraham did, and say to your son, *"God will provide for Himself the lamb for the burnt offering, my son"* (Gen. 22:8, NASB). And you will be able to say to the servants at the bottom of the mountain, *"Stay here with the donkey, and I and the lad will go yonder; and we will worship and (we) will return to you"* (Gen. 22:5, NASB).

In the literal sense Abraham knew that Isaac could be burned to ashes. But *in his spirit he knew that God would put those ashes back together and that they would walk back down that mountain together.* So, what was Abraham living in? Was he living in the ashes? Or was he living in the walking back down that mountain? Abraham was able to look beyond the present and see what God saw.

In the Gospel of John, the Pharisees told Jesus that they were of their father Abraham. Jesus responded with, *"If you were of your father Abraham, you would do the works of Abraham"* (John 8:39). Jesus went on to say that *"Abraham rejoiced to see my day"* (John 8:56). What was Jesus talking about? Thousands of years before the incarnation of Jesus, Abraham was called on to sacrifice his son. That sacrifice contradicted God's plan, God's promise, and God's provision. But Abraham, somewhere out there, got to seeing things as God saw them. When he did, he saw the Lamb of God who would take away the sins of the world. Abraham saw it and rejoiced. Why did he rejoice? Because if Jesus was to ever come as the Son of Man, Isaac had to live. Whatever called Isaac to nothingness was just a vehicle for enlargement, enabling God's perfect will to be done. Abraham was able to handle this because he had eyes that were anointed with the eye salve of the Spirit of God. He was able to see as God saw. And just as with Abraham, you have something that God wants sacrificed. It's not your money. It's you!

Manley concluded his message by referring to the Apostle Paul's admonition in Romans 12 that we present our bodies, ourselves, as living sacrifices on the altar. In that presenting of ourselves we have the picture of our submitting to the purifying work of God's fire. Whatever then is resurrected from the "ashes" of that altar will be pure gold that can be used by God to meet the poverty of those who come to us for help. From those ashes will be resurrected a "white-robed saint" clothed with the glory of God. And through that purging process we will have had the salve of the Holy Spirit applied to our eyes, enabling us to see as God sees.

As he was being helped down from the platform that morning, Manley did not know this would be the last time he would speak at Bellevue Baptist Church. In just a few hours he'd be flying back to Dallas to check into the same hospital room he had left the day before. The nurses were waiting for him. The doctor who had reluctantly agreed to give him a "one-day pass" would continue to attend to his needs. Nor did Manley realize that in less than six weeks he would be returning to that same hospital for the last time.

28
Faith Week's Final Visit

*"The Lord in unfailing wisdom has appointed a time for the outgo-
ings of His gracious power, and God's time is the best time . . . the
Lord will keep His appointments. He never is before His time;
He never is behind."*
—Charles Haddon Spurgeon [32]

Manley stayed in the Dallas Medical City Hospital through
the weekend before returning to Grapevine. He always found
getting back home to be good, though this time, as was often the
case, he would be there for just a few days. Those regular treatments at the nearby Dialysis Center were constant interruptions
and reminders that life was but a vapor.

Soon Manley and Marthé were off again to the airport, this
time for a flight to Fayetteville, AR, where they would be picked
up and driven to Siloam Springs for *Faith Week*. Manley looked
forward to this annual event as much as anything he did. He had
only missed one year since its beginning in 1974. That was due
to his being in the hospital. Attending *Faith Week* that year was
one of his *preacher boys,* Harry Layden, whose life had been
profoundly affected by Manley.

A Testimony

"Manley Beasley is one of my spiritual heroes. I was one of
those fortunate young men who got to travel with him from time
to time. I would sit at his feet and just listen to him talk about
the walk of faith. Those years shaped the course of my life and
ministry.

"Several weeks before Manley went to be with the Lord I had one of my greatest thrills; for one last time, I got to be a servant to Manley. When he arrived, I could tell that he was in severe pain. He had had another finger amputated and his feet were turning black due to the circulatory problem that limited the blood flowing to them. I recall going to his room to rub his feet to help relieve some of the pain. He was so weak physically. Yet I recall how this did not affect his spirit as he pressed on in the strength of the Lord.

"As I was rubbing his feet one day he said, *'Son, I know you desire to be a man of faith, but if you are going to have the kind of walk you desire, there is a principle you are going to have to learn; we all have an Isaac.'* I asked him what he meant. He then told me the story of Abraham and his test of faith. He said, *'Son, if you desire to walk with God with a faith that pleases Him, you cannot hold anything back'* He said, *'We all have something at the bottom of Mount Moriah that we need to get to the top if we are going to experience what faith is all about. We all have an Isaac.'*

"That day changed my life. *Faith Week* was where I said goodbye to my mentor and is the place where I began to build an altar of faith. Eight months later God revealed to me my own personal Isaac. He has used it to touch and challenge countless others in their walk of faith. I met God in a life-transforming way in that room that day."

—Harry Layden
Harry Layden Ministries, Tulsa, OK

Though Manley appeared to be becoming increasingly aware of the brevity of time, he did not anticipate it would be so short when he faced the Faith Week staff that Wednesday morning. He shared what would be his last message with these who had become like family to him and to Marthé.

Manley's Message

Faith Week has always been a real challenge and blessing to me. Over the years I have done everything there is to do here, except to take out the garbage. It has been a rewarding experience for me as I go across the country and have people walk up to me and say things like, *'Aren't you Manley Beasley? I was at Faith Week one year when you ministered to me.'* The reward for getting old is seeing some of the fruit from your years of service. For me *Faith Week* has been one of those most fruitful places. I had made plans to come and stay all week. Then two weeks ago my doctors changed the dialysis process. It has affected my whole system. I have not been able to adjust to the change. Also, I have had another finger amputated and infection has set in, so we'll have to return home tomorrow to have the stitches removed and for the doctors to see what they can do.

Though Marthé and I have known almost all of you for a long time, a few of you are meeting me for the first time. You may not know that in 1970-71 I came down with seven different diseases, three of them terminal. I was not supposed to have lived. Then two years ago I had another bout with death. The doctors again said that I was going to die. I actually stopped breathing; my heart quit beating on six occasions. Then a month ago I overdosed and almost died (At this point Marthé speaks up to say that Manley did not overdose but that it was a nurse who overdosed him with one of the medications). It's been quite an experience. Now, I may look weak and feeble, but the Lord has promised me all grace, all sufficiency in all things at all times, unto His good work. I anticipate fighting the battle and running the race well. I will be ready to go when it is all over.

Three years ago I was with Dr. Stephen Olford in a conference in Denver, CO. In one of his sermons he was addressing different kinds of ministries that function in the Body of Christ. He surprised me by saying, *'Now, you take Manley Beasley; he has the ministry of suffering.'* This baffled me at first, but then I began to understand it. When I was with Dr. Olford this past week in Memphis, he elaborated on his statement. *"Manley,"* he said, *"the church needs people to go through suffering to show the rest of us how it is done."*

I believe I can say that suffering does not bother me as much as it challenges me. A concern I have—and a temptation I face—is whether or not I am going to be faithful in the midst of my suffering. If suffering is my lot, then I want to be a faithful witness to those who are watching me. I want to be a witness to the faithfulness and sufficiency of God, because the first thing that a Christian is called on to be is a witness. I want to be the kind of witness who makes the invisible visible. What I mean is that the invisible message found in the Word of God might be worked out in my daily life for people to see."

We're going to read Hebrews 3:8-19. These are verses that deal with a portion of Israel's history and the temptation Israel faced to believe a lie. In verse 11 the writer talks about a *rest,* a rest that refers to Canaan. The Bible says that we are to labor that we might enter into that rest. Entering into that rest does not mean passivity. It refers to our cooperating with God in whatever He initiates so that through His power we experience victory. In verse twelve we read that when a man has an evil heart of unbelief, he depends on the flesh. This means he goes first to man to handle his situations and not to God.

Our text is found in verse 19 where we read, *"So we see that they could not enter in because of their unbelief."* My outline, however, will be taken from the 13th chapter of Numbers. We know the story of Israel's 400 years spent in Egypt and how God used Moses and Aaron to lead them out of captivity. We know how God got the attention of the Egyptians through miracles and finally through the sign of the blood at the Passover. In typology this scene represents our salvation, the washing away of our sins by the blood of the Lamb.

When the Israelites left Egypt, however, they were not only leaving their bondage behind them, they were leaving with God's commitment to them that His presence would go with them—the cloud by day and the pillar of fire by night. What a sight that must have been—being led by a cloud and a pillar of fire. Now, if you know your geography, you will realize that God did not lead them directly into Canaan, even though that was His ultimate objective since the land of Canaan represents the overcoming life. It is God's objective for every saved sinner to be led into that land where they will be overcomers—where they will walk in victory.

Why is this important? It is important because unless you are living an overcoming life, why should anyone believe you when you tell them that you have been saved by grace or that you have been delivered from the bondage of sin? For example, if I walked up to you and said that I am saved, but you see me living a defeated life—if I am not overcoming sin and if I am not living in victory—why should you believe what I say? But if I tell you I have been saved and by my life I demonstrate that He Who is in me is greater than he who is in the world; if you see me living an overcoming life, even though I face one battle after another, you will know that I have something that you don't have. So, God's objective is to teach us how to be over-comers. Amen?" (Manley would often lean toward the audience while cupping his hand to his ear to solicit a response).

God was leading the Children of Israel into a *School of Faith,* and in this school they were going to face ten crises between Egypt and Canaan. Let's look at two of them. The first was the Red Sea. How did they get across that sea? By faith! When Moses did what God told him to do, they saw the mighty hand of God at work. Then there was the lake of bitter water. They cut down a tree and at God's command they put that tree in the bitter water and the water became sweet. That tree represents our Savior. And figuratively speaking, when they got themselves properly related to Christ, God would provide a lake for every tribe. Why didn't God lead them right to those lakes in the first place? Why didn't He take them right into Canaan? Because God was trying to teach them how to walk by faith, He was trying to show them that man shall not live by bread alone but by every word that proceeds from the mouth of God.

Looking ahead to the New Testament we find that Jesus not only taught His disciples the principles of the Ten Commandments, He was constantly testing them to see if they were getting it. They were, however, forever flunking—that is, until Peter walked on the water. For Peter, that was the first glimpse of what Jesus was trying to teach him. How about you? Do you have skirmishes every day? Are you facing problems, challenges, difficulties? Do you see them as part of what God wants to use to teach you to turn to Him, to trust Him? And one of the amazing things about all this is that God sometimes allows the devil to be the delivery boy for these problems.

Now, going back to Numbers 13, we find God's people, who had been heirs of Canaan for 400 years, arriving at Kadesh Barnea. They are almost home! Here was the land that has been promised to their forefathers. The land that was rightfully theirs. It lay just ahead of them. God tells them to check it out. They did. They sent twelve messengers who came back with a glowing report on the beauty of the land and how fruitful it was. But they also described walled cities and giants that made them feel like grasshoppers. "*So what*," said two of the messengers: "*don't worry about the walled cities and giants. Let's go up there and conquer the land because God is with us.*" The remaining ten, however, said that the opposition was too great; the walls were too high and the giants too big. God's people chose to believe the ten. In Hebrews 3:8 this response is called a *provocation,* or a *rebellion.* It is a picture of rubbing a raw sore. God's children had rubbed the sore one time too often. They had murmured; they had griped; and now they were rebelling. What was now clear was that it had not been their faith that had gotten them as far as they had; it was the faith of Moses. But now they were faced with the choice of trusting the power of God or looking at their own weakness. A time arrives when God no longer lets you live on the coattails of someone else's faith.

So we find them refusing to believe God, so the glory departs. God turned them back into the wilderness. All except the two who believed God were condemned to die, never to see the promised land. Verse 19 says that they were unable to enter the promised land because of their unbelief, which means they believed a lie. The moment we choose not to believe the truth, we choose to believe a lie. If the devil can get you to believe a lie about the Word of God, you die. That is what happened to all but Caleb and Joshua. And one other thing: some say that they believe the truth while not acting on it. God says, *"fear lest a promise having been left you, you fail to discover it."* In other words, fear that you fail to put into practice the truth that you have heard.

What do you think would have happened that day at Kadesh Barnea if God's people had confessed their weakness and lack of faith but said, *"sink or swim, win or lose, we are going in because God is on our side?"* Unfortunately they didn't do that. Instead they believed a lie—in spite of the truth that the land was theirs and all they had to do was to take it. That day, they died.

For us, the fundamental issue is the Word of God—whether or not we are going to believe it, whatever the situation may look like. God is looking for men and women who will live by the Word not just by what they may see, smell, taste, feel, and hear. For this kind of living we must come to the place where

God's Word is our absolute authority. *And when the Word of God is mixed with faith it becomes an active, living Word. When not mixed with faith, as was the case with the Children of Israel at Kadesh Barnea, it is of no profit. It has to be believed and acted on to profit us.*

Manley went on to say that when we believe a lie, we forfeit our intimate relationship with the glory of God. We cease to be an instrument through which God can get glory. We forfeit the blessing of getting in on the riches that God has for us. It is a costly thing to believe a lie. He pointed out that those ten "negative" messengers saw the blessing of Canaan, but they took their eyes off the Blesser when they were overcome by the sight of the walled cities and giants. At that point they began to believe the lie of the enemy.

Manley continued: In Christianity today, there are three levels of activity—those who do things *for* God such as *"I prayed a prayer to get saved"*—those who *live by principles* that when executed, the principle will get them results, and then there are those, thank God, who *walk with a person,* and His name is Jesus. A believer has no trouble with faith when he sees Jesus. *A glimpse of Jesus will save you, but it takes a gaze to sanctify you.* That is why the enemy will do everything he can to keep you out of this book, the *Word of God,* because this is where we see Jesus.

When we take our eyes off of Jesus, the walled cities the devil throws up in front of us will look impossible to conquer. When we get our eyes off of Jesus, the problems we face will look as big as giants and we'll give up. The interesting thing is that the Bible tells us that the walled cities had no defense. Years later Joshua and the Israelites faced the walled city of Jericho and did what God told them to do. God jerked the molecules out of the stones in those walls and they came tumbling down. Yes sir! And when Caleb and Joshua, who had kept their eyes on

God, came across those giants when they were checking out the land, they saw them as big old loaves of bread—bread to eat.

It is right and good to see ourselves as 'nothing.' That is commendable and scriptural. But if you do so and not remember that God takes the weak and uses their weakness to take the prey, you are going to miss a great deal in your Christian life. I spent several of my earlier years saying *"I can't,"* because I could only see myself as a grasshopper. I couldn't see how God could use me. But one day I learned, as I have said before, that God has to make us *nothings* before He can make us *somethings*. God can take a *nothing* and so fill him with His glory that he will be equal to any task that God calls him to do.

Remember Gideon? God said: *"Thou great man of valor."* Gideon said, *"Who, me?"* Gideon saw himself as nothing, but Gideon, in the hands of God, was more than a match for any enemy he would face. If you see yourself only as a "nothing," you are believing a lie because in the sight of God you are a "something." Glory to the Lamb! Whew . . .. When I get a glimpse of how God sees me, I want to move on. Praise God! Yes, sir . . .. Praise the Lamb! Amen and Amen . . .. Glory to God! Let God show you what you are. There's nothing wrong in seeing yourself as a grasshopper if you don't forget that grasshoppers hop. Just think of how many "nothings" have been raised up over the history of the church to be used to glorify God and touch the world.

Manley closed his message with an illustration from the life of Jacob who had believed a lie for twenty years—the lie that his son Joseph was dead. Immediately following the message he and Marthé began a hurried trip to Tulsa for their flight to Dallas, where another dialysis treatment awaited him and where the doctors would remove the stitches from the finger amputation that had become infected. As they drove away, waving goodbye to Ruffin and Melissa Snow, to Harry Layden, and the many others whom Manley and Marthé had grown to love over the years, none of them realized—or at least, none of them wanted to entertain the thought—that this would be Manley's final farewell to Faith Week.

Back home in Texas, Manley stayed just long enough to attend to his medical needs before heading straight for Louisiana's Tickfaw River and the summer home of his friend Jimmy Robertson. The Tickfaw runs through the Maurepas Swamp and is the habitat of many species of wild life and water dwellers. It was the kind of setting that Manley had grown to love over the years. The river created a wetland where you find Hardwood and Cypress trees, Snowy Egrets, Great Blue Heron, beaver, coyotes, possum, raccoons, and squirrels in abundance. And of course there were the alligators, which provided one of Manley's favorite delicacies, alligator tail.

He had been here many times before. Now sensing the need to "get away" before going on to the Southern Baptist Convention in New Orleans, he knew he could just sit back, put up his feet, wear his jeans and riding hat—or if he wished lounge all day in his PJ's—surrounded by long-time friends. And of course, it was a time for eating his favorite foods. And eat they did! Jimmy was one of ten children. All his siblings loved Manley. And so they came. All of them! And their children, too. It was like a "homecoming." And the food! Though the whole Robertson family knew their way around the kitchen, Jimmy's wife, Francis, was one of Manley's favorite cooks. And she knew what Manley liked to eat most—anything that came out of the water: catfish, shrimp, frog's legs, soft shell crabs, gator tails, oysters (raw) and oh, the gumbo! The fellowship and food were like a prelude to heaven, which as they all would soon discover, Manley already knew was just around the corner.

29
The Last SBC

*"Every time I think of Bro. Manley, Hebrews 11:6 comes
to mind: 'Without faith it is impossible to please God.'
At the beginning of my Christian life, at the age of 28, Manley's
message of faith and revival gave clear direction to my spiritual
journey. Never have I seen strength made more perfect
than through his physical weakness. I recall his reminding me
that when you come to the end of yourself, God is ready
to use you. For many of us he has been our pastor and our prophet.
His godly wisdom has helped us through dark days
in our professional and personal lives."*

—Morris Chapman [33]

Sunday Evening, June 10

June 1990 was a watershed year for the Southern Baptist Convention held at the New Orleans Superdome. At this time and place more than 22,000 messengers would gather to vote for a president whose election would set the SBC's direction for decades. At this Convention the study course *Experiencing God,* written by Henry Blackaby and Claude King, would be introduced. On a more personal note, this was the time and the place Dr. Blackaby would ask me to pray about joining him as his associate in the *Office of Prayer and Spiritual Awakening* at what was then the Home Mission Board, in Atlanta, GA.

But even as all these matters affecting our futures were taking place, Manley Beasley, whose name had become synonymous with faith and adversity, would stand for the last time to address thousands of fellow ministers at the SBC's annual Pastors' Conference. This was Sunday evening, June 10, exactly one month before his home-going. Though now very weak and in much pain, he would take the podium to preach the message God had put on his heart.

Manley's Message

It's good to be with you tonight. It is always good to be with God's people. I would like to be able to stand on the front porch for about thirty minutes and then preach. I don't expect many of you have any idea what I'm talking about, but that's alright.

A man's behavior will be along the line of his belief. If you want to find out what a man really believes, watch his behavior. James puts it a little plainer. He says if you say you have faith but don't have corresponding action, your talking about faith is futile. In the eighth chapter of John we hear Jesus making this very plain when some Pharisees approached Him and said, *"We are of our father, Abraham."* Jesus said, *"If you were of your father Abraham you would be doing the works of your father Abraham."* Dear friends, we can talk all we want, we can say all we want, but when we look at the behavior of man, we find out what he really believes.

People ask me all the time, *"Preacher, what is happening to you? We hear that you are in the hospital more than you are out."* Well, God told me that the outer man had to perish that He might renew the inner man day by day. So, I tell you, I'm having a good time with what is going on, whether you understand it or not.

If I had a title for this message it would be: *The Day a Man Dies,* or, *The Day a Church Dies,* or, *The Day a Denomination Dies.* Long before you have a funeral, death sets in. We seem to have the idea that death only occurs when we have a funeral. We miss the fact that death is a long-time process in the life of an individual, a church, or a denomination. And spiritually speaking, when we misinterpret what death is, we cannot make the corrections necessary to return to God so that His glory might once again be among us.

In Hebrews 3 we read the account of the Children of Israel being delivered out of Egypt by the precious blood of the Lamb, the Crucified One. But they didn't leave Egypt alone, because as we read they were accompanied by the almighty presence of God—a cloud by day and a pillar of fire by night.

Note: In light of Manley's having shared this basic message a few days earlier at *Faith Week,* we refer you to the previous chapter for a more complete record of this sermon. We will only touch on a few highlights in this chapter.

Manley continues: New believers, at the beginning of their walk with God, are not equipped to stand in the land of Canaan, a land that represents to us the life of an overcomer, the life of service. They have to be led through a process in which they discover their own inability to get the job done, and that it is in and through the ability of Jesus Christ, the Son of the Living God, that anything lasting is accomplished. This was an educational time for the Children of Israel as God led them through ten crises between Egypt and Canaan. In these crises they discovered their own inability and that God alone had the answer. This is a picture of a legitimate 'wilderness experience' where God teaches His children how to walk with Him.

During the 40 years I have been preaching—thirty-five of them on the road, traveling from place to place, from church to church—I have been observing people. Though I may not have the theological education that some have, God has been preparing me to know man—but most importantly because I have been born again—God has been preparing me to know Him. I may not be acquainted with the original languages of the Bible, but I tell you I know the Author of this book. I walk with Him and I talk with Him. Bless God, He is alive and well. He can handle any issue we face. This was what God was teaching the Children of Israel. He was wanting them to get to know Him, not just to know about Him. I know a lot of people who know about God, but I wonder if they know Him. I don't see any behavior that favors Him.

And so we find God's children finally arriving at a place just outside Canaan. Let me say again: though some song-writers treat Canaan as though it is heaven, it is not. No giants and walled cities exist to conquer in heaven. Canaan represents a level of service where you are so cooperative with God that He is able to accomplish His ends through you—and you get the benefit.

Up until the time they arrived at Kadesh Barnea God had been working *for* His children. When they possessed the land forty years later, He began working *through* them. In fact, up until then they had been depending on Moses. If it hadn't been for him, they would have been in pretty bad shape. But here they are, looking at the land that had been theirs for 400 years and if they had only obeyed God, if they had only trusted Him, every one of those who had been delivered out of Egypt would have experienced the promised blessing. But rather than believing the word of God, they decided to question it. Because of their unbelief, they chose not to take the land that was theirs.

Now, listen carefully: unbelief is not doubt. Doubt can be a legitimate place for you to be temporarily while you decide whether you are going to believe a lie or believe the truth. That day, they did not go in because of their unbelief. When you refuse to believe what God says, whether you understand it or not, you make a choice to believe a lie. That day their doubt became *unbelief* and the sentence of death was placed on every one of them, except for Caleb and Joshua. That day, death began its work. That day the glory of God began to depart.

Today, the enemy is doing everything he can to get people to believe a lie, to doubt what God has said. An attack is occurring on this book today. A battle is going on. It is an effort to discredit this Word of God. Well, they reached me too late, because I have gotten to know the Author and He is alive. Yes sir. I could bring 15 doctors in here today who would say that I am supposed to be dead. They would tell you "that man's God is the only explanation for his being alive." My desire is that He will get glory through this body, whether in life or death. I am such a fanatic when it comes to believing this book that I even believe the jots and the tittles will shout glory. I have run into Jesus in the valley of death. I've been with Him on the mountaintops. I have met Him on the slopes of danger.

Some people try to approach this book like a scientist approaches a problem. They do an investigation so they can get understanding—so they can have faith. But if they would read what the Bible says they would realize that the Bible teaches it is by faith that you get understanding. If you understood everything about the Bible, that wouldn't be faith. There is a lot about this book that I don't understand. That doesn't bother me, because I know that I am not as smart as God. I am willing to leave it up to Him to explain it in His good time. I would rather have the behavior that is like Him than to just know all about Him.

You say, *"Manley, that is mystical."* Well, let me tell you, ever since I got saved, I have been a mystic. I am inhabited by the Holy Spirit! How mystical do you want to get? I am not looking to the things which are seen, but I am looking to the things which are not seen, for the things which are seen are temporal, but the things which are not seen are eternal. When you begin to see things that way, those giants begin looking like loaves of bread.

Many well-meaning Christians pray, *"Oh God, make me usable, enlarge me, bless me."* Then God lets a piece of bread, I mean, a big old giant, run across their path and they head for the hills. They run out on their problem. The moment you believe a lie, you remove yourself from being usable to God and to His Lordship in your life. You cease to be a vehicle through which the glory of God can be expressed. What happens is that everything you do from then on can be explained by human ingenuity.

When you choose to believe a lie, you miss out on all the blessed promises of this book. You miss out on being made rich in Christ Jesus. The day a person, a church, a denomination chooses to believe a lie, that day the sentence of death is pronounced on them. They are turned out into the wilderness to wander until that generation dies off and God raises up a new one. God grant that we will be a people who take God at His word and refuse to ever believe a lie.

Love Expressed

In the days following Manley's message a constant stream of friends, fellow ministers, lay people, and denominational leaders visited him in his hotel room. These visits were interrupted by dialysis treatments and an occasional trip to sit in on a session of the convention. One of Debbie Beasley's assignments was to accompany her father wherever he needed to be or wherever he wanted to go. Her primary view of the Convention, as she put it, was from behind her Dad's wheelchair as they went back and forth, back and forth, across the walkway that connected their hotel to the Superdome.

Visitor after visitor came to thank Manley for his life of service—for the ministry he had had to them over the years; for the example of his perseverance in the midst of adversity; for his faithfulness to Scriptures; but perhaps as much as anything they came just to express their love for him. Some knelt on the floor so they could look into his eyes as he was stooped over in his wheelchair.

How do you explain this kind of affection toward a man who dropped out of school at the age of thirteen, whose early years were spent in pursuing a life of sinful pleasure, who faced the challenge of dyslexia throughout his life, who for twenty years carried in his body multiple diseases, three of them terminal? The explanation is found back in the message Manley preached at Faith Week two weeks before.

"One day I learned that God has to make us 'nothings' before He can make us 'somethings.' God can take a 'nothing' and so fill him with His glory that he will be equal to any task that God calls him to."

And so it was with Manley Madison Beasley.

30
Countdown to Heaven

"It is a mystery no words can tell, but known to those who in this stillness rest; Something divinely incomprehensible, that for my nothingness, I get God's best!"

—selected

Being as close to Zachary as he was, following the New Orleans Convention Manley decided to visit with his friends at the Milldale Bible Conference Center again. He wanted to walk once more on the grounds where he had seen God move so mightily through the years. This was the place of so many precious memories. Jimmy Robertson recalls Manley's last visit.

"After the New Orleans Convention Manley came to stay with us here at Milldale. He was planning to spend several days before returning to Texas. When he arrived, however, he became very sick. The pain in his feet and hands was so excruciating that it was almost unbearable. My wife, Francis, got hot towels, soaked his feet in basins of hot water, rubbed him with everything that she could find. None of it seemed to help. I told him, *'I've got some pain medicine here, why don't you take it?'* He reminded me that he never took pain medicine because his body could not throw it off. Then he decided he would go ahead and take it, if I promised not to tell Marthé. He took two of the pills but soon realized that he was going to have to get back to his doctor in Texas. We began trying to get him flight reservations back home. Several hours later he asked if I had any more pills. He said he was in the worst pain he had ever experienced.

I told him I had several left and that he could take all of them with him if he'd like.

"I'll never forget those last hours we had together, and I'll never forget the moment he said to me: *'Jimmy, I believe God is going to take me soon. He has not given me any fresh vision for the future. It won't be long now.'* That was the last time I saw him. He was gone a few weeks later."

About that same time, Sonny Holland recalls the phone ringing.

"Bubba, it looks like I am going to be leaving you all."

"What are you saying, Manley?"

"God has not given me any Scripture or anything to indicate that I will be staying any longer. I think God is fixin' to take me on."

We started to weep, to cry, and to reminisce. We had a great time on the phone just looking back over the many precious years of ministry we had had together. The last thing I said to him was: *"Manley, I'll see you in heaven."*

The flight from Baton Rouge to Dallas seemed unusually long that day for Manley and Marthé. They were met by Debbie and taken directly to the Dialysis Center for another treatment before going home. Then in spite of Manley's weakness and pain, on Saturday they were back on a plane headed for Lubbock, TX.

A surprise awaited them there. Manley would be expected to preach in two morning services at the First Baptist Church, not just the one service that he had planned on. Then there would be the evening service as well. Nevertheless, Manley agreed—never wanting to turn down an opportunity to preach and trusting God to again provide the supernatural strength that he had experienced so many times before.

The services on Sunday, July 1, were the occasion for all the musical stops to be pulled out in celebration of

Independence Day. Due to this, Manley did not have enough time to complete his message in the early service so he announced that he would be finishing it in the 11 o'clock hour. The sanctuary was packed, as many from the first service returned to hear the rest of the message that God had laid on his heart. But Manley was beginning to struggle. Marthé recalls how much weaker he was in that second service. Yet he persevered. There was yet another service that evening. Marthé wondered how he was going to make it.

That evening, after a period of exciting musical celebration at First Baptist, Lubbock, led by John Lee, Manley was assisted up the steps to the pulpit where he chose to stand, rather than sit on a stool, for what would be the last message he would ever preach.

Manley's Last Message

Well, amen! That's the kind of singing that would make an Episcopalian shout! I praise God for this choir. (Reaching down to get a glass of water, he continued) My sermons are sometimes dry, so I have to add a bit of moisture to help them. I'm not going to preach all night, though I could. Ever since I had to go on dialysis three times a week and limit my preaching engagements to Sundays, it has been a new ballgame because I have so much I would like to say. I've about quit preaching by the clock and have started to preach by the calendar. Now, I am going to say something tonight that may shock you. I'm not going to give the Scripture reference at first, because I don't want you turning to it and working up your own sermon while I am getting to my point.

Some disciples came to Jesus one day and asked him what they needed to do in order to work the works of God. If someone asked you that question, what would you say to them? Most people would say that you need to go to church, that you need to read your Bible, pray, witness, and if you are a Baptist, that you need to tithe. That's probably all many would say, don't you agree? But listen to what Jesus said: *"This is the work of God that you believe on Him whom the Father has sent.'"* Isn't that interesting?

How many of you believe on Jesus whom the Father has sent? Probably everyone here tonight would say they do. But have you considered what this really means? Jesus is saying that this is what they should be doing if they were going to do the works of God: they were to believe on Him. Jesus understood something about believing on Him that we have missed in our day. *Jesus is saying that if we are going to do the works of God, our behavior will be exactly in proportion to our belief. Our actions, our character, our service will be in direct proportion to our faith.*

In Romans, Paul says you can't do a thing to get saved, except to trust God to save you. And James says that if you have real faith, corresponding action will follow. Think about that for a moment. That is heavy. In other words, sanctification, service, your living, will be in direct proportion to your faith. This is what Jesus taught. You remember when those Pharisees came to Jesus and told Him that they were of their father, Abraham. Jesus' response to them was that if they were of their father Abraham, they would be doing the works of Abraham. Don't you see how this connects with what James is saying? A lot of error is being preached in the churches of our country these days. People are hearing that they are to have faith and works.

I recall one time when I was explaining what faith is how a man jumped up at the end of the service to tell me that he now thoroughly understood what faith was. He said, *'Let me tell you a story.'* He went on to tell of a man who wanted to cross a river in a rowboat. Now I knew what book he had read it from, the page and paragraph, but I just listened to him. He talked about two oars; one that said *works* and the other one that said *faith*. The man started rowing with the oar that said *faith* and the boat went round and round. He then switched to the other oar that said *works* and the same thing happened. Then he decided to use both of them at the same time and guess what? The boat went straight across the river. *"Boy,"* he said, *"now I understand what faith is. You have to mix faith and works together."* When he got through, I said, *"Friend, that is not what I said."*

The faith that Jesus was talking about is the kind of faith the disciples experienced when Jesus stepped into their boat and they had neither oars nor wind, but it says that they were immediately at shore. Come on now! Come on! The Bible teaches a faith that works, not faith and works. *If I want to know what kind of Christian you are, all I have to do is observe your behavior and I will know immediately the level of your faith.*

You ask, *"What are you trying to say to us, Bro. Manley?"* Well, I'm trying to say this. True Christianity is a life that can only be experienced by faith. It is not a life that you live by your emotions. It is not a life that you live by your intellect. It is a life that you live by faith. Your mind and emotions are of course involved, but we are a people of revelation and we walk by the revelation of this truth, God's Word. You can understand as much as you want intellectually and not be living the life of a Christian.

You can have experiences that cause you to hang from the chandeliers. You can speak in a thousand tongues, but if your life does not find its roots in the revelation found in this book, and if this is not the reality of your life, then all you have is a "religion" that is called Christian. And I guarantee that that is all a lot of people have today.

You can recognize people like this when you ask them how they are doing. They may say they are doing well. But when you ask them what they mean, they will say something like this: *"I'm doing the best I can with who I am. I'm trying my best, for after all, all that God expects out of me is that I do my best."* That, my friend, is not scriptural. God has not called on you to do something you can afford to do. He is calling on you to do something that you cannot do, and that is to trust Him for your salvation; that is to trust Him for your sanctification; that is to trust Him in your service.

If what is going on in this church can be explained by human ability, I don't care if you are the biggest Baptist church, the most prestigious church in the world, I've got news for you, *that's not Christian, that is Baptist religion.* Your behavior as an individual or as a church reveals what the level of your faith is.

Romans 4:16 says that *it must be of faith that it might be of grace.* Isn't that wonderful? In the old times, years ago, preachers preached for change in the life of people. Today they preach for commitment. Have you made your commitment? Have you prayed the prayer? I've never heard anything so ridiculous. When you believe on the Lord Jesus Christ there is going to be a change in your life; a moral change. As you trust Him in your daily life, you will experience a continuous change that makes people know that the only explanation for your life is God. That's Christianity. A lot of people have religion, but so few know how to be Christian. It is by faith. Jesus understood this. He said that if you have your faith right, your works will be right, your actions will be right. If you have your faith right, your substance will be right. If you have your faith right, everything in your life will be in correspondence with your faith.

I was one of the preachers at a conference where about 6,000 were in attendance. One of the speakers spoke on soul-winning and challenged everyone to commit to winning one soul between then and Easter, which was several weeks away. I became convicted that I was not the soul-winner that I needed to be. Beside me sat one of the best-known preachers in evangelism. He started talking out loud to God and I couldn't help hear what he was saying: *"Oh God, I am making a covenant with you tonight to win one soul between now and Easter."* I realized that I could not make that kind of covenant with God, but that I could ask Him to make me a soul-winner right then, not sometime up the road. *"God,"* I prayed, *"make me a soul-winner right now."*

The "Amens" were pronounced and by the time I reached the end of that pew a doctor of Islamic background walked up to me and asked me how he could be saved. Do you catch the difference between religion and Christianity? You see, I was convicted that my works were not right, so I repented and believed by faith that God would make me the soul-winner I needed to be.

Often in our churches today we try to pump people up to get them to do something, because we know that if we don't keep pumping them up, they'll quit. But if you get them full of God and faith, they won't need pumping up. They will do it. Most of our church members, however, aren't full of God, so you have to motivate them, manipulate them, and today we find ourselves in the biggest motivational business in the history of the church. Listen to me. You can fill churches and you can have all the money in the world, and Jesus Christ not be anywhere around.

I'm going to close with one more illustration. Mark 11:24 says: *"Whatsoever things you desire, when you pray, believe that you receive them and you shall have them."* My friends, that means that **when God speaks to you out of His Word and you have an intellectual understanding of what God wants for you, and with this is a stirring in your heart that you want God to do this particular thing, there will then come that moment when you have to make a choice to believe His Word, in spite**

of what you may see, smell, taste, feel and hear. When you make that choice, you place yourself at the disposal of God to work in you, through you, and for you.

Now to the illustration. The first time I went on dialysis, the doctors had to teach Marthé and me how to operate a relatively new version of the procedure that is called CAPD. This procedure makes it possible for dialysis patients to administer it themselves in their homes or even on the road. Our instructors said it would take us 13 days to learn how to do it. I told them I would like to learn it in five days because I had a conference engagement up in Canada. Well, that threw them into a fit when they heard that I was going to be leaving the country. Anyway, at the end of five days we took the test, passed it, and headed for Canada.

In the meantime, the Canadian pastor who was putting this conference together heard that I had gone on dialysis. He began to worry that I might get up there and die on him. Well, it just so happened that he ran into an accountant friend of his and the pastor brought up the subject of my being on dialysis and that it was some kind of new version of CAPD. The accountant said, *"You may not believe this, but one of my clients is Dr. Dimitrous Oreopoulos who invented this version of CAPD. I'll call him to see if he would be available to assist if the Beasleys need help."* Can you believe it? This doctor said he would count it a privilege to make himself available if we were to need him.

Well, we had only been at this conference for a few days when I got a call from my office in Port Neches, TX, saying that we were going to need $4,000 by Monday morning and that we didn't have it. That same day my office in Euless, TX, called and said that we were going to have to have $6,000 by Monday and we didn't have it. Now listen carefully. We needed $10,000 by Monday. I was returning home on Saturday. So if I had been able to make some kind of arrangement with the bank, I didn't have the time. The Lord spoke to me and said, *"Why don't you trust me?"* I said, "What *do you mean exactly? I believe you can do it."* He said, *"But you don't see the substance, do you?"* *"No."* *"Well, if you had faith there would be substance."* I said, *"But Lord, I want to trust you so badly that I will do anything if you will just handle this problem."* I discovered that God was not sympathetic. He would not make bargains. The only check He would cash was faith.

After having taught for years that you have to believe first and then receive, after seeing God perform so many miracles, after having built my whole life on this principle of faith, here I was still fighting the battle of faith. God then reminded me of a paraphrase I had made of Hebrews 11:1: *Faith is acting like it's so, when it is not so, in order for it to be so, because between God and you, it is so.* By 11:30 that night I had discovered afresh that *God has given us all things that pertain unto life and godliness*—and that *"has"* means that He has already given it. I realized that I already had the $10,000 even though I could not see it, smell it, taste it, feel it, or hear it. I was ready to take God at His Word.

During my message the next morning I shared with the people that the day before I had wrestled with the Lord over a problem and that at 11:30 that night I got peace. I received peace that you can believe this book and stand on it when God gives you His Word on a matter. Now listen. I did not even hint that I was trusting God for $10,000. In fact, most of the folk thought it had to do with something physical, like my kidney problem. At the close of the service a man and his wife walked up to me and said: *"Brother Beasley, that problem you mentioned, was that a financial one?"* It so shocked me that I lied about it, at least I didn't answer him directly. I said, *"Somewhat."*

That's all there was to that conversation. He and his wife walked on. A bit later, my wife and I stopped by a little tearoom and there sat these two people. This man saw me and called me over to their table. He said, *"Manley, God has given me the gift of giving. I want to know how you handle your ministry, financially? Do you have a budget and a board that underwrites your needs?"* I said, *"No, we trust God to put it in the hearts of people to give to the ministry as He wants them to. We feel very accountable with this and we don't beg and plead for support. We know we are trusting a God who will meet all our needs."* He said, *"My wife and I have been impressed to give you something. We will pray this afternoon and will have a check for you this evening."* It was now Friday and we were leaving for home the next morning. As Marthé and I walked away, I said: *"Those folk have no idea what our need is, and anyway, here we are up in Canada where no one knows us, and we need $10,000 by Monday and . . .."*

Well, we met the couple for dinner that night. This brother said, *"You need to understand that the Lord would not let us give you any more than what this check is for. I was prepared to give whatever amount the Lord told me to give. And furthermore, you need to know that my wife and I have been in the process of retracing our honeymoon trip that took us across Canada and up into Alaska years ago. We had not planned to stop here, but we believe God had us route ourselves this way so we could be here to give you this check. We have decided that this is the main reason we made the trip, so we are heading back home to Florida tomorrow."* He handed me an envelope and said, *"Go ahead and open it."* Inside was a check for $10,000.

Dear friends, what I am trying to tell you is this: At 11:30 the night before, I had rendered present that for which I had hoped and acknowledged how God was going to accomplish it was His business. ***It was my business to believe on the Lord Jesus Christ, whom the Father has sent, with more than an intellectual belief and with more than a passing emotional*** *experience. It was also my business to believe on Him in a discovery of the truth of God's Word that would lead me to make that choice, the choice to step out on His truth, in faith.* So you see, what I am saying: as we do this, we position ourselves for God to perform a miracle by which the only explanation for our lives is God. We are then believers whose behavior matches what we profess to believe. That's the Christianity that is more than adding church attendance to your life, or trying to read your Bible, or occasionally praying, or giving. That's the Christianity the Bible teaches—a Christianity that leads you to a whole new level of faith and trust, a level where you will hunger after these things as they become more and more the priority of your life.

Now, let me close with this: *"Whatsoever is not of faith is sin, and without faith it is impossible to please God."* With that, Manley had the congregation bow their heads as two men assisted him down the steps to his wheelchair.

It surely is no coincidence that Manley would end the last sermon he'd ever preach with those words of admonition and warning—words by which he had lived, for so many years. Words that summed up his life and message.

31
Home Again

"Rarest gems bear hardest grinding;God's own workmanship are we."
                                                              —selected

It had been a restless night. Manley was needing another dialysis treatment, which he could not get until he was back home. As he and Marthé were checking in at the airport the next morning, they were surprised to see John Karl Davis, a fellow evangelist who had just finished a meeting at another church in Lubbock. John Karl was thrilled to see one of his "heroes"—one who had had a profound influence on his own life and ministry over the years.

With Manley being in a wheelchair, he and Marthé were extended the courtesy of boarding the plane first. As the attendants were helping Manley back to his seat in coach class, someone began taking special notice of him. After he and Marthé were settled in, a stewardess stopped at their row, carefully looked at Manley, then blurted out: *"I know who you are. For a minute I did not recognize you. You're Manley Beasley. I was saved in one of your meetings twenty years ago. Listen, you are not going to be comfortable in these cramped coach seats with all that medical stuff. Let me see if I can get you moved up front."* A few minutes later, Manley and Marthé found themselves in the comfort of first class.

When the stewardess learned that John Karl Davis knew Manley and was anxious to talk with him, she also invited him to move up front. John Karl has special memories of that Monday, July 2, 1990 flight.

A Testimony

"I draped myself over the back of the seat in front of Manley. I had planned on telling him how difficult my ministry had become. I figured that no one would understand the discouragement and pain I had been going through as much as he would. Little did I realize that in eight days Manley would be gone. As I looked at this great man of God, now so physically frail and just a shell of what he had once been, I asked him if he was still "counting it all joy," a message that I had once heard him preach. He smiled and said, *'Not yet son, but I'm headed there.'* I then told him that I'd heard of a time when he was very, very ill, how the Lord had allowed him to have some kind of vision of heaven. I asked him if he would mind sharing with me some of what he saw. I was not prepared for his abrupt answer. *'NO,'* he said. *'But why?'* I asked. In a softer, tenderer tone, he replied, *'Because I love you, my brother, and I want God's best for you. God has given you His Word that contains everything you need to know. If I told you, you might be tempted to depend more on what I say or saw than on what God has already said.'* Later, in looking back on those treasured moments with my brother, I recalled a statement I had heard years before: **'Real love is giving people what they need, not always what they want.'** This was another lesson that I learned from Bro. Manley."

—John Karl Davis, evangelist
Fort Worth, TX

"Please take your seats, stow your trays and fasten your seat belts. We are making our final approach to the Dallas airport."

Debbie was waiting with a wheelchair, ready to take her father as quickly as possible to the dialysis center for his Monday treatment. The treatment had been so much easier when they had been able to do this at home, but for months now, due to the deterioration of the kidneys, Manley had to have it administered at a Dialysis Center.

Home again for five days—five days in his favorite chair; five days of watching his daughter, Debbie, and daughter-in-law, Shirlene, copying the "Tape of the Month Club" cassettes; five days of phone calls; and five days with family. He was looking forward to the arrival on Friday of his three sisters— Henry Mae, Joyce, and Pat. Then there was the anticipation of next Sunday's preaching engagement in Nacogdoches, TX. Unknown to Manley, however, Marthé had wisely cancelled as soon as they'd returned from Lubbock. She knew he would be upset and did not plan to tell him until later in the week. And of course, there was Jonathan, his youngest, who would be leaving in a few days for his first full-time church staff position as minister to youth.

Jonathan Remembers

"I had packed my car on Friday, July 6, planning to leave early the next morning to drive all the way to Sherwood Baptist Church in Albany, GA. I was excited. My plans changed, however, when Dad called Friday night: *'Jonathan, why don't you phone Michael Catt to see if he would not mind your delaying your arrival by one day so you can spend tomorrow morning with me. Your mother is getting her hair done in the morning. We could have a few hours to talk about what lies ahead.'*

"When I arrived, Dad was sitting in his favorite chair. He motioned for me to sit down in front of him. I knew why. He needed someone to massage his feet. I had done this so many times before. It helped relieve the pain he was constantly in due to a vascular problem causing a lack of circulation in his extremities. As I rubbed his feet, we talked about the church and the youth ministry that I would have in Albany. Then, after a while, to my surprise, he said, *'Son, now let me tell you what some of my plans are.'*

Dad then began sharing with me what his goals were for the next year. Here he was, 58-years old, on dialysis 3 times a week, looking like death warmed over, talking about his vision for the next year. In retrospect, however, my brother, Manley Jr., and I think that Dad actually had a premonition of what was going to happen to him, but that did not stop him from dreaming. We talked and talked. I would share things that were on my heart. He would share what was on his. Sometimes he would grimace and occasionally give a yelp when I pressed too hard against a sore spot in his feet.

"As I look back, I would not trade those few hours with my father for anything. They were just what I needed. I took three things away with me that morning. First: I learned that you are never too old or too sick to have dreams and plans for the future. Second: you are never too old to learn. No matter how old you are, you must remain teachable. Third: methods may change, but the truth never does. He told me that I would have to use different methods than he would use in order to reach my generation. He said that was alright with him. He never told me what to do, but he emphasized staying with the truth and keeping balance. Dad had faced this from time to time when he felt that some of his closest friends were getting out of balance. Though Dad remained sympathetic and loyal toward them, he never did waver from his own commitment to live and preach what he saw to be a balanced gospel.

"Then it was time to go. Dad walked me to the door. I said, *'Hey, I'll call you when I get to Albany.'* He gave me a hug and said, *'I love you, son.'* I said, *'I love you, Dad.'* I got in my car, waved, and started driving toward Georgia, little realizing that the next day he would be taken to the hospital for the last time. When I arrived in Albany on Sunday afternoon, I called home. I was told Dad had been taken to the hospital but that he didn't seem to be doing too badly. I must admit that I was not all that concerned. Dad's being taken to the hospital was almost routine. It had happened so many times before. God had always raised him up.

"Monday morning, I drove to Atlanta with one of the other ministers of the church to buy supplies. When we got back to Albany about 3 p.m. a phone call from my brother, Manley Jr., was waiting for me. He said that I needed to make plans to return home as soon as possible.

"Normally when Dad would take a turn for the worse—when he would go to the hospital or when he would end up in intensive care—the Lord would quicken a Scripture to my heart that he would be alright. That is something Dad had taught us all to do, so that night I prayed and began searching the Scriptures for a word, probably more for my comfort than for Dad's. I used the Bible that I had marked with dates written in next to Scripture promises regarding Dad that God had given me over the years. All the old ones were there, but this time nothing seemed to speak to my heart.

"I was on my knees praying that whatever was best for Dad that God's will would be done. I finally climbed into bed. I lay there, in and out of consciousness, not able to really sleep. I remember looking at the clock around 3:30 a.m. About that time I began having a kind of vision. Dad was in heaven. I saw him trying to walk toward Abraham, who was one of his favorite Bible characters. Abraham was a distance from him. I heard Dad calling to him and trying to reach him, but he was having a struggle to make any headway. The picture then began to widen. Suddenly I could see why Dad was having such a hard time. He was surrounded—almost up to his shoulders—by what I realized were crowns of life. They were so thick around him that they were impeding his progress. I fell into a peaceful sleep, that is, until the alarm awakened me. I had a 6 a.m. flight to catch."

32
Final Hours

"Faith must be tested, because it can be turned into personal possession only through conflict. The test will either prove that your faith is right or it will kill you. There is continual testing in the life of faith, and the last great test is death."

—Oswald Chambers [34]

When Manley had been rushed to the hospital Sunday afternoon, the first thing medical personnel did was put him on dialysis. The toxins had built up in his body at an alarming rate. His kidneys were shutting down. These little "fist size" organs process 100 percent of the body's blood supply every five minutes, during which time they filter out all the waste products and excess water from the blood, leaving cleansed blood in the body while discarding waste products. But they also have other functions without which the body cannot go on.

Normally, a three-to-four hour hemodialysis session—the kind Manley was then on—would take care of the toxins for about three days. This time, however, doctors were faced with an emergency. He was entering the ESRD stage of renal disease. If they could not get his body cleansed, if they could not get the kidneys to function even on the limited basis as they had been, he would only have a few days to live. The Sunday session was not successful. The doctors decided to try one more time on Monday morning. It, too, failed. His lungs were now beginning to fill up with fluid.

Manley had asked that nothing be kept from him.

Following the final hemodialysis, the family gathered around his bed, where Dr. Aladdi gave them the news that other than putting him on a respirator nothing else could be done.

"Thank you doctor, but I don't want you to do that."

"Daddy, do you understand what that means—that you can't live without it?"

"Mama, I know that. I've made my decision."

"That's yours to make, Daddy."

They prayed. He slipped into a coma.

Manley loved his family very deeply. The bonds of love and trust were so strong. They had walked with him through the valley of the shadow of death so often. They had always been there. Was that why, when his only brother, Kenneth, whom he had not seen for some time, walked into his room late Monday afternoon and said; *"Manley, this is Kenneth. I've come to tell you goodbye,"* that Manley opened his eyes, and smiled? Was that why, while the family was momentarily standing outside the door of his room, he came out of his coma long enough to ask the attending nurse to dial the phone number of his sister Joyce. *"Joyce?" "Manley, is that you?"*

But so often he had faced death before. So many times his family and friends had gathered around his hospital bed to say their final goodbyes. So many times he had been raised up to preach again and again and again. Forty years of faithful service on earth. Would it not happen just one more time? Mixed with his desire to be with the One who had rescued him from the depths of sin—the One who had called and commissioned him to preach the gospel and the One who had promised he would live to see his children's children—Manley longed to see the revival he had prayed for and believed was going to occur. He also desired to stay just a bit longer, to preach one more time.

Could he not have a few more weeks to fulfill his promise to his son Jonathan to preach at his ordination service? Just a while longer? A few more days to gather around him those he loved so dearly? A few more days? Would he never preach again? Was it really time? *"Joyce?" "Yes, Manley." "There is no easy way to go home."*

Manley knew. His family knew. His friends knew. Family and friends took turns holding his hand. *"Daddy, we know you can't say anything, but if you can hear us, can you give us a sign?* An ever so slight squeeze of a hand. Tears flowed. Peace transcended. Bubba slipped away. It was time to meet Jonathan at the airport. As arranged, he would wait for his brother at the Delta Airlines curb-side parking.

The connecting flights in Atlanta had been on time and now Jonathan was flying back home. He had been away only for three days. Would this be just one more of those many near-death experiences his Dad had faced over the years, only to be raised up to preach again? But this time he had not experienced any encouraging word from Scripture. And what was the meaning of the dream? Jonathan would soon know.

"I walked out to the curb where my brother was waiting in the car. I opened the door, looked at him, and said: *'He's gone, isn't he?'* **Dad had left at high noon!"**[35]

Manley's Final Instructions

"I don't want to be carried off in a black hearse. Do you understand me, Marthé? No black hearse! Make sure you find a red, white, or blue one; anything but black. And I want the family to dress in bright colors. It's not to be a sad time. I want my home-going to be a celebration of my life. Understand?" These were the instructions Manley had given the family on one of those earlier occasions when his death had seemed imminent.

They were soon to discover, however, that dressing in bright colors would be a lot easier than finding a bright colored hearse. With Jonathan calling regularly to check on his progress in finding the right vehicle, the funeral director soon realized how important it was that he find an alternative to the black hearses they used for "normal" people. The funeral director assured him they would find one or he himself would not show up at the funeral. A *white hearse* was found in a little town outside of the city. At Marthé's request, the funeral home also provided a white limousine for the immediate family.

In the meantime, while the family members were making their own plans, the news was spreading by word of mouth, phone calls, faxes, emails and telegrams. When the time arrived for the *Celebration Service,* the church was full. Perhaps as meaningful to the family as anything that day was the number of Manley's fellow preachers who attended. Though not officially counted, estimates were approximately 500 seated in a section reserved for ministers.

When the funeral director told Marthé in addition to the "official" pallbearers she could have as many "honorary" ones as she desired, he did not know what he was getting into. Marthé extended an invitation to all the preachers who wished to be an honorary pallbearer, to participate. There may never have been so many "honorary" pallbearers at a funeral in Texas history. Lined up, four wide, hundreds of Manley's preacher-boys processed behind his casket into the late afternoon Texas sun.[36]

33
Come Celebrate

<u>Tribute by Michael Gott, President of the *Texas Southern Baptist Evangelism Conference,* at Manley's death</u>

Manley Beasley was unusually used of God in Southern Baptist life. The impact of his unique ministry as both a revivalist and evangelist will be felt for decades.

Few men among Southern Baptists were honored as a prophet of his stature. He was a man with unflagging devotion to Jesus Christ and His church. He longed for true revival. It became the passion of his life. He studied the Bible to discover its principles of revival and the personalities in history whom God anointed for this purpose.

Spurgeon once said that God recruited His finest soldiers from "the highlands of affliction," and so it was with Manley Beasley.

Manley's "thorn in the flesh" became a throne of the Spirit as he was driven again and again to fall before God, thus deepening his relationship with God in an extraordinary way. It was evident to those who knew him best that an anointing was upon his life which was intensified by his physical weaknesses and sickness.

Nevertheless, through years of ill health, he kept a schedule that would have tired a young man. He seemed to draw from a secret source.

Young preachers sought his advice and prayers. He

preached the faith. He walked and walked the faith he preached. He was a man molded and fashioned by God to be conformed to the image of Christ.

It seemed to many that he would return from periods of sickness, having been in the "secret place of the Most High," physically weaker but spiritually renewed, mounting up on eagle wings. Often he spoke of his life being extended by God for a purpose. He fulfilled that purpose in his ministry that called Christians to personal renewal and the church to biblical revival.

He faced death as he lived life—with a testimony of God's sufficiency and with a spirit of divine adventure and confidence.

For Manley Beasley, to live was Christ and to die was gain.

Come Help Us Celebrate the Life of Manley Beasley

So read the announcement on the marquee of First Baptist Church, Euless, TX, that Friday, July 13, 1990. And they came. They traveled from across America and beyond. Men and women, old and young arrived at the service to pay tribute to a man whose life and message had changed the course of their own lives. They arrived in person, made hundreds of phone calls, sent scores of telegrams and letters. People from every walk in life expressed gratitude to God for having had Manley's life intersect with theirs. Among the many testimonies shared at the Memorial Service was the following tribute and message by Adrian Rogers, then-pastor of the Bellevue Baptist Church in Memphis, TN, where Manley had preached less than two months earlier.

"I first met Manley in 1962 in Fort Pierce, FL. I had heard

about him and decided to attend a meeting he was leading at the Fairlawn Baptist Church. He was a stunningly handsome man, hair black as a raven's wing. He talked in mystical ways. I knew then that I was listening to a man who was walking a different track than most people. Over the years I learned to tune in more and more to what Manley Beasley said. I can honestly say that I have never known a man more in love with life and yet not at all afraid to die than was Bro. Manley.

His life makes me think of the Apostle Paul and the letter he wrote to the church in Philippi. You recall what he said in the first chapter, verses 21 to 24. *"For to me to live is Christ, and to die is gain. But if I live in the flesh, this is the fruit of my labor: yet what I shall choose, I know not. For I am in a strait betwixt two, having a desire to depart and to be with Christ; which is far better: Nevertheless to abide in the flesh is more needful for you."*

Paul is writing from prison. He is facing a trial for which he does not know the outcome. He doesn't know if he is going to be exonerated or executed. He is saying, *"I may live, or, I may die."* Then he begins to muse on that. *If I live, then for me to live is Christ; if I die, to die is gain.* It's as if he is saying, *heads I win; tails I win.* It makes no difference to Paul, for to live is Christ and to die is gain.

I believe that what Paul is saying in the first part of this statement is that the very *source* of his life was Christ. He said in verse 6 of this same chapter that, *"he that hath begun a good work in you will perform it until the day of Jesus Christ."* Paul was one who did not just have God simply working around him and with him. He had God working "in" him. And so it was with Manley. Manley had God working in him. Manley knew that salvation is not getting man out of earth into heaven but it is getting God out of heaven into man. This is what it was for Paul. This is what it was for Manley; **the source was Jesus.**

But not only was the **source** of his life, Jesus, the *subject* of his life was Jesus. In verses 12 and 13 of this same chapter, Paul says: *"But I would you should understand, brethren, that the things which happened unto me have fallen out rather unto the furtherance of the gospel; so that my bonds in Christ are manifest in all the palace, and in all other places."* Don't be sorry for me, Paul is saying. The fact that I happen to be in the palace prison is giving me the opportunity to preach the gospel. These body guards think that I am chained to them, but they are really chained to me. And I have been able to share about the Lord Jesus Christ because of these bonds. If you were ashamed of Jesus, you would not want to be around the Apostle Paul. If you were ashamed of Jesus, you would not have wanted to be around the man called Manley.

But not only was the *source* of his life Jesus and the *subject* of his life Jesus, but the *standard* of his life was Jesus. In the 14th verse of chapter 3, Paul says; *"I press toward the mark for the prize of the high calling of God in Christ Jesus."* Paul had his eye on the goal and his goal was this: *"I want to be like the Lord Jesus. I want to be conformed to His image."* Never once have I heard Manley Beasley say one un-Christlike thing. Manley was human and therefore not perfect, but I have never seen anything in Manley Beasley that was not like the Lord Jesus. The *standard* of his life was Christ.

In this day when man needs a hero, Manley was that hero to many. He was for me, and he still is, because I want to follow him as he followed Christ. The prayer for my life today is that I might finish well. I thank God that Manley Beasley went out in a blaze of glory, for the *standard* of his life was Jesus Christ.

But that is not all. The very *song* of his life was Jesus. In Philippians 4:4, Paul says: *"Rejoice in the Lord always, and again, I say, rejoice."* Let's not forget that Paul was in prison waiting to be executed when he writes this. The whole letter to the Philippians was a letter of triumph. You feel the breezes of heaven blowing through this letter when you just open it up. Manley may have had his down moments, but for us who watched him, we knew that the *song* of his life was Christ.

Then the *satisfaction* of his life was Christ. In Chapter 4:11 Paul writes, ". . . *I have learned in whatsoever state I am, there-with to be content."* I don't need anything else, Paul was saying. I have Jesus. In him I am satisfied. This is what I saw in the man named Manley; the *satisfaction* of his life was Jesus.

Going further, we read in Chapter 4:13 that Paul can do all things through Christ who strengthened him. The very *strength* of his life was Jesus. The last time I saw Manley was at a Bible conference we had at Bellevue, where he and Ron Dunn were speaking. He was so weak that I thought he would never be able to get up to the platform, much less preach. But then, when he began to preach, the Spirit of God quickened his mortal body. I have never heard such a sermon like he preached that night. I am still living in the fragrance of it right now. The *strength* of his life was Jesus.

And finally I must say that the *supply* of his life was Jesus. Paul said: *"But my God shall supply all your needs according to his riches in glory by Christ Jesus"* (Phil. 4:19). We sometimes confuse wants with needs, but God always knows what our needs are. He has promised to be our supply.

Now, let's turn it over and look at the flip side where Paul says: ". . . *to die is gain."* Then a few verses down he says, *"I have a desire to depart and to be with Christ which is far bet-ter."* I am not a Greek scholar, but I've read that what the schol-ars say Paul is doing here is piling one comparative onto anoth-er. He is saying that it is not just better but it is very, very, very much better to depart and be with Christ.

The word *"depart,"* is such an interesting word. It's a word that has the idea of unraveling, or untying, or loosing something. It was a nautical term. Sailors would use that term when they untied a ship from its mooring and the ship would begin to go out to sea. That was called a "**departure.**" I was born by the ocean in West Palm Beach, FL. I would sometimes go and watch the ships as they'd sail out. You'd see a ship being untied. Then it would begin making its way across the waters. Eventually it would drop over the horizon. Those standing on this shore would say, *"There she goes."* But people standing on another shore would say, *"There she comes."* The same ship that drops out of sight here appears in sight over there on that distant shore.

The word *"depart"* was also a military term that meant to strike a tent, that is, to loosen the tent pegs, to untie the ropes that hold the tent. I think also that this is what the Apostle Paul had in mind when he said, *"to die is gain."* He was saying that I'm going to take down the old tent that I have been living in. I have fought the fight, I have kept the faith and now the battle's over. I am going home.

And so it was with Manley, this man of faith. Some might say; *"but if he had so much faith, why wasn't he healed?"* Well, number one, he is healed. We are the ones who are sick. With His stripes we are healed. Today he is perfectly healed. I tell you this: in this life it takes far more faith not to be healed and serve God than it does to be healed and serve Him. Thank God for the faith Manley had. He fought a good fight and won it.

"Depart" was a political term. When they would take the shackles off of a prisoner, loose his chains, open the prison door and set him free, it was called a "departure." That is what happened to Manley the other day. All of us down here are still in chains of some kind—physical chains, emotional chains, financial chains, or whatever they may be—but now our dear friend Bro. Manley is leaping and dancing and praising God, completely free.

"Depart" was also an agricultural term. It was used when, at the end of a long, hard, laborious day a yoke of oxen would have the heavy wooden yoke loosed and lifted off their shoulders by the farmer. The oxen would lay down their burden, loosed from the heavy weight of the yoke. We lay down our burden, down by the riverside. That's what Paul did. That's what Manley has done.

"Depart" was also a philosophical term. When a philosopher faced a problem he could not resolve, could not understand, or could not see through, and when suddenly he could see it, he could understand it, the unraveling of the problem would be called a *"departure."* That meant he was able to see clearly. Some folk are looking forward to getting to heaven where they will get all their unanswered questions answered. I expect, however, when we see Jesus, we are going to say, *"What questions?"* We will have no questions when we see Jesus. We will know as we are known. Face to face with Christ our Savior! All of that and so much more is meant in this word, *"depart."*

So, the day finally arrived for the Apostle's departure. The guard said:

"Paul, it's time to go."
"Where are we going?"
"Down to the Tiber River. Down to the Executioner's bloc."
"Well, all right. I am ready. Let's go"
"You don't seem to be afraid, Paul."
"No. I'm not afraid."
"You're not the least bit afraid?"
"No, not really."
"Why aren't you afraid, Paul?"
"Well, you see, I've done this before."
"Oh, no, Paul. A man only does this once."
"Oh, friend, I have done this many times. I die daily."

"OK. I understand. You are a fanatic. What is that, Paul? Is that a song you are humming? I've never heard that tune before, Paul. What is it?"

"Oh, it's just a little song. 'It will be worth it all when we see Jesus.'

"Paul, put your head down here on this bloc. Are you ready?"

"Yes, I'm ready."

"Is there anything else you would like to say, Paul?"

"Yes, I would like to say one more thing."

"What is it, Paul?"

"Jesus Christ is Lord!"

The axe falls and the next scene is heaven. Paul is face to face with Jesus. I don't know what he said, but I have an idea what he said. It went something like this. *"Lord, I wasn't big. I wasn't wealthy, but Lord, you saved me, You called me, You commissioned me, You sent me, You empowered me, and I followed You, my Lord. I have been faithful to the fight. I have been faithful to the faith. I have been faithful to the finish."*

I don't know exactly what Jesus said to him, but I think it went something like this. *"Well done, good and faithful servant. You have been faithful over a few things, I'll make you ruler over many."* Then in that resurrection day, the Lord will place a crown on Paul's head. I don't know what Paul will do with that crown, but I think I know. I can see him now as he takes the crown from off his head and lays it at Jesus' feet.

I would have loved to have been an angel standing around when Manley Beasley arrived in heaven the other day and as he looked into the face of Jesus for the first time. So many times we've been praying, *"Lord, let him stay."* But there has been another who has been praying, *"Father I pray for them whom you have given to me, that they may be with me where I am; that they may behold my glory, the glory that I had with You before the world began."*

Do you know what Manley is doing right now? He is beholding that glory. Think of it. He is beholding that glory! *"For to me to live is Christ but to die is gain."*

Farewell for a while, Manley. We'll see you in the morning.

Appendix One
Index of Testimonies
(See Appendix Two for additional testimonies)

Appendix Two
Additional Testimonies

A tribute written by Michael Catt
in the Sherwood Baptist Church, Albany, GA,
newsletter the day of Manley's funeral

"*On Tuesday Manley Beasley* went to be with the Lord. He served God faithfully in sickness and health. Since 1971 Manley had never known a healthy day as you and I would describe health. He lived longer than any of his doctors ever imagined.

"*The Messages of Manley Beasley* were born out of his personal walk with God. No one else can preach his messages, because they are born out of his experiences. When he preached on suffering, you knew he had been there. When he preached on the glory of God, you sensed he had seen it.

"*Many believers have wanted* the faith of Manley Beasley, but they have not wanted to pay the price he paid. Stephen Olford said that Manley had the 'gift of suffering.' In our selfish, self-centered society that does not understand suffering, Manley was an example of how a believer should suffer.

"*Manley Beasley was part* of a dying breed. He was a prophet. I heard him preach three times in June; twice at Faith Week and then to nearly 20,000 at the Southern Baptist Pastors' Conference in New Orleans. To the end, he was a prophet and revivalist. Even as his outer body was decaying, his inner man was being renewed.

"*Men like Manley* cannot be replaced. They are cut from a different mold. Their calling is unique. They move through this world preaching God's message, and then they are gone.

"If God were to rewrite Hebrews 11, He might include Manley Beasley in the Hall of Faith. His whole life's testimony was, 'by faith.' He was one of whom 'the world was not worthy.' His life and ministry can only be characterized by the word *faith.*

"We have lost far more than a man. We have lost an influence, a presence, and an insight into God. We have lost a prophet—and God knows how desperately Southern Baptists need a prophet today.

"You can't ignore a prophet. He won't let you. Unction is his middle name. His words ring with the authority of heaven. You can't get rid of a prophet, because his voice cries out across the valleys of depravity. No one ever meets a prophet and leaves the same as he came. When you are with a prophet, you know it's time to paint or get down off the ladder. In essence that was the last thing Manley said to Southern Baptists: 'It's time to paint or get off the ladder.'

"Manley Beasley bore in his body the marks of adversity, pain, trial, and suffering. Today they will bury the outer man, but the inner man is walking the streets of gold. No scars, no pain, no hospital beds, no surgery, and no dialysis. His funeral is being preached by Manley Jr., Adrian Rogers, Ron Dunn, and Bill Stafford. Today, Manley Beasley is more alive than he has ever been. His joy is Jesus. He is bathed in the glory of God. He sees Him as He is! Manley, enjoy yourself, thou good and faithful servant!"

Stephen Davis, pastor, First Baptist Church, Russellville, AR
"When I think of Bro. Manley, Hebrews 11:6 comes to mind; *'Without faith it is impossible to please God.'* At the beginning of my Christian life at the age of 28, Manley's message of faith and revival gave clear direction to my spiritual journey. When I met Jonya Wright, our first date was to go and

hear Manley Beasley. Then after we were married, we saw our faith tested when Jonya was diagnosed with some of the same blood diseases that Bro. Manley had. He loved us, encouraged us, and prayed for us during those difficult days. Our entire church in Russellville, AR, has been impacted by his message of faith and revival. He loved us and led us with a Spirit-controlled balance. We miss him now but look forward to seeing him again on the other side."

Peter Lord, conference speaker, author, Titusville, FL

"Manley was the first person who challenged me to think outside the box of traditional Baptist ideas and thinking. He taught me what real faith was and encouraged me to practice it. For me, it began when I invited him to hold in a meeting in my church. At that point the Lord proved to me that what he was preaching was truth. Things began to happen. I am grateful our paths crossed when they did. He is one of those people whom the Lord Jesus Christ has used to bless and challenge my life."

Bill Bozeman, evangelist, Savannah, GA

"Few men have impacted me like Manley Beasley did. I cannot imagine what it would have been like if God had not placed him in my life. Soon after graduating from seminary I began collecting every sermon tape of his that I could find. I would listen to them in the car. I would listen to them when I went walking each morning. God has used them to teach me how to trust Him during some very difficult times in my own life. One of the greatest moments in my ministry was when I was privileged to talk with Bro. Manley on a plane in May 1989, about a year before God took him home. I felt like Elisha must have felt with Elijah. I asked him so many questions. Most of them were about prayer, including his own personal prayer life. I am eternally indebted to Manley Beasley and his influence and his message that to this day continues on through my own ministry. "

Bobby Moore, pastor emeritus of Broadway Baptist Church, Southaven, MS, and author of *Your Personal Devotional Life*

"I was praying with Manley and others prior to a meeting at a youth camp in Macon, MS. I will never forget his asking me, *'Are you talking to God or to the people in this room?'* It was a question I needed to hear. It is a question I have never forgotten."

Karen Dutton, a neighbor

"We were privileged to know the Beasleys in a way that not many others did. Our son, Kevin, a good friend of their youngest son, Jonathan, spent a lot of time in their home. Bro. Manley truly lived what he preached. He was a great encourager. He spent energy encouraging you rather than judging you. Though he associated with many well-known and famous people, he always treated you as if you were just as important. I never heard him complain even when he was extremely ill. He knew God better than anyone I've ever known. We loved him. We miss 'The Preacher.'"

Jerry Spencer, evangelist, senior pastor of Sharon Baptist Church, Savannah, TN

"In 1960 I met Curtis McCarley, a brilliant Camp Meeting preacher from North Carolina. Soon after he had received his master's degree from Southwestern Baptist Theological Seminary in Fort Worth, he moved to Camp Zion in Myrtle, MS, where he and Manley Beasley became best friends. Curtis had memorized much of the Bible and was truly a theological scholar. He told me that his friend, Manley Beasley, had a sharper mind than his and had spiritual insights beyond any preacher or professor he had known.

"Hearing this genius man of God talk about Manley Beasley in such glowing terms made me more that a little eager to meet him. Over the next few years I kept hearing about Bro. Manley. Finally in 1969 I drove from Orlando, FL, to Zachary, LA, to attend a Bible Conference at Milldale Campgrounds. When I walked in, the person at the podium was introducing Manley Beasley as the next speaker. I was thrilled and mesmerized. Strikingly handsome, he spoke with clarity and power. He walked all over the platform, gesturing with his long arms, and filling the air with his resounding voice. He spoke with authority under the anointing of the Holy Spirit. His message titled 'Spiritual Eyes' both convicted and convinced me. At the close I found myself along with scores of other men and women weeping on the altar, broken before God in repentance and commitment.

"Until his home-going, we were fast friends. He preached in every church I was pastor. We preached together on many occasions in conventions, conferences, and camp meetings. When I served as president of the Conference of Southern Baptist Evangelists, I held the program at First Baptist, Dallas. Manley was one of my preachers. Later when he was president of the same conference, he asked me to be the closing speaker at our convention in Norfolk, VA. It was one of the great honors of my life to have him invite me to preach on his program.

"Our families had some great times together. Manley loved my wife, Sue, and she loved him. She saw Jesus in Bro. Manley and he made a permanent impact on her life of faith. When my family and I lived in Houston, the Beasleys lived in San Antonio. Manley called me on July 2, 1974, and asked me to bring my family to his home for the 4th. I'll never forget our shooting fireworks together. Manley was feeling weak, but he insisted on standing outside as we watched the kids shoot fire-crackers, bottle rockets, sparklers, Roman candles, etc. I still laugh when I remember the 'fireball' from a Roman candle that landed in Bro. Manley's hair. Boy, did he jump, dance, and shout as he frantically wiped the fire out of his hair. Everyone got a big kick out of that special scene. Manley too was laughing as he jested, 'Well, that's one time I was on fire for God.'

"A few months before he died, Manley and Marthé were visiting in the home of our mutual friends, W.C. and Earline Jones in Crestview, FL. They all drove to Vernon, FL, one night to hear me preach. We ate together in the church dining room. This was our last supper. After the meal, standing in the parking lot, Manley pulled up his sleeves and showed me the calcium deposits on his arms. He asked me to feel the size of these deformities. They were like small eggs under his skin. He told me they were all over his body as a result of his connective tissue disease.

"I talked to him on the phone several times after that, but I saw him only once more in New Orleans at the Southern Baptist Convention. We were waiting to be seated in the hotel restaurant when I heard someone call my name. I turned around and Homer Lindsay, Jr., pastor of First Baptist, Jacksonville was pushing Bro. Manley in a wheelchair. Adrian Rogers was standing beside him. Manley told me he wanted to preach one more time in our church in Dothan, AL. We set a date. Then just before Homer rolled him away he said, 'Jerry, lean over and let me whisper something to you. Son, when the Lord calls me home, I want you to sing *I'll Walk With the King* at my funeral.' In just a few short weeks, I honored that last request.

"I miss Manley Beasley. I miss all those men he and I preached with at Milldale—Curtis McCarley, Hyman Appelman, J. Harold Smith, Ed Greig, R. G. Lee, etc. I remember how Manley used to say: 'If you don't see it before you see it, you won't ever see it.' Well, I can see Manley and those men fellowshipping up in Glory. It won't be long until we'll see them again face to face."

Michael Gott, evangelist, Keller, TX

"Once, when Manley discovered that I was leaving the country for an extended evangelistic ministry, he insisted I drop by his home to see him. He would not take no for an answer. I could not understand why he was so insistent. Since his home was near DFW Airport, it was not a problem.

"He was home alone. He met me at the door as if he'd been awaiting my arrival. We sat down in a relaxed manner, exchanging typical conversation. Then he paused dramatically, looked at me, and said: *I am going to die soon!* I had often heard about his being very ill, even in critical condition, but he had always bounced back. Possibly my body language indicated that I hadn't taken him seriously because he looked at me and said, *Listen, I'm serious!* He then showed me his enlarged veins in his arms and legs and said, *'That's what they say will take me, but the doctors are wrong. God will take me, and He's about ready.'*

"He then paused to gaze out the window. Without looking for sympathy or being sentimental, he said, *'I wanted a quiet, meaningful farewell with you. I wanted to commission you to be faith full.'* Notice, he said *'faith—full,'* two words. Then he preached a little sermon. I did not actually record Manley's words, or take written notes, but I listened and I can almost repeat his words verbatim. He leaned forward. With an intensity commensurate with the moment, he said:

"Really knowing, believing, obeying, and proving God with faith is the only Christian way of life. It is an illusion to think that nominal church life today even slightly resembles the spirit of the early church. What is usually happening in churches today makes very little, or no difference, to one's thoughts about

God, one's relationship to Him, and one's daily practice and walk in faith. What is actually at stake is whether or not we desire authentic New Testament Christianity and how far we are willing to go to learn the secret of supernatural living that is pleasing God.

"For him the life of faith was not a subject to be pondered. It was a life to be lived. He did not teach us to believe in God as an end but as the means to the end. The end was a life that could not be explained in any way outside of God alive within. Preaching the faith-life was not 'his line.' It was his life. Faith was never the obsessive object of his message. The object was Jesus, his overriding subject. No one could better explain the distinguishing marks of a life lived by faith. That day I walked away, never to see him again. Today we are all in his debt."

John and Judy Rownak, Fayetteville, AR

"Early in 1974 we first met Manley at a conference at Eastwood Baptist Church in Tulsa, OK. Over the next sixteen years we had the privilege of not only hearing him preach over 200 times but getting to know him and his family well. During that time—and even today—his teaching on faith has grounded us in the assurance of God's faithfulness.

"Much preaching and teaching is soon forgotten, but teaching backed by life is lasting. Manley's life was defined by his faith. His life is still a great encouragement to us. Hebrews 11 lists the 'Roll Call of Faith' by introducing each person with the phrase, 'by faith'. When speaking of Manley's life, it could be introduced by those same two words. He is surely a part of that 'great cloud of witnesses'.

"Manley Beasley truly was a man of faith, an instrument of revival."

Endnotes

Chapter One
[1] From *Prodigals and Those Who Love Them* by Ruth Bell Graham, Baker House.

Chapter Two
[2] Words by Ron Owens from the song, *Each Step of the Way,* ICS Music.

Chapter Three
[3] Years later, that teacher, now in a nursing home in Texas, saw Manley preaching on a local church TV program. She got in touch with him and he went to visit her. She asked his forgiveness.

Chapter Four
[4] From the hymn, *All the Way My Savior Leads Me* by Fanny Crosby.

Chapter Five
[5] Attributed to Barbara Bush.

Section Two
[6] Author unknown. Edited by Ron Owens.

[7] From Daily Readings, *Cheque Book of the Bank of Faith* by Charles H. Spurgeon.

Chapter Six
[8] From *Principles of Spiritual Growth* by Miles Stanford, published by Back to the Bible, Lincoln, NE.

Chapter Seven
[9] From *With Christ in the House of Prayer* by Andrew Murray, Baker Book House.

Section Three
[10] Words by Ron Owens from the theme song for Manley's radio program, *Living Faith.*

Chapter Ten

[11] Major W. Ian Thomas, Founder, *Torchbearers International.*

[12] For further writing by Manley on this subject see his booklet, *"Is Your Salvation Real or Counterfeit?"*

Chapter Thirteen

[13] March 29, *My Utmost For His Highest* by Oswald Chambers.

Interlude

[14] Steve Graves is founder and director of *Coaching by Cornerstone* and co-founder of the *Life@Work Company.*

[15] From the song, *The Process* by Ron Owens.

Chapter Fifteen

[16] From *The Valley of Vision,* a collection of *Puritan Prayers and Devotions.* Banner of Truth Trust, 1975.

Chapter Sixteen

[17] F. J. Huegel to Manley on the occasion of Manley's visit to the Huegel home in Mexico City.

[18] From Ron Dunn's book, *When Heaven is Silent.*

Chapter Seventeen

[19] Dr. Bob Bender was pastor of First Baptist, Ada, OK, at the writing of this letter.

[20] James Alexander Stewart.

Chapter Eighteen

[21] Attributed to A. T. Pierson.

Chapter Nineteen

[22] Source unknown.

Chapter Twenty-One

[23] J. Edwin Orr, author and historian on the subject of revival.

Chapter Twenty-Two

[24] J. Edwin Orr, author and historian on the subject of revival.

Chapter Twenty-three

[25] Johnny Hunt, pastor of First Baptist Church, Woodstock, GA.

Chapter Twenty-four

[26] James Alexander Stewart, Scottish Revivalist and founder of *Revival Literature Crusade*, Asheville, NC.

Chapter Twenty-five

[27] From the poem, *Lord, Come Upon Your Church Once More* by Wesley Duewel, author of books on prayer and revival and former director of OMS International.

Chapter Twenty-six

[28] From *In the Day of Thy Power* by Arthur Wallis.

Section Six

[29] From the hymn *My Savior First of All* by Fanny Crosby.

Chapter Twenty-seven

[30] This message, preached at Bellevue Baptist Church less than six weeks before Manley's home-going, is available on CD and DVD.

[31] The other two occasions were at Manley's birth and when he was two years old. In both cases the doctors said he would not live. See *Section One* for details.

Chapter Twenty-eight

[32] From Daily Readings, *Cheque Book of the Bank of Faith* by Charles H. Spurgeon.

[33] Morris Chapman is president and CEO of the Southern Baptist Executive Committee,

[34] From *My Utmost For His Highest*.

[35] Manley's home-going at "high noon" created an interesting conversation piece for the Beasley family in light of Manley's love for the "Western" way of life: ranches, horses, cowboys, and the significance of "high noon" in some of the tales of the American West.

[36] Internment took place at *Bluebonnet Memorial Park*, Colleyville, TX.

Photo Album

Manley Beasley
September 10, 1931—July 10, 1990

Early Years

The Beasleys in Rockport, MS,
before their move to Texas

During Manley's
Merchant Marine days

Kenneth and Manley in front
of Grandpa Harris' home

At the age of 16
the "cool" owner of
an Indian Chief motorcycle

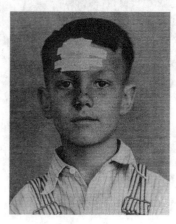

Vera Mae: "Manley, do not
light those firecrackers!"
Crack—crack—crack. He turns
to run . . . right into a tree.
Next day—school picture

Parents and Siblings

Vera Mae with all her children: Joyce, Kenneth, Manley,
Henry Mae, and Pat, Christmas 1982

Together for their father
Henry's 85th birthday

Kenneth and Manley
with their mother

Manley's favorite picture of his
mother, Vera Mae, taken during his
"prodigal" days. This is the only
photo she ever had made by a
professional photographer.

Family and "Promises"

Portrait while living at Milldale

Portrait while living
in San Antonio

Together at Vera Mae's graveside service in Port Neches, TX

Manley with all five of his "promises"

With one of his
"promises", little
Micah. This is last pic-
ture taken of Manley.

Manley and Marthé

Faith Week in 1981

Anniversary service at Hillcrest
Baptist Church, Nederland, TX,
where Manley was pastor for four
years at beginning of his ministry

Wedding bells, December 20, 1952,
at Central Baptist, Port Neches, TX

Photo taken in 1980 during period
when Marthé was miraculously
healed of cancer

21st wedding anniversary in 1973
while living in San Antonio, TX

311

Milldale Years

Jimmy Robertson, Manley, and Sonny Holland

REV. LEONARD RAVENHILL (second from left) is pictured with (left to right) Rev. Sonny Holland, Rev. Jimmy Robertson and Rev. Manley Beasley during the Milldale Baptist Church June Bible Conference. Rev. Ravenhill held the audience spellbound nightly with his dynamic deliverance of the Word of God to the largest audiences ever assembled at the Milldale Bible Conferences. Reverends Holland, Robertson and Beasley, along with other revivalists, will bring the messages at the August 4-8 Milldale Baptist Church Bible Conference.

Copy of original newspaper clipping about conference

GUEST SPEAKERS

MANLEY BEASLEY   JAMES A. STEWART

Milldale Conference on Revival
November 21-25, 1966

Copy of original announcement

Manley and Marthé with
Oswald J. Smith

International Congress on Revival

INTERNATIONAL
CONGRESS ON
R E V I V A L

BELGIUM: Our greatest desire is that as many pastors as possible live the moments that we did in Les Diablerets, so that they, too, will return with the conviction that what Belgium needs is REVIVAL; that this is most urgent and that we must be willing to pay the price.   Baptist Union of Belgium

WEST GERMANY: Please accept our thanks to all who support this ministry. We serve as missionaries/pastor of a German-speaking congregation in W. Germany. I attend conferences with our German Baptist Union, but we don't have anything like the ICR. God is using the Congress in my life. It always comes at a very important time. We are the only Baptist witness in an area with 250,000. Thank you for letting us come on scholarship.   SBC Missionaries

THE SOVIET UNION: Please do not take lightly the doors that have opened for the International Congress On Revival. These doors may not be open for very long. If you do not respond now, you may look back and be sorry. The ICR has the opportunity to do things other large organizations cannot do.
Superintendent of Churches in USSR

SCOTLAND: We greatly appreciate the sacrificial giving of those who made it possible for us and many others to attend. God spoke to my wife and me in a deep way, and as I visit many Baptist churches in Scotland over the next months, I shall be trying with God's help, to convey something of the burden and urgency of the teaching and inspiration we received at the Congress.   President, Baptist Union of Scotland

CZECHOSLOVAKIA: We need revival. Thank you for getting our attention back on this most important thing. We remember what God did in our country many years ago when James Stewart visited us. Lord, do it again.
President, Baptist Union of Czechoslovakia

FRANCE: Our churches are small. Sometimes we feel discouraged. Thank you for helping us and making it possible for us to come to the wonderful Congress this year. Our churches need revival.   Pastor

The International Christian Center (Hotel Rosat) in *Château d'Oex*, Switzerland, where Manley's vision for revival in Europe was birthed

Manley, far left, and Ron Owens, far right, with Baptist leaders from Eastern and Western Europe at 1988 Congress on Revival

Delegates from 22 nations attend an *International Congress on Revival* in Switzerland

313

Final Convention

Manley with Adrian Rogers, center, and Tom Elliff, right,
after having preached at the 1990 SBC Pastors'
Conference in the New Orleans Superdome 17 days
before his home-going

Manley talking with Adrian Rogers
in New Orleans. Note missing fingers
on Manley's hand.

Miscellaneous

Manley with his cousin, W.C.
Beasley, a WWII decorated hero
whose testimony played   a significant role in Manley receiving
Jesus as Savior

"Cowboy" Beasley pauses for
a photo on his
Milldale "ranch"

Mack and Dottie Kearney with
Manley, Christmas 1979

Chef Manley in the backyard of
their home in Euless, TX

315

Hospitals, a Second Home

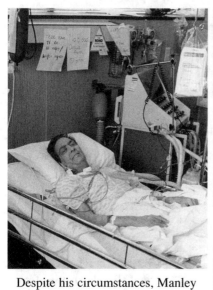

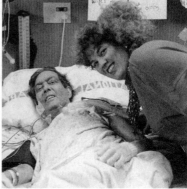

Manley with daughter Debbie

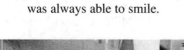

Despite his circumstances, Manley
was always able to smile.

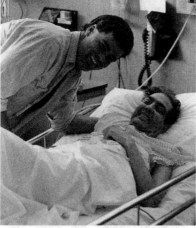

Manley Jr. and Manley Sr.

Manley with a sculpture of Moses,
one of his favorite Bible characters.
Though still pressing on, he is at
this time not far from "home."

To order additional copies of this book, visit

www.beasleybiography.com

www.hannibalbooks.com

www.amazon.com

www.barnesandnoble.com

and other online and physical bookstores

A Closing Word

We invite you to visit our website,
www.beasleybiography.com

where
- you can share what the book has meant to you
- read what others are saying
- purchase additional copies
- learn about other Manley Beasley resources

If you believe that *Manley Beasley: Man of faith, Instrument of Revival* is relevant and needed in our day, we encourage you to think of ways to get this message into as many hands as possible. "Word of mouth" has always been the best distributor. If you have a website or blog, you might consider writing something about the book and setting up a link from your site directly to *www.beasleybiography.com*. Or, if you have a mailing list—snail mail or email— a personal testimony of how Manley has touched your life is the most powerful promotion. Or, you may wish to purchase multiple copies, at a volume discount, to give as gifts or make available through your own ministry.

An **Audio Book** of *Manley Beasley: Man Faith, Instrument of Revival* is scheduled for a May 2009 release.

Other books by the author are available at
www.owensministries.org

Return to Worship . . . "With all the wisdom and skill that can come only from wide experience, serious study, and sincere devotion to Christ and His Church, Ron Owens gives us the counsel we need in this troubled hour. I wish every believer, pastor, church musician, and worship leader would read this book and take it to heart. It calls us back to God-centered worship that is based on truth, not trends, and that brings glory to the Master, not applause to the servants."—Warren Wiersbe, author and speaker

They Could Not Stop the Music . . .
"I couldn't put it down and I was stirred to tears as I read of Georgy Slesarev, first violinist of Moscow's Bolshoi Theater. His personal commitment to Jesus Christ and his refusal to allow 'the music of his testimony to be stopped' cost him his life. Read this incredible story. It will be a soul-searching experience. I enthusiastically commend it to you." —Cliff Barrows, Billy Graham Evangelism Association

Worship: Believers Experiencing God, a six-week course for personal or group study, co-authored with Dr. Henry Blackaby

Contact information:
Ron Owens
PO Box 54553
Hurst, TX 76054